SPIRITS OF THE STONES
Visions of Sacred Britain

SPIRITS OF THE STONES

Visions of Sacred Britain

Alan Richardson

Illustrations taken from Edward Duke's book, *The Druidical Temples of Wiltshire* reproduced by kind permission of County Local Studies Library, Wiltshire Libraries and Heritage

First published in Great Britain in 2001 by

Virgin Publishing Ltd
Thames Wharf Studios
Rainville Road
London W6 9HA

A catalogue record for this book is available from the British Library

ISBN 0 7535 0414 6

Phototypeset by Intype London Ltd
Printed and bound by Mackays of Chatham PLC

This is dedicated to all those unsung pipe-and-slipper men who, from the apparent inertia of their armchairs, travel to the bleak edges of Time and Space . . .

CONTENTS

ACKNOWLEDGEMENTS

A great many people took time out from their busy lives and their own labour-intensive projects and went out of their way to help me with this book. It could never have been written without them. Those who are happy to have their names mentioned include, in no particular order:

Uri Geller, Chris Arnold, Basil Wilby, Herbie Brennan, Poppy Palin, Edna Whelan and Rowan Greenwood. Canon Anthony Duncan, Chris Thomas, Melusine Draco, Patrick Godfrey, John Crabtree, Flora, Asha and Esther Colmar; Murry Hope, Dot and George Warminiec, Cairistiona Worthington, Evan John Jones, Sian Bottomley, Mary Fink, Lewis Shepherd and the Dusty Millers; plus a special thanks to Judith Page, who organised so much! John and Elizabeth Fox, Bob Stewart, Dolores Ashcroft-Nowicki, Tammy Ashcroft-Nowicki, Angela Barker, Richard Eastburn-Hewitt and Monique Michaud. Janet Bord, Heather Shaw, Tim Perry, Adam Wilson, John Billingsley, Helen Belot, Peter Larkworthy, Jan Holden, Arthur O'Neil, Simon Buxton, Rae Beth and the Hardins of Louisville. Stuart Johnson, Colin Wilson, Ray and Cass. Mark Aldridge, Clive Harper, Jenny Dent, Isobel Drinkwater, Laura Jennings-Yorke, Marcia Pickands, David Owen, Andrew and Carol Maxwell, Wor Pat and Tony McCarroll; plus the Oldham, Fuge and Johnson families.

My coarse chums at Ashton Street, especially: that pitiless pair Caroline Hancock and Debbie Haldane, who sat (without shame) and watched me do *all* the work; Unique Monique for her Canadian chic; my kind, wise and near-faultless line managers; and Kerri Sharp of Virgin, who encouraged me right from the start.

ACKNOWLEDGEMENTS

Very special thanks to Jill Forsey and Annie Tod – unto the ages of ages, worlds without end. Tony Heyes, Caroline Williams, Jo Chant, Alison Cotton, Richard Hook, Helen Cazelet, Jenny Straffon and Lettie Bannister. Nicky Higby, John McHale and Chris Seton-Smith. We had some laughs in the snake pit, eh?

Logan Lewis-Proudlock of the College of Psychic Studies helped me to believe the project was worthwhile during a period of darkness and doubt, and also gave me a great deal of practical help and advice.

And, as usual, Billie John, who has always kept things going during hard times.

An important part of this project involved visiting particular sites in company with mystics, mediums and magicians of very different traditions, as will be described within the narrative. Quite apart from the psychic experiences that were triggered off in different ways within all of us, we also had – far more important in my estimate – a lot of laughs. Some of them were complete strangers or distant acquaintances beforehand, but have since become firm friends: Mike Harris and Wendy Berg, Iris Scott and Paddy Slade. In addition, my old pal and that most gifted of mediums Ray Bailey chipped in with some important insights and some much-needed help at a crucial time.

But, as ever, it means nothing without the constant background of my daughters, who hold the secrets of *real* magick: Zoë, Kirsty, Jade and Lara.

Apart from these there are a lot of magicians, now long since dead, who taught me things when I was a very young man, and whose strange auras and talents for passing on wisdom at subliminal levels contributed in no small part to the present work, many years later. Foremost among these has to be William Gray and his wife Bobbie; Christine Hartley, WE Butler; and Francis X King. The brightest of blessings to all of them.

While all of the above gave me permission to make use of their material, they will not necessarily agree with my own interpretations of it. And I am sure they will let me know in their own inimitable ways. All quotations, where not attributed, are from direct personal correspondence.

Not everyone wanted their real names used. In these cases I have used pseudonyms or 'witch-names'. Not everyone wanted the exact locale of their especial magickal sites revealed, either, so where requested I have been vague – though not inaccurate – with details. Enough clues have still been left so that anyone with a poignant urge to find the locations will be able to do so, with a bit of effort in research.

In fact, if any reader wants to make contact with any of the individuals or organisations mentioned within the text they should write to me c/o of the publishers, including adequate return postage, and I will forward their messages – although I cannot give any promise that they will get a reply.

This project is ongoing. If any of it strikes a chord with readers who feel they may have relevant experiences and insights to share then – again – if they write to me personally I will value what they send, and if appropriate fit it into any future edition.

Alan Richardson
Wessex, 2000

FOREWORD

Let me lay down a challenge, with a mischievous smile. In his introduction, Alan Richardson suggests, 'there is no need to travel to Stonehenge, Avebury or Silbury Hill to touch upon their magick.'

What he says is true. I have visited sacred sites psychically, as well as military establishments, as part of the CIA's remote viewing program in the Seventies. I let my mind fly and drew the essence of the place into my soul, without ever leaving the lab. But the experience, when a site is the source of immense psychic energy, is far greater than the mind can comprehend. To step inside a Neolithic circle or a pre-Celtic tomb is to be overwhelmed with impressions and knowledge without words.

The greatest glory of the British Isles, and one of the most secret, is its network of ancient sites. The barrows and circles, the spectral stones and the Iron Age furrows – they are poems written in the landscape. To travel by train from London to Bristol, as I sometimes do, is to watch prehistoric Wessex history through the video screen of a first-class carriage window . . . or so I like to fantasise. I see the burial grounds of kings and the temples of fabulist priests who guarded libraries of myth in their eidetic memories. I hear the song of bards and the miracles of healers flickering across the man-made slopes, which have remained unchanged since England's ancestors dug the earth. All of this so long ago that, in the land of my own ancestors, the ink was still snaking across the parchments as Moses wrote the divine language of the Torah.

There are other countries where the echoes of past lives take shape on the surface of the earth, like the scars of forgotten waves in the sand of a deserted beach. I have walked on the pyramids of Chichen Itza in Mexico and in the stone tombs of Ellora in India. I have climbed to Masada and sailed the Nile. These places can mould your soul. The stones and mounds of Britain are uniquely powerful. To stand on Fish Hill, overlooking Broadway in the Cotswolds, is to feel witchcraft boiling up from the ground in dizzying, sulphurous clouds. To stalk the Rollright Stones, counting again and again and always finding a different number, is to walk through a glittering mist of ancient magick.

Take this book and devour it. It is compulsively readable – I swallowed it at a sitting. Alan's enthusiasm is electrifying, his knowledge encyclopaedic and his theories breath-taking. But do not stay content in your chair when the book is closed. Get in your car. Catch a boat or take a flight. With *Spirits of the Stones* as your guidebook, plunge into the lake of prehistoric energies. On the other side of the mirrored surface, you will find yourself in a world of undreamed mystical depths.

Come stand with the stones.

Uri Geller, Sonning on Thames, July 2000

INTRODUCTION

This is a book about those megalithic remains that are still scattered across the countryside thousands of years after being built, and whose meaning – like dreams – is often the subject of intense and varying interpretation. It is also a book about ordinary folk who have unexpectedly been touched by the ancient sites, had the most inexplicable experiences and felt their own lives enlarged. Ordinary folk who, in many cases, also think of themselves as witches, magicians, mediums, Free-masons, shamans, Rosicrucians, Christian Mystics, druids, seers – or just plain bull-headed speculators after the truth.

My approach to the work was quite simple. As well as plundering published sources, I sent flyers off to every interested party I could think of, taking in the full range of New Age beliefs. I asked them to send me details of their experiences at the ancient places, asked them to ask their friends, and assured them that I was not going to put them in competition with other contributors or mock or scorn what they had to say. On top of this I also recruited the talents of several individuals from very different traditions (of whom more later), and went around specific sites with them, recording what – if anything – they 'saw' at each place. I assured them that they would not be, at any point or in any way, under any pressure to perform psychically. Nor did we ever meet up as a group until after the project was finished.

If confession precedes revelation, then I must admit I was motivated by a long-standing jealousy. Many years ago I read Grace Cooke's account of her visits to random sites in the south of England, where she tuned in to the inner energies of each and wrote up what transpired in her book *The Light in Britain*. Being a very young man at the time, and full of the

1

sneering omniscience of youth, I was not always impressed or convinced by some aspects of what she 'saw', but I would have loved that kind of talent anyway. Over the years, with more discoveries and greater insight, I have come to accept that Grace has proved more right than wrong. If I still have occasional illusions of omniscience, at least I no longer sneer.

It seemed to me, however, that she approached it all from too narrow a viewpoint, and tended to impose her own essentially Christian emotions on sites that predated Christianity by thousands of years. So I was always determined to throw this open to the wider public, then visit these places in company with mediums and seers with pagan as well as Christian leanings, from magickal as well as mystical backgrounds, men and women of vision who have tried and tested their talents over many years, and who have nothing to prove.

This is the essence of the book.

Structurally, it is based upon the scheme outlined in 1846 by the Reverend Edward Duke, who fancied that our ancestors, in their own geocentric way, reproduced the solar system through sites in the Wiltshire countryside. Thus Silbury Hill was the Earth, the linked circles at Avebury the Sun and orbiting Moon, and so on at appropriate intervals, until Saturn touched down at Stonehenge.

While there may be obvious logical objections to his scheme, his 'meridianal line' encompassed the whole range of megalithic culture from single unhewn standing stones, through harvest hills, sacred wells, faery hills, long barrows and tumuli, to the mighty trilithons at Stonehenge. I have used his scheme, therefore, in a thematic rather than literal sense. The structure of the chapters is not offered as any kind of unified esoteric system: it is simply a means of dealing with a range of remarkable experiences which lap and overlap one another, and which seem to spiral outwards from a central source.

So, by linking astrology/astronomy with the 'spirit of place', we can create a simple map of the psyche wherein major psychological and spiritual landscapes can be shown to have earthly signposts. When we look at Avebury, for example, we can also look at the concepts and energies behind all stone circles, as experienced by individual occultists across Britain and Ireland, and not restrict ourselves to the Wiltshire landscape that Duke once surveyed. In such a way we can hope to see how the light of the stars and planets once found expression in the land around – and how they can still be touched. In this way, *Spirits of the Stones* treats these mysterious sites and remains not as dull remnants of a dead culture of ancient Britain, but as vital places within the psyche that can be accessed by anyone, anywhere, from any land. The realm of the megaliths is not so much a geographical location with historical overlays and archaeological remnants, as a very deep stratum of consciousness inside us all. And if there is one thing that all the people within this text have taught me it is this: there is no need to travel to Stonehenge, Avebury or Silbury Hill to touch upon their magick. They are symbolic gateways to levels of consciousness and universal energies within our minds that we can all reach, simply by travelling *within*.

During the first draft of the book, my thesis was that the stone circles acted upon the consciousness of the individual like Rorschach ink blots: what each person 'saw' was simply an expression of things within their unconscious. But as more material came in I had to revise my ideas rapidly and completely. Quite simply, the amount of similarity and agreement was so striking that this metaphor became crass. The differences between the insights were less due to psychic ineptness than to individuals experiencing the same place under the different circumstances and usage of widely separated eras. What was true of a site in Neolithic times was not necessarily true in the same way by the end of the Bronze Age.

As I got deeper and deeper into the images and energies behind the hitherto private experiences of many quite remarkable individuals, I found myself becoming strangely moved. It was as if a part of me, long since lost at the back of my mind, were being made to remember things that I should never have forgotten. Hopefully, this book will have a similar effect upon those who read it, and who allow the pictures to rise from their own unconscious.

Instead of mocking the approach of mystics and magicians, we should listen to them very carefully. These people have spent so long back-pedalling in the face of several decades of rationalist onslaught, and it is only very recently that they've once more been allowed a platform. Their insights have already proved no less durable than the dour theses of their academic detractors, many of whom would have looked askance at the very suggestion that magick might be the most crucial discipline of all.

More, there is a poetry, cohesion, poignancy and hope within the tales of the occultists (to use a dreadful but probably necessary term), which the work of the measurers and gluers of shards can never hope to equal. Tales that are extraordinary. Experiences that are disturbingly believable. Insights from the remote past (using dormant faculties that we all have and can reawaken) that can influence the futures of us all. For the astonishing thing is not that there are secrets buried within the countryside, which the mystics, mediums and magicians can help us find, but that there are secret places within the mind that are aligned to stars and planets, energies and entities, and that – apparently – can take us across time and within ourselves.

CHAPTER

ONE

THE REVEREND DUKE AND THE ANCIENT DRUIDS

In 1845, at the age of 66, the Reverend Edward Duke left the rambling splendour of his home, Lake House, in the heart of the Woodford Vale in deepest Wiltshire, and ordered his servant to drive him – at a speed commensurate with his dignity and status – towards the village of Avebury, some 25 miles to the north. He took with him in the carriage enough clothes for an overnight stop, a compass, a bundle of local maps and the obligatory drawing pads and pencils. At that moment he felt himself to be in the hands of a higher power, and nothing was more important than getting to Silbury Hill, on the edge of Avebury, where he could begin his great work. To him that day, the mundane world scarcely existed. It was not important that his church was in turmoil over the dread threat of Roman Catholicism in England, or that a truly devastating potato famine was sweeping through Ireland, Belgium and Holland – nor yet that the government under Peel was deeply and fatally divided over those Corn Laws and Enclosure Acts that would affect the land (and the spirit of the land) for generations to come. All these things were merely temporal. All these things left him untouched because he had had . . . well, a revelation!

Of course it was all too soon to risk sharing this with anyone else. The other fellows in the Archaeological Society, and – even worse – his parishioners, would think it decidedly odd for a vicar to be in the grip of visions – even if they did come from a slightly higher source of inspiration than Magdalen Hall, Oxford. But (and here he could hardly contain himself) he had glimpsed something hidden within the landscape of Wiltshire that no one else had seen! A secret that, he felt, would transform the way his peers had looked at (and sneered at) the pre-Christian heritage of standing stones that still littered the fields, like so many redundant and equally tiresome farm hands.

As his head boiled from both the sun and his ideas, all sealed up by the tight rims of his hat and collar, he soon made the steep climb up the man-made slopes of Silbury Hill. Halfway to the top he paused to catch his breath and also say a brief prayer for the spirit of King Zel, who the locals said was buried within; then he pressed on, ever more breathless, but ever more excited. At the summit, sitting on a small folding stool that his servant had hefted up with all his other paraphernalia (for he was a gentleman before he was a vicar), he consulted his map and compass in order to look almost due south, over Milk Hill and the Vale of Pewsey behind it, over Wilsford Down and then Knighton Down, in the direction of his own parish and mighty Stonehenge itself. Then, casting a glance over his shoulder towards the nearby stone circles in Avebury, which had endured (mute as his congregation and scarcely less responsive) for thousands of years before Christ, he *knew* that his revelation was indeed correct . . .

What the Reverend Edward Duke 'saw' was not the sort of ley alignment that would so interest his descendants a hundred and fifty years later, but a series of orbits. Using the geocentric model of the ancient world, Silbury Hill was nothing less than the Mother Earth around which all else turned. Or, as he was to write, Silbury was: ' . . . a centre, around which the planets, represented by their temples, were supposed to revolve, and for this . . . when viewed from a distance, [Silbury] did aptly answer its intended purpose, that of representing the Earth.'[1]

Which meant, in modern prose, that Silbury was the Earth; the Sun and encircling Moon were found within the nearby stone circles of Avebury; the serpentine avenues of stones touching them represented the ecliptic, or the sun's passage through the zodiac. Moving further outwards, the circle of stones at Winterbourn Basset fell on the orbit of Venus. The orbit of Mars could be found at the Roman Temple of Marden. That of Jupiter lay on Casterley Camp. While the orbit of Saturn was unmistakably represented by Stonehenge.

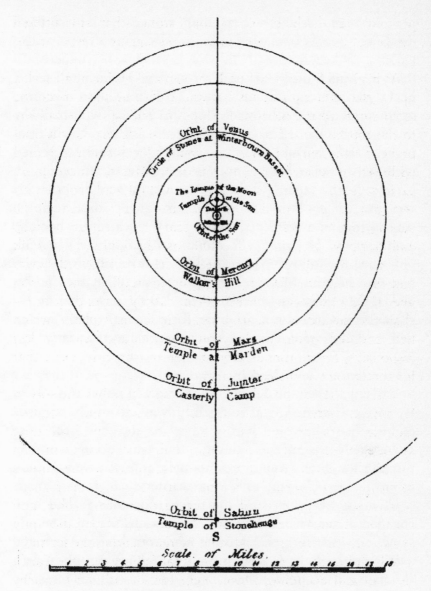

DUKE'S MUNDANE SYSTEM

He expressed this revelation in a remarkably simple diagram, and one that – as far as he was concerned – virtually proved the fact that the heavens could be found on Earth amid some Wiltshire fields.

But who, sir, asked the coachman, was responsible for these marvels?

Duke looked fondly at his young servant, for underneath that low brow there lurked a surprisingly keen intelligence. Leaning over conspiratorially, their hat brims almost touching, he looked both ways before telling him in a half-whisper: The druids were responsible! he said, perpetuating the current idea. None other! Mr Duke was in no doubt whatsoever, for he had used the winter nights to hone his arguments often enough on his young wife Jayne. All these ancient sites were, he patiently explained to his loyal and honest servant, druidical temples. And saying this even helped to give him the title for the book he would write, *The Druidical Temples of the County of Wiltshire*, published the following year. As he was driven from the ever-pregnant belly of Mother Earth to visit the other sites on his orbits, then ultimately back towards Lake House, that ghost-ridden home of his not far from King Saturn's place, he felt that he had opened a lost and secret door into the past.

Duke's journey and the subsequent book were one of the very first to crack open the door of what became known as the New Age perception. As a vicar still tightly swathed in the wrappings of his Christ, he could hardly have imagined the free, loose and nakedly pagan consciousness that was to come surging through the door a century or so later, and that we will look at in some detail in the following chapters.

It was not the first time the reverend gentleman had been engaged in such work, however. In previous summers he and some fellows had ripped into the numerous barrows scattered across nearby Lake Down with all the enthusiasm of modern children tearing open Kinder Eggs – and for much the same reasons. Local traditions that this could bring bad luck, that it could result in the release of ancient and angry spirits into the world, held no fears for him – the good reverend was a scientist, after all, and had no truck with mere superstition.

Yet were he to make the same journey today from the top of Silbury Hill to the centre of Stonehenge, and thence home to nearby Lake House, he might find the summit of the hill crowded with bare females celebrating their women's mysteries on one of the 'sacred days'; or young folk of either sex standing silently at the megaliths of the nearby circles listening to their inner song. He would pass near-empty churches struggling against decay while fleets of luxury coaches from all over the globe carried passengers towards the ancient sites and their accompanying fast-food outlets. The fields might be empty of labourers but they would be, in places, thronged with earnest souls who sought corn circles, or power places, or primordial terrestrial zodiacs that could be seen only by those who could fly; and many of these people would be self-styled witches, wizards, urban shamans, gurus, dowsers, ley hunters, neo-druids, eco-warriors, or plain and simple seekers after the truth, with nary a gentleman or a Freemason in sight. And all of these ordinary people would be trying, in their own ways, to link these ancient sites, stones and circles with something they perceived as greater than themselves. So perhaps the spirits of the barrows have been more active than the Reverend Edward Duke might care to imagine. And, even if his own ghost then looked for solace in the enduring, ancient architecture of his beloved Lake House (reputedly once the home of Sir Lancelot), it would have even more shocks. He would find it lived in today by a man calling himself simply Sting, who practised tantric sex, who cavorted with savages while saving rain forests, created ungodly songs, and who (as an actor) had played a host of unholy characters including the Devil himself.

Although it would be easy to use the image of Duke to poke fun at his whole era, the fact is his book anticipated the computer-aided studies of Gerald Hawkins and Professor Alexander Thom by over a hundred years. His intuition that the stones within Avebury and Stonehenge were linked with stellar, solar and lunar cycles has been confirmed by the very best of modern technology; and his belief that the ancient Greek, Roman and contemporary British commentators on the druids (especially William Stukeley, 1687–1765) were drastically off-target in their statements has also gained a lot of credence by our own time. More, his perception that the stars above could be mirrored in the sacred landscape below was echoed by the separate researches of Robert Bauval and Mark Vidler over 150 years later, and their respective books, *The Orion Mystery* and *The Star Mirror*, are currently turning all previous ideas about the ancients on their heads.

Yet the overriding question today is not who built these wonders, but why?

The arguments have been firing back and forth with such vehemence for so many years now that it needs a radical new viewpoint, yet one that is actually the oldest viewpoint of all: that of the seers – people with odd and highly developed perceptions who can, with varying degrees of accuracy, look back and forward through Time. Witches and magicians, mediums and mystics . . . yet of the people and very much for them, in ways that the good reverend with his inherent elitism might not have understood. For if there was anyone who might have been able to tell Edward Duke something more about this infinitely varied 'inner history' of the stones, then it may well have been his trusted servant over an ale or three in the smoky bar of the Druid's Head, in Lake itself.

Not that his servant was a member of any arcane or secret group, but simply because he was one of the common people, one of those ghost-obsessed observers, preservers and remem-berers, witch-descended, whose oral wisdom was passed down through the generations with a kind of fearful delight and who had, or understood, that quality of Second Sight that was once common among the country folk. Unharmed by education, he was one of the tillers of fields, 'Brothers to the Ox', whose working life was spent next to or among the stones, at all seasons and in all weathers, dawn to dusk, and who could feel their actual presence in a way that day-trippers with letters after their names could not, and who knew when the stones were asleep, and when they were very much alive . . .

In his book *Megalithomania*, John Michell records an extra-ordinary story in this respect, taken from Callanish, on the Isle of Lewis, where even into the last century certain old people and their families were held in special respect and esteem as 'belonging to the Stones'.

The old man also told him that when the sun rose on Mid-summer morning *something* came to the Stones, walking down the great avenue heralded by the cuckoo's call. He had described the *something* by a word [which] was probably pre-Gaelic, and from a root common to the British group of languages. It meant, they thought, the Shining, or Pure, or White one . . . and had probably been the epithet of a god.[2]

It is this kind of magickal, mystical, fantastical response to the stones that concerns us here rather than their measurement, mapping and scientific analysis; for at the end of the day, unless they are channels for unusual energies, straight lines are merely straight lines, even if they *do* connect with planets, stars or local features.

A similar vision to that at Callanish, and one that has entered into the folk memory of Wiltshire lore, has it that, at sunrise on the longest day, the great barrow of West Kennet is entered by a 'priest' followed by a huge white hound with red ears. Intriguingly, such a beast is neither unique nor simply the product of one man's fantasy, because phantom white hounds with red pointed ears are common throughout the country in their role as 'fairy dogs'. And the notion of the 'fairy' in this context is not the Victorian one of Arthur Rackham – of tiny creatures living amid the flowers – but of wild, ancient, potentially dangerous other-than-human spirits that are linked with both natural energies and our most distant ancestors. Thus the white hound of West Kennet might well feel completely at ease with the *'something'* that visited Callanish.

Another story of this ilk, contemporary with the Reverend Duke, relates to the tumulus at nearby Hackpen Hill, which was seen as akin to a gate into the underworld. Again, however, the underworld of pre-Christian communities was not envisioned as a place of dreadful night and suffering as he might have warned, but a timeless realm of light, laughter, freedom and music. The lower slope of Hackpen is still known as Fiddler's Hill and from here, it is said, hypnotic, otherworldly refrains can still be heard under the full moon, on certain nights in May and August, tempting mere mortals to step bodily into another dimension entirely. And as we listen to the inner songs

11

invoked by the experiences of the modern mystics, who have gone into places like Hackpen Hill with their eyes wide open (all three of them!), we might start to dream of our own gates, leading towards our own inner music and freedom. That is the power behind the stories that will follow.

During that frantic period in the eighteenth and nineteenth centuries, however, when the barrows were being opened by all manner of often well-meaning academics, new lore was being created by the locals – all of whom felt that such plundering brought bad luck to the community. When the large bowl barrow at Manton, near Marlborough, was excavated they found the crouching skeleton of an old and obviously important woman, who had been buried with an amber-pommelled bronze knife, beads of gold, bronze and more amber, as well as two incense cups. However, an obviously fey widowed lady who lived near the barrow later complained that since the exhumation the spirit of that 'old creature' came out of the mound and squinnied at her window almost every night.

We will hear many more stories along these lines as we enter that folkloric stratum of consciousness that is intimately connected with the land, and the notions of 'Spirit of Place', for the actual creation of folklore is as continuous as a fountain of water, and by no means the preserve of bygone generations. We all play a part in it. In fact, one of the purposes of this book is to create a new generation of folklore, looking at the perceptions of those people who would have known *exactly* how to deal with that wretched 'old creature' – though not before entering into a thoroughly productive communication with her on mediumistic levels.

The ancient sites (not all of which are still potent or even awake, according to general opinion among the witches) can provoke a wide variety of experience and vision. For example, a retired colonel named Charles Seymour had, in 1939, a disturbing vision of human sacrifice at Avebury that he felt must date back three or four millennia.

> . . . there was a long altar stone in the middle and over it had
> been built a sort of a roof of leaves that looked like beech. It

was very early in the morning just after dawn and I think it was about May Day . . . I noticed the dew on the grass. Then came two priests one carrying a gold hilted bronze (?) sword about 2½ feet long. This was a big man heavily built with a wide face, a big mouth, large teeth with very prominent and pointed eye teeth. The other was a smaller thin man and fanatical looking who carried a large gold cup. Following them were men carrying a rough litter on which lay a young woman about twenty or thirty. Fair hair blue eyes. She was naked with finger nails, toe nails, and nipples painted red. She was not bound . . .

Then the woman was placed on the altar stone with her head (face) facing N.E. looking into a notch in the hills where the sun would appear. This woman was paralysed below the neck – hypnotised or drugged. But she could move her head a little and her eyes rolled and she was fully conscious. The big priests stood behind her head waiting for the sun to rise to plunge the sword between the painted nipples. The smaller priest with the bowl squatted at her feet to catch the blood from a runnel in the gently sloping stone of sacrifice. The whole temple space was filled with figures. The sun came up after a long wait and the priest raised the sword to stab . . .[3]

In contrast, at around the same time, a medium named Grace Cooke had the first of a series of visions relating to the mysteries of ancient Britain, which she eventually published as *The Light In Britain*. Like the Reverend Duke, she was drawn to Silbury Hill, first, even though she knew nothing of its fame.

Gradually my etheric vision awakened and I saw that the area about the hill was filled with nature spirits of all kinds, and I realised that I was watching a ceremony of the 'rogation' or the 'blessing of the seeds' taking place . . . Then I felt a tremendous heat all around me on the hilltop and saw with amazement an immense altar upon which a great flame arose – it burnt quite unlike an ordinary fire, for it seemed to need no replenishment; and I felt that it had been burning there in the etheric world for unmeasured time. Great beings who seemed to be the high priests were serving at this altar . . .[4]

Her own vision of the Avebury complex was in sharp contrast to the dark and almost demonic events seen by Seymour.

To her the whole area was one of light and goodness, thronging with happy, gentle, childlike and presumably vegetarian folk who worshipped under the aegis of priests from Egypt, as well as some god-men from a lost continent who looked like Mayans. It was all done in a perfect harmony of mind, body and spirit, and, if there was darkness or evil anywhere within the land, then the stones themselves, acting like spiritual cleansing machines, would transmute it into light, light and yet more light.

For those who feel uneasy with the raw visions of the occultist, the point of the present book is not whether such visions or experiences are historically right or wrong, or else little more than telling projections from the unconscious. The point is whether any of them strike a chord within ourselves and help us to glimpse . . . *something*. Perhaps at very least that is the metaphor we can derive from the experience at Callanish: the energies behind the stones can enable *something* within ourselves that is very odd, old, bright and pure to enter the avenues of our consciousness.

The measurers and mappers have surely done as much as they can with their uncompromising craft of lines and alignments. Instead let us look at both the *non*rational faculties of the mystic and the medium, as well as the experiences of supposedly ordinary people – the unlearned, unlettered and unknown – whose ideas have been coloured by superstition and the thrill of ancient magick, and whose insights derive from the rough and unexpected gnosis of the passer-by. Through these, if we are to believe the messages from the megaliths themselves, as told to the initiated, we can help awaken energies for the future, so that we may all, in our own way and at our own pitch, hear the song of the stones.

TWO

THE SACRED HILLS, MOUNDS AND SILBURY

The history of ancient, and not so ancient, places
may be recovered by the perception of 'place
memories' or by direct communication with the
spirits of that place. To understand this one has
to realise that death is not a closed door, time is
not the 'linear' phenomenon we suppose it to be and
space is by no means a material fixture. Time, space
and events, those parameters of our outer world,
take on an easy flexibility in the quantum world
behind appearances. Mortal consciousness has the
same inherent flexibility.
– Mike Harris, *co-magus of the Avalon Group*

When we feel the first stirrings of wonder for the earth mysteries, and follow whatever tradition or practice gives us the
kick inside (which tells us that something altogether new within
us is alive and growing), then we find ourselves at Silbury Hill,
or somewhere akin to it in spirit. This is the place, wherever it
happens to be geographically, where things develop and take
shape. It does not have to be the actual huge and enigmatic
cone of that name in Wiltshire: any numinous place – particularly any sacred hill or mound – can become the still centre of
the turning world.

The Reverend Edward Duke's notion, and the essence of this
book, was that:

> ... our ingenious ancestors portrayed on the Wiltshire Downs,
> a Planetarium or stationary Orrery [which is] located on a
> meridianal line, extending north and south, the length of sixteen
> miles. The planetary temples thus located, seven in number,
> will, if put into motion, be supposed to revolve around Silbury
> Hill as the centre of this grand astronomical scheme. Thus

Saturn . . . would in his orbit describe a circle with a diameter of 32 miles . . . The Moon is represented as a satellite of the Sun . . . while the Sun himself pursues his annual course in the first and nearest concentric orbit. Venus, Mercury, Mars and Jupiter . . . were all located at due distances from each other [and] the relative proportions of those distances correspond with those of the present received system.[1]

There are obvious and logical objections to this scheme, but logic is not always healthy, and frequently lacks the poetry from which true magick can spring. In fact, what Duke has given us is a map of the psyche, using physical locations as signposts to inner realities. The astrological qualities represented by the earth, sun, moon, Venus, Mars, Jupiter and Saturn represent a totality of consciousness, and by linking them with the sites, and the impulses and energies behind the sites, we can go some way towards experiencing the axiom, 'As above, so below; as without, so within'. And in an odd way it also echoes and honours the modern druid cosmology that depicts a series of concentric circles, representing the realms known as Annwn, Abred, Gwynvid and Ceugant – the dimensions of existence the soul experiences as it makes its way towards immortality.

In beginning the exploration of the earth mysteries at Silbury Hill – or any sacred hill, mound or barrow in your own locality – you begin to align your psyche with forces larger than yourself, yet integrally part of you at the same time, as we shall see when we look at the experiences of mediums, mystics and magicians of all persuasions, ages and aptitudes. This is not something that is easily explained by recourse to modern psychobabble, but more intensely felt by that power of intense imagination that verges on actual psychism. DH Lawrence, writing what was almost the last prose of his short life, summed it up thus:

I am part of the sun as my eye is part of me. That I am part of the earth my feet know perfectly, and my blood is part of the sea . . . There is nothing of me that is alone and absolute except

16

my mind, and we shall find that the mind has no existence by itself, it is only the glitter of the sun on the surface of the waters . . .[2]

In differing ways, everyone in this book – whether Wiccan, Druid, Spiritualist, Rosicrucian or whatever – has something of that understanding. Lawrence's final paragraph in his final book, *Apocalypse*, reads:

> What we want is to . . . re-establish the living organic connections, with the cosmos, the sun and the earth, with mankind and family. Start with the sun, and the rest will slowly, slowly happen . . .[3]

In our case, finding our centres and using Duke's scheme, which so perfectly mirrors the process of 'stumbling into awareness' that everyone has upon the spiritual paths as we find our centres, we can paraphrase it to read instead, 'Start with the *Earth . . .*'

It all springs from there.

The medium Grace Cooke founded the White Eagle Lodge in 1936 in order to channel the teachings of its eponymous Native American spirit guide. Visiting Silbury Hill almost a century after Edward Duke, she too sensed the peculiar quality that seemed to make Silbury the natural centre of a universe, the perfect meeting point for man and his gods, and the *axis mundi* around which all else turned. If the Reverend Edward Duke liked women at all, he might have liked Grace. As she climbed the hill without any previous notions as to its history or archaeology, her stated intention was to use her psychism to discern something of the inner life of ancient Britain. As Duke had felt, this was clearly the place to begin.

> I felt a magnetic attraction towards this hill; it was drawing me and I wanted to climb to the top and hastened to do so. Once up there, a magnificent view of the surrounding country-side opened out, but most striking to me was a bird's-eye view of the lines of stones of Avebury which looked as though they had first been laid out in the form of a curving serpent. From above it was apparent that many of the larger stones were missing,

but sufficient of the smaller monoliths remained to give me the impression that this may have been the site of some so-called serpent-worship of prehistoric time, about which I had once read. We felt a power so strong that we had to linger at the top. For some reason, in spite of the cold March day, it no longer felt cold or blustery . . .[4]

She was not the only one to have been struck by the odd atmosphere that surrounds this mound, springing up as it does from beside the busy A4, and into your awareness like something rising from the sea. Paul Devereux, the level-headed, judicious and often inspired researcher of the earth mysteries, also felt that the key to unlocking the whole Avebury complex was held by Silbury Hill, and was aware that the place became his teacher, often feeding him with information and illuminations just below the threshold of consciousness, and once actually speaking to his inner ear the words, 'In this Mystery shall we dwell.'

The voice, he felt, was feminine.[5]

As I browsed through the existing literature on visionary experience at ancient sites, Silbury's pure and bewildering image tended to linger in my mind long after the books were put away, and I had turned my conscious mind to less esoteric topics. It seemed to lurk, for lack of a better word. Rationally, in a world where we know that the earth revolves around the Sun, there seemed little advantage in adopting Duke's scheme, where the Sun orbited the earth. But, as Paul Devereux sensed, Silbury became the key to everything. If it whispered to him, 'In this Mystery shall we dwell' it seemed to whisper to me, on the edge of sleep, 'Look here. Begin *here!*'[6]

As Mike Harris, the magus of the Avalon Group, emphasised, you don't always need to be at these places in the flesh for them to affect you. Speaking in purely magickal terms he noted:

I was 'inwardly persuaded' some years ago that one does not have to necessarily be *at* prehistoric sites [to work magick]. As long as one can intuitively locate a suitable location (meridian?) one simply needs to set up a pattern of milky quartz (small bits, no JCB necessary) and get on with it. Our Celtic forefathers realised how you could do this 'in miniature' playing Bronze Age games of sovereignty on a Gwyddbwyll board in doors out of the rain!

Playing games with quartz on a Gwyddbwyll board is not something I am ever likely to do, but I have no doubt from my own experiences, as well as those of many others we will meet throughout this book, that certain places can force themselves into your mind in quite unexpected ways. He added:

> We can learn a lot about this from our ancestors, not least on a technical level. They had, for example, a profound knowledge of geo-physics and the relationship between the human physical and psychic constitution and the earth's electromagnetic field. In fact one may find oneself drawn to, for example, a Bronze Age site . . . to receive instruction. Such instruction may be 'on site' not simply because the appropriate inner contact is located there, but because the site itself has the technical facility and power linkages through which 'hands on' experience may be provided . . . a bit like teaching physics in the school laboratory as opposed to the classroom!

Now the term 'inner contact' tends to be used by magicians to describe a psychic, mind-to-mind link with discarnate entities. Through this type of awareness it seems that we can learn, as mystics and magicians have always insisted, the universe within us. The best way to explore it is by turning inward, and travelling inside.

And it quickly became clear that if there was any logical and outer place to begin an irrational study of the inner and illogical history of a landscape, then it had to be at Silbury Hill.

People learn about Silbury almost coincidentally. They come to study the huge stones at Avebury but inevitably end up staring mutely at the conical riddle of the largest man-made mound in Europe.

And, oddly enough, despite almost unanimous agreement among modern mystics that this was the main focus for the mysteries of the whole area, there is very little folklore attached, and almost nothing in the way of haunting – except for the usual one about King Sil (or Zel, as Wiltshire folk pronounced it) riding headless around its base. In fact a number of psychics, while offering visions of other sites, felt that there something about the hill that actually inhibited spontaneous vision. Almost as though the hill itself stopped it, soaked it up. Intriguingly, the psychic Olive Pixley insisted that this was actually the very essence of Silbury's purpose: it had been built by those who wished to disintegrate evil 'magnetic influences'.

Of which more later.

Silbury is odd – even in the context of the megaliths that saturate the area. It sits next to the busy A4, still known as the London Road, a short distance from the Avebury complex of stone circles and avenues and six miles (10km) or so from the busy town of Marlborough – whose college contains a large Silbury-type mound which some enthusiasts believe to be the true site of Merlin's grave.

Statistically we can make short shrift of it: Silbury is a man-made truncated, flat-topped cone in shape with slopes of 30 degrees, 40 metres (130 feet) high with a single terrace 5 metres (16½ feet) below the summit, and a diameter of 160 metres (525 feet) at the base. In all, almost half a million tonnes of chalk was used in its creation, covering an area of 2.2 hectares (about 5½ acres).

Facts that work upon the mind and conjure up . . . nothing at all.

In terms of myth and legend, which touch upon the main concerns of this book, locals have insisted for several hundred years at least that the golden-armoured King Sil was buried in a gold coffin, or on horseback, deep within. On certain nights, usually when the moon was high, he could often be seen riding around his hill. The standard sort of haunting, in fact.

In terms of etymology, the whole notion of King Sil within, smiling upon such antics, may well be a red herring. It has been argued that this being was created in recent centuries by the need to find a rationale for the mound, and that 'Zel' or 'Sil' is derived from a range of languages from Old Norse, through Old Teutonic, to one of the British Celtic tongues, and

20

meaning variously Harvest Festival, Happy, Blessed or Holy. Another idea is that 'Sil' is derived from 'Suil', or 'Sul', which is Celtic for 'eye' or 'seeing', making it, in a sense, a 'hill of vision'.

In terms of archaeology, evidence suggests that Silbury Hill was built in the twenty-seventh century BCE,* during what has been defined as the Late Neolithic period. This makes it older than the stone circles at Avebury and Stonehenge, and contemporary with the 4th Dynasty pyramids in Egypt. It is older than the Temple of Ceres in Paestum and the Temple of Apollo in Corinth; and, by the time the Temple of Saturn was first erected in Rome, Silbury Hill was already 2,000 years old

In terms of its modern history, the antiquarian John Aubrey visited the mound in 1623 and felt that it was an ancient mausoleum. William Stukeley drew it some fifty years later and told how a rotting male skeleton was unearthed from under the summit, which some believed to have been Zel himself. Then in 1776 the Duke of Northumberland hired miners to dig a shaft into its core, which yielded nothing but an old piece of timber. In 1849, meanwhile (possibly watched by Edward Duke, although no one knows for sure), another attempt was made to unearth the 'secret' by digging a tunnel into the base of the hill, where they found no more than an inner mound some 2 metres (6½ feet) high and 20 metres (65 feet) in diameter.

No gold-clad king. No riches.

But this particular excavation provoked a spectacular and violent thunderstorm which crashed and echoed among the hills with a terrifying intensity, the likes of which no one could recall in their lifetime. The common folk, who watched from the sidelines when Silbury (or any ancient barrow) was being raped, smiled because they knew that supernatural forces were always unleashed when you did this – even if these forces had been, as the vicars constantly preached, superseded by the powers inherent in Christianity.

Even the architect John Wood experienced something of this

* Before the Common Era, an often preferred term to BC.

21

in 1740 when he tried to make a plan of the circles at Stanton Drew in Somerset, commenting:

> A storm accidentally arose just after, and blew down part of the Great Tree near the Body of the Work, the People were then thoroughly satisfied that I had disturbed the Guardian Spirits of the metamorphosed Stones.[7]

In fact one of the common and almost primary experiences of almost all my correspondents was this unleashing of storms when the sacred sites were, in some way, touched. Far from being a curious side issue, it seemed to me that these sudden and freak explosions of unlikely weather were an integral part of those Earth Energies that we will look at more and more as our journey progresses, and that it might be wise to start by looking at these sorts of experience first. Rather like descending towards a planet through its atmospheres, and understanding its storms. Then, as I sat wondering which and how many of such examples to use, I received a letter from a man in Essex who used the pen-name 'Gareth Knight', which just about summed it up.

Gareth Knight is a magician. He has been practising High Magick of an essentially Christian kind for an exceedingly long time, now. His many books on the Qabalah, on Ritual Magick, Merlin and the Holy Grail will prove in the decades to come to have had a subtler and far greater impact on the spiritual life of the late twentieth and early twenty-first centuries than current observers realise.

I first saw him working magick at the Hawkwood College in the mid-1980s. And during the rite, when under the full flow of the Merlin archetype, he looked at me. He looked right at me and into me, and through me. But it wasn't Gareth Knight from Essex behind his eyes. It was, I *knew*, the Merlin himself. The Merlin of Britain. And I *saw* forests and wild lands, and hidden glades, and forgotten worship, and felt the staggering sense of age, and Ages stretching backwards, and I was startled by the sense that this blunt being behind the mortal eyes was not quite human, or more than human, and that it somehow knew me, from a long time ago.

'Gareth Knight', however, is a very straightforward, very human mage, and like all real adepts he is immensely down-to-earth. His letter touched upon his own excursions to particular sites and the experiences he and his family had.

On one occasion I went, accompanied with my wife and children, to seek out the original site of the bluestones that comprise the innermost circle of Stonehenge. They form the horseshoe formation at the centre of Stonehenge in contrast to the local Sarsen stones that form the bulk of the monument of trilithons and marker stones. The bluestone outcrop occurs in the far west of South Wales in Pembrokeshire, near the end of one of the oldest green trackways in the British Isles . . .

We struggled up the ancient track that led to the heights where the blue-green outcrops of intrusive igneous Ordovician dolerite are to be found. Eventually we reached the top, and making our way along the ridge finally arrived at the site of the bluestones. As we did so, the heavens opened!

Such a squall of wind and rain lashed into us that within seconds we were soaked to the skin, despite protective clothing. It was a literal baptism almost by total immersion.

Such was the strength of the storm that as it swept across the Irish Sea it completely wrecked many vessels in the famous Fastnet yacht race. It was the most severe storm that had been experienced for years. However, it was the timing of it that most impressed me. For just at the moment we reached the rocks so it hit us in the face. I only hope that those poor yachtsmen were not wrecked simply as a consequence of my having a windy and watery greeting from Merlin.

On the way up the mountain I had wondered why it was that the heather had not grown over the path, for it seemed not to be overmuch used. On the way down, I realised why; on rainy days the path was a raging stream.

I rest my belief on causation being on another level. It was not me that caused these storms, nor the storms that caused me subliminally to act in sympathy with their coming, like animals getting edgy before an earthquake. Rather I think that some level of causation was acting upon me and upon the weather at the same time.

On another occasion, he and his wife were researching a curious, myth-ridden outcrop on Alderley Edge. At a place where the face of the magician Merlin is carved into the rock, and a spring drops water from the rock into a shallow pool below, they had no sooner read the carved words,

> Drink of this and take thy fill
> For the water falls by the Wizard's will

than on an otherwise bright April day it suddenly started to snow, and thickly too.

He cited other remarkable experiences too, in New York and Paris, all tied in with particular inner work or intentions of his at the time, but he finished with the comment:

> We live, in other words, on the plane of effects. What causes these effects remains a matter for metaphysical conjecture. Just on occasion, it feels as if one might be a pawn in some other higher being's chess game. And the burst of bad weather might be the way by which some higher being announces 'Checkmate!'

In the same vein, when Elizabeth Anderton visited Arbor Low on 1 May, or Beltaine, she started fooling about on the central stones – and immediately regretted it, as she wrote to me:

> ... something made me turn and from the north was a dark black wall, and in seconds we were engulfed by darkness, a howling wind and a storm of rain and very large hailstones. There was no shelter, I tried to shield behind a larger stone but it felt as if I was being flayed by the hail ...

And quite apart from numerous local examples of storms coming out of nowhere when tumuli were opened, or sacred places pried into, Howard Carter's team had the same experience when they opened the tomb of the boy Pharaoh, Tutankhamun, and all Egypt seemed to suffer.

So the first and simplest observation to be learned is that certain ancient sites are somehow connected to energies – earth and sky energies if you like – which can make themselves felt in the most dramatic of ways, and always unexpectedly.

Silbury obviously had the same lurking effect on the collective consciousness of the archaeologists as it had on me when I started this book, because the digging continued even after nothing was found. In the 1920s the great archaeologist Sir Flinders Petrie turned his attention from Ancient Egypt and made an attempt to find the entrance to the inner chamber within Silbury, but had no luck. Then in 1968 Richard Atkinson, sponsored by the BBC programme *Chronicle*, went further into the core than anyone and found . . . nothing very much at all: a large tooth plus a piece of vertebra from, it was thought, a bull, pieces of twine, insect remains, snail shells. This may not seem very much but Gareth Knight, again, pointed out that the significance of the snail shells is within their internal spirals, wherein we find:

> . . . a revolution or unwinding out of a central point to bring forth life. And to go back to consciousness of origins one can follow the spiral in reverse direction, boring a contemplative hole to the very origin of the centre of things. This is not a lesson that lends itself easily to verbal description, but those who wish may find a surprising amount of revelation if they take the trouble to contemplate an actual snail's shell – studying the lessons and patterns of nature as our remote forerunners did.

At the heart of the mystery, in the centre of this odd cosmos we are trying to explore, lie some spirals and a piece of a bull. Remember those two images in the chapters to come.

In fact, if we use the image of the spiral rather than the rigid meridian of Edward Duke, and start to curve out from the heart of Silbury, we will notice that certain themes and images return again and again, but on differing levels each time, and in such a way that we might find ourselves being taught things, at odd and subliminal levels. The reader might find, as I did, that images and atmospheres relevant to geographically distant sites come creeping into the back of their mind and lurk there.

But, of course, those people who ripped into the belly of

THE KING IN THE HILL – OSIRIS IN THE SACRED MOUND

Silbury Hill in the full glare of the television cameras, hoping to pull the golden figure of Sil out into the light of another aeon, made one mistake as far as the modern capacity for creating and re-creating myths went: they did not go below ground level. That is, they allowed the possibility that Sil might yet be there, below ground level, still sleeping and dreaming and waiting to be reborn, safe within the amniotic fluid of our collective unconscious: the God within the Hill, waiting.

Although we will come back to this idea of the Sleeping God, or the God within the Land, later, the real irony can be seen from Sil's angle: while Duke, Petrie, Atkinson and others like them went on to or into the hill in search of his remains, in a sense it was almost as if he were the one who, by circling the hill in spirit like some ancient magician, summoned, stirred and called *them* up – all those diggers and measurers and visionaries who, through their researches into Silbury, were to make the land pregnant once more with the New Age mysteries.

This, I believe, is the real significance of Sil, and that priest with his strange dog who came into the West Kennet Long Barrow at dawn, and all those bright and dark spirits and gods glimpsed at these sites by the occultists that follow: they wake up something within ourselves that draws us to the sacred places. As we shall see, it is not so much that we are going looking for them, but that they are summoning us.

So in many ways, used as we are to the presence of gigantic, mysterious structures around the world, both ancient and modern, and often unconsciously holding the notion that the potency and wonder of a structure are directly proportional to its size, this treasureless Silbury can be a disappointment. No one and nothing of obvious material importance was found within. Nor does it have any of the staggering features that the more famous stone structures can summon. The fact that it is the largest man-made structure from that period in Europe can fall flat under the perception that here is something that was obviously well within the technology of Neolithic society.

The question 'how?' that is provoked by the Great Pyramid and Stonehenge is rarely asked of Silbury Hill, because the engineering skills demanded at Silbury were both obvious and attainable. Magick, levitation, extraterrestrial energies and intelligences never came into the equation, because, quite simply, chalk was taken from the encircling quarries using deer-antler picks, shovels made from wood or the shoulder bones of oxen, and transported a short distance in baskets using what we suppose to be willing labour.

Playing number games, it has been determined that four hundred people working ten hours a day could have finished it in ten years. Or, more realistically given the hunting, farming and herding needs of the community, four hundred people offering three months of work on it every year would finish such a hill in forty years.

An impressive amount of labour, yes, but nothing compared with the work involved in building Stonehenge, or the Pyramids. No real mystery there at all, except when we start to wonder why and try to deal with the niggling effect that primal and evocative image of Silbury Hill can have upon our consciousness: the gleaming white stepped cone rising from the green levels, the causeways crossing the surrounding water-filled moat, and the whole structure catching and reflecting the light from the sun, moon or stars, depending on the rite . . .

For as we, on the brink of another age, summon up that potent image we cannot help but catch a sense of the wonder they must have felt when it was finished, and how it would

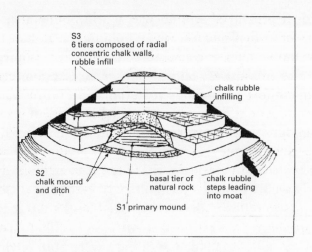

S3
6 tiers composed of radial
concentric chalk walls,
rubble infill

chalk rubble
infilling

S2
chalk mound
and ditch

basal tier of
natural rock

chalk rubble
steps leading
into moat

S1 primary mound

BLOCK DIAGRAM OF SILBURY HILL

have seemed to them the most futuristic structure in the world, hinting at consciousness yet to come.

Hinting at ourselves.

And really, this is where the true Mystery begins ...

There has been a long tradition among occultists, psychics and visionaries that, in brief, links ancient British sites with what might be termed Outsiders: usually Atlanteans from the West, or Egyptian astronomer-priests from the East. Not all have this belief, but a surprisingly high number do, as we shall see – and not all have gone looking for it.

Perhaps, using an unconscious kind of psychometry of the sort that can find lost objects, they were intuiting the inner structure of Silbury Hill itself. Terence Meaden described this in his book *The Goddess of the Stones* as a 'gleaming white stepped cone with a broad flat top, surrounded by a ditch nearly ten metres deep spanned by two chalk causeways...'[8]

Silbury, in brief, is a hidden pyramid. It is contemporary with the great pyramid-building era of Egypt itself.

Now, although I had read everything I could about Silbury over the years, this was one obvious fact that had eluded me, and clearly refused to register at the time. I knew, for example, that barrows are invariably built in a specific way, using alternative layers of organic and inorganic materials around a

28

specifically constructed central core. But I assumed that Silbury was another such structure, though on a huge scale.

So becoming aware of the inner nature of Silbury quite startled me, and in the synchronistic way of things seemed to trigger all sorts of outward events pointing in this direction: letters from people who had – like Grace Cooke – seen Egyptians, or mysterious Outsiders who may have been Egyptian, at the Silbury/Avebury complex; chance findings of obscure books and texts that sought to advance this thesis; folklore about Gypsy Lanes really being 'Gyptian Lanes, or whippets being derived from Wepawet (the Egyptian god known as the Opener of the Way); and even dear old Edward Duke loomed up to flaunt his learning by trying to show (wrongly) how certain local place names were derived from Egyptian god names.

There seemed no end to it at one point, and as I sat brooding in my Wiltshire home I found that a large portion of my psyche was locked into the realms of Nuit and Geb, the Star Goddess and Earth God respectively.

For example, I received a letter from someone who chose to use the pen name Jack Green, who described himself as a follower of the Wiccan path, and who told me of a persistent vision relating to the top of Silbury, when he 'saw' a group of men crouching on the top step.

> I don't know *what* they were doing. They wore heavy fur cloaks, so I suppose it must have been winter, and they were looking out to the north-west, I think. They were crouching in the teeth of a stiff wind. The whole air was that they were checking something out to see if the thing [Silbury Hill] was working, somehow. Don't know how. It was almost as if they were engineers of some sort, making sure everything was just right. I had a feeling that at least one of them wasn't from this country. Egypt? Can't say . . .

Then, in Trowbridge Reference Library, Paul Devereux's book *Symbolic Landscapes* almost literally fell off the shelf at me when I was looking for something else. Used to this kind of serendipity by now, I opened it to find a rather odd connection between Silbury Hill and its biggest contemporary, the Great

Pyramid itself: 'The angle of slope of the Great Pyramid is between 51° and 52°. Silbury's location is between 51° and 52° of latitude. Conversely, Silbury's 30° angle of slope echoes the Great Pyramid's line of latitude at 30 north . . . [and] the coincidence does not end there.'[9]

In fact the whole notion of Egypt-within-Britain came to obsess me to such an extent that I was in danger of losing track of my original aim: to present the visions of people from a wide range of traditions, without imposing my own ideas.

So although these Outsiders – whether they are Atlanteans, Siriuns, Martians, Egyptians, Mayans or even a mysterious race of technologically advanced beings known as the Watchers – will necessarily crop up again, I have studiously tried to stop them from building any firm foundations in this narrative at least.

Besides, it has to be said that Ross Nichols, the former Arch Druid, firmly rejected *any* idea that the ancient British sites were built by anyone other than the ancient British. In fact, in keeping with that spiral pattern that underlies all of the present themes and their manifestations through time, and that sees old turnings spin into new truths, there is always the possibility that our guide, the Reverend Edward Duke, may have been right about the Druidic origin of the megalithic sites: there is an increasing conviction that Druidism is actually pre-Celtic, and was adopted by the Celts of Gaul and Britain from the earlier peoples among whom they settled. One theory is that the word 'Druid' is derived from 'derw' (oak) and 'gwydd' (man of wisdom). Another is that is derived from the Irish 'drui', which is invariably translated as wizard or magician. So, as viewed by the Roman commentators, the megaliths were built by the magicians of those people who lived around them.

Psychologically, sacred mounds or hills in any tradition, whether man-made or entirely natural, are places where Heaven and Earth can touch, where humanity can ascend towards divinity.

But again, what are these sacred mounds actually for, other than collective worship? Are the 'spiritual mechanics' involved in their creation no more than deeply felt but largely symbolic gestures towards the god or goddess of the tribes? Or did they actually do something? Why are so many of such mounds essentially empty? Did they – do they – represent in purely psychological (i.e. sub-magickal) terms the sort of sterile, barren earth that we need to fertilise and reseed through our powers of magick and imagination? In practical terms the lives of the people in those distant times were so short, so hard, and the labour required so intense that it is hard to imagine so colossal a task being undertaken without a tangible and measurable benefit to the tribes in the entire area.

Is that an entirely modern, selfish attitude? Or can we, by using the atavistic yet eternal talents of vision, come a little closer to the truth?

I mentioned earlier the psychometric opinion of the late Olive Pixley, who felt that Silbury had been raised by those who wished to disintegrate evil forces that had been induced and practised there. Olive Pixley was a friend of John Foster Forbes, the writer and broadcaster, who took another talented medium, Iris Campbell, to visit various sites throughout Britain, and recorded her psychometric impressions, being careful not to fill her with too much – if any – information about what Olive had already seen. Now Iris's vision related not to Silbury as such but to the Bass of Inverurie or Dun Abbas, meaning 'Mound of Death' – a large and conical mound with a smaller one lying next to it in the heart of Aberdeenshire. Forbes felt that this was 'in no way dissimilar' to other such mounds at Durham, Windsor, the Tower of London, Oxford, Bishop's Stortford and Silbury itself. According to Miss Campbell's vision, here was a site where malign magick was practised by a race of people akin to the semi-human Firbolgs of Irish mythology. These people were in themselves monstrosities, she felt: 'Men with huge exaggerated bulging bodies, especially round the middle, tiny heads and small arms and hands, taking on strange and hideous forms'.[10] They created two structures which used and magnified the magickal energies found in the elements of earth and water, to summon, almost hypnotically, like the Morlocks in HG Wells's novel *The Time Machine*, humans and animals from miles around, like flies to a spider's web, whereupon they were slaughtered. But this is where Silbury comes into it again. We might imagine the evil structures of these basses as akin to the round tumulus at the heart of Silbury. Because according to Miss Campbell's continuing vision, the Druids came along and managed to:

> overlay in a circular form a great mound of super-imposed earth so as to frustrate and dissipate the evil magnetism . . . On top of these mounds the later Druids wrought their own white magick and closed over forever the evil influences beneath these mounds. And so they remain inviolate to this day, for all efforts to unlock their secrets have failed; no burials have been found, no altars to past gods, and so they will remain until the end of this age.[11]

Iris Campbell and Foster Forbes were having their own respective visions in the late 1930s. They would not have been able to draw upon the analogy of Chernobyl to describe the need to cover and thus suppress the demonic, mutant, uncontrolled energies radiating blackly and bleakly from the cores of these now sacred hills.

So according to Messrs Campbell, Pixley and Forbes, these places certainly did something in the first place. It was only later, when their influences were undone, that they became places of worship in the more usual sense.

Visions, of course, which are what this book is about, can be perceived through intellect and feelings, as well as the *ajna chakra* – the 'third eye' – of the mystic. They can be poetic and artistic as much as magickal, and have a far-reaching impact upon society at large.

It was Michael Dames who, almost single-handed, imposed his vision upon Silbury Hill and presented it to a feminising world that was entirely ready to accept it. To him the 'vision' of Silbury Hill was one of unity – of the land and its people – with the huge sloping mound clearly seen as the pregnant belly of the Great Mother. He presented this image of the pregnant belly so elegantly and persuasively in his book *The Silbury Treasure* that this has become accepted almost without question, to such an extent that women's groups devoted to the mysteries of their sex regularly dance naked on the summit, in honour of the goddess.

Yet as we have seen he was not quite the first to give the hill a determinedly feminine character, for our friend Edward Duke saw it as Mother Earth, at the centre of the cosmos, with the moon, sun and stars encircling her . . .

Which makes us ask of folk tradition and modern magick whether Silbury Hill and other Hills of Vision are inevitably centres of the goddess, as much of the New Age movement in the latter part of the twentieth century has insisted.

Folk tradition, which is inextricably linked to the Second Sight, is quite clear on this matter and records the sacred hills, hill forts and stone circles as having been created by the Old Gentleman, Old Nick, the Dark Man. The Devil himself. According to local tradition Silbury was built with supernatural speed, 'while a posset of milk was seething', which might well be a dim echo, passed down through the generations, of tribal smugness over how quickly the mound had been created, millennia before. In one of the tales the people of Devizes and Marlborough have quarrelled, and the Devil agreed to help the latter by dropping a mound of earth on Devizes. However, thanks to the help of the wily St John, who happened to be passing Devizes, the Devil was tricked into dropping the load in open countryside – hence Silbury Hill.

Oddly enough, this almost exactly matches the creation stories of the eldritch Meon Hill, in the Cotswolds, and Cley Hill, near Warminster. Both places were once crowned by substantial hill forts, and both were linked in Christian eyes with the Devil and/or witchcraft. Cley Hill was believed to contain a golden ram in contrast to the golden figure of King Zel. Once again the Devil was on his way to drop a huge load of earth on to the hapless and presumably Christian folk of Devizes, but was duped – once again – into dropping it before the intended target, thus forming Cley Hill.

All such hills are, in effect, 'Devil's Earth', and linked to worship that was ancient when Christianity first came to this country, but that in subtle ways still affects us today.

Witches once danced on these places, secretly, silently.

They still do. But sometimes they use ghettoblasters, and go for every sound bite they can get.

Arthur O'Neil was one person who was drawn into the mysteries of a particular 'Hill of Vision' sharing this same provenance, and who found himself involved in synchronistic events leading him to climb the pagan centre of the aforementioned Cley Hill on the edge of the Longleat Estate in Wiltshire. His journey, which was dominated by the image of a lunar crescent that appeared time and again in striking but unexpected ways, culminated in an exquisite vision when he sat atop the hill on the barrow, which (unknown to him at the time of writing) was said to be the home of Bugley, the King of Faery:

> The cool air was like nectar. The pain in my head had subsided and it felt now as if a pair of hands were pushing fingers into the back of my head. I had a sensation of having a golf ball under each armpit. I closed my eyes and immediately I received a 'vision'. I was amazed because I had never had anything like it before. It was objective enough to convince me that it was not being produced by my mind. I 'saw' a spider's web which was huge and at the centre of the web was a rose, partly opened and I think the colour was pink. I say 'think' because I didn't know enough at the time to write it down and now the colour evades me although it was fresh in my mind for a few years after. A name was whispered to me. 'Ariadne', which I didn't know so I tried to change to Ariane because I had heard of a French rocket of that name. I described it out loud to the others as it was happening. It felt like a gift by way of compensation after suffering that bloody massive headache for a large part of the day. After a short while we returned to the camp site where two horses neighed at each other all night long.

Ariadne? Or more truly Arianrhod – whose name means 'silver wheel'? Robert Graves felt that they were one and the same, with the 'silver wheel' being an image of the spider's web.

I think I may have seen her myself, sitting on the same barrow on top of what is traditionally the home of the Horned

God. In fact it was he I wanted to summon: Bugley, whose name is a corruption of bwcca/pooka/pook/Puck. The barrow itself, when opened in the last century by Richard Colt-Hoare, contained nothing but some ears of wheat, in keeping with many such structures. No great god-king was ever buried there, yet, as with Silbury Hill, local tradition fills it with a very powerful spirit indeed.

When I went there to experience the sunrise on 1 May, Beltaine, I saw the mists covering the lower land as the shallow sea had once done in the most ancient of days, when ichthyo-sauri swam under the waves. And when the rising sun and setting moon were level in the sky and forming the two 'eyes' of heaven I had the fullest and most unexpected vision of the goddess within the little hill below, which I privately thought of as the Moon Place. I had glimpsed her briefly before, and thought of her as having oddly grey hair – the hair of an old, old lady – despite her young features and immensely attractive presence. This time I realised it was actually silver hair, flowing, the colour of the moon, as the mound seemed to open and she appeared at its gate for a while, beautiful. There was no name, no voice, no inner voice, no other revelations beyond a sense of acknowledgement.

I came down from the heights, and I was lost for words.

Paganism, in the broadest sense, is one of the most proliferating forms of worship today, yet in Duke's time any overt forms of this worship had long since disappeared. Even so, Silbury remained the focus of celebrations on Palm Sunday which attracted folk from miles around.

'The roads for some little distance at the foot of the hill were occupied with stalls, on which were for sale such articles as toys, sweets, nuts, ginger beer, and more particularly flat round gingerbread cakes not gilded nor of human shape . . .'[12] They sat on the slopes and ate cakes, or figs, and drank sugared water (or ale if the vicar wasn't watching), and youths of both sexes and rival villages would race down the slopes on crude wooden sledges, ripping their kecks to pieces when they weren't indulging in traditional Wiltshire pastimes such as wrestling, racing or heavy petting amid the gorse. And, if the common folk knew who (or what) was the real power within the mound, they also knew that the Old Ones at least didn't frown upon fun and joy within their holy places.

Other 'holy hills', such as Cley Hill near Warminster and Martinsell Camp between Oare and Wootton Rivers, boasted very similar festivities – all of them appealing to the common folk, and with a very strong tendency to what the clergy felt was rowdiness and bad or lewd behaviour. On the steep slopes of Martinsell Camp, for example, youths raced each other down on toboggans made from the skulls or jawbones of horses, in a clear echo of the pagan horse cult that dominated this area for thousands of years.

All these places are what might be termed 'places of power', and seem to have inner lives of their own and, as we shall see, can trigger off bewildering experiences within the individual at the most unexpected times. Like the Glastonbury Festivals of today, they also held attractions for young people that established religion could not match, and who were often drawn to them with a delight and passion that the clergy both envied and feared.

In many ways, as the Reverend Edward Duke rightly surmised, Silbury was the focus of it all, and the place where ancient trackways ended and began.

So as we touch upon the heart of the Earth Mysteries we might do well to remember that the ancient peoples did not always see the Sun as male and the Moon as female, or regard the Sky and Earth as eternally male and female respectively. There is folklore from all nations equating the Sun with the feminine principle, whereas the term 'Man in the Moon' is too well known to need comment. Early Egyptian lunar deities such as Thoth, Khonsu and Osiris were all masculine, as was Geb the Earth God. The sky, in contrast, was ruled by the goddess Nu, or Nuit.

Two dowsers who recently followed what they perceived as a ley line stretching across the country had a glimpse of Silbury at dawn on 1 May. As they stood tuning into the energies and atmosphere, aware of extraordinary weather effects caused by the showers and shafting sunlight, they became aware of this sexual ambivalence of Silbury. One moment it was a 'great green breast rising from a shifting, shadowy body', the next a 'golden cone glowing in the sun'.[13] Perhaps that is the true nature of this enigmatic mound: 'male/female, quintessential One'. Like the hermaphroditic freshwater snails whose shells were found placed in abundance atop Silbury's inner mound, the most ancient deities were often complete within themselves; they impregnated and they also gave birth. Like the archetypal Primeval Mound which once emerged, glistening, from the pure darkness of everlasting night, Silbury Hill should not be limited by mere gender and agenda.

In this enigmatic place of the earth, and therefore that centre of the mind from where the earth mysteries themselves could be said to spring, it may be appropriate to look at how one influential writer defined the very notion of 'earth force'.

It was Guy Underwood, from the small Wiltshire town of Bradford-on-Avon, who proposed that there was 'some powerful cosmic force which covers the surface of the earth as do gravity and light.'[14] This was the 'geodetic' law as he termed it – recognised by early man but almost completely ignored in this scientific age. He believed it influenced animal, vegetable and human life, and that early man used it to create the prehistoric monuments of Britain. Underwood died in 1964 at the age of 81, and today (as with many frontrunners in the rediscovery of the Mysteries) his ideas are largely ignored or even derided – perhaps because they are too complex in their expression. A reassessment of his important book *The Pattern of the Past* is well overdue. I first read the book in America, when it came out, and retained over the years a hazy memory of the 'geodetic forces' he described. When I reread it twenty years later, I was stunned to find that he had found his first 'blind spring' through dowsing, almost at the end of the street in which I lived.

His inner perceptions found expression through the rod of the water diviner rather than the Third Eye of the psychic. He learned how to locate underground streams by tuning into the lines of influence above them. But with practice his sensitivity went a stage further, and in the course of his trials two further types of line emerged, which were similar to water lines but took independent courses. These he called 'aquastats' and 'track lines', with the generic term for all three types being 'geodetic lines'. He came to believe that all prehistoric tracks and roads were aligned on track lines, whereas the aquastats were most involved in the layout of religious monuments. Practically every detail of the latter structures was governed by aquastats. 'For example, aquastats dictated whether the enclosing ditch of a monument should be outside the mound (as at Stonehenge) or inside (as at Avebury). They also determined the position, size and shape of every stone, and whether it should be standing, recumbent, or tilted.'[15] When he progressed to the discovery that aquastats and track lines produced secondary linear effects which sometimes affected the layout of temples, he felt that he had become involved not so much in archaeology as in ' . . . some strange, complex, and incomprehensible branch of physics.'

These primary lines (water, aquastat and track) had much in common, he felt:

> . . . they appear to be generated within the Earth; to involve wave-motion; to have great penetrative power; to form a network on the face of the Earth; to affect the germination and manner of growth of certain trees and plants; to be perceived and used by animals; to affect opposite sides of the animal body, and to form spiral patterns. They are controlled by mathematical laws which involve in their construction the number 3; and in their spiral patterns the number 7. They played a prominent and possibly fundamental part in the religion of many widely scattered peoples.[16]

What confuses the whole issue is when these energies, these geodetic forces, become subject to religious considerations. As we have seen, where the ancient sites could not be taken over and Christianised, they were usually regarded as direct creations of the Devil. And so the questions of Good and Evil came into play, and still come into play now as Christians who warn against the Satanic origins of Silbury Hill conflict with modern pagans who laud what they see and feel is its obvious sanctity.

One curious story comes from the reminiscences of William Ernest Butler, widely regarded by all who knew him, or who could read between the lines of his writing, as a magicians' magician. He once described one of the supreme moments of his life as when he first stood forth in the Body of Light ' . . . and knew myself to be the being who used the physical body as his instrument, but the limits of my space have been reached.'[17] He was a subtly influential and rather elemental figure, his unusual books *The Magician – his Training and Work* and *Magick and the Qabalah* exerting a great if unacknowledged impact upon the few hardy souls who kept the light of the native Earth Mysteries alive in the 1960s and 70s.

As a boy of nine, growing up in a small and remote Yorkshire village in the early part of the twentieth century, his first practical experience in the occult arts was when, in 1909, he decided to summon up the powers of a remote and holy mound using an invocation he had found in a magazine. The article was an account of the classic sacrifices offered to the gods, and this awoke in him a fierce desire to offer such a sacrifice in the Roman manner. But where?

He does not name the place but described it as being a tumulus, on top of which was a large unhewn stone, which was said to be the burying place of some old British chieftain set in the moors not so many miles from his (unidentified) village.

Arriving there very early one summer morning, he used the stone as an altar and set alight the paper and twigs. This is how he described it:

> The tumulus lay north and south, and it was to the south I faced as I lit the altar fire and commenced the fairly long invocation. It was now, as the rhythm of the words began to affect me, that I found certain changes taking place in my mind. At first it seemed as if some subtle shadow passed across the sky, and the brilliance of the sun was slightly dimmed, but when I looked up quickly there was no trace of cloud.

Now I became aware of a curious reduction of my personality, as though, in comparison with something which, though not visible, was present with me, I had somehow shrunk in stature. First came the curious dulling of the light, then this curious change of personality, and, following upon these, a feeling of utter helplessness. The fire was almost burnt away, but the red-hot embers on the altar-stone still sent vagrant whiffs of aromatic smoke into the air . . . By now however the bold boy of nine who had dared to invoke the Olympian deities had become a frightened scrap of humanity, around whom veil after veil was falling. The brightness of the day was dimmed by these half-seen shadows, around there pressed the living presence of Evil – fierce and ancient – and the words of the invocation faltered and ceased.

Finding himself surrounded as if in a thick fog, he ran, falling down the tumulus in his haste, and with it the spell broke and warmth and light came back to the moor, leaving a frightened, sweating little boy who, 'though he knew nothing of the Real Presence of Good, had become very conscious of the Real Presence of Evil.'[18]

Much later on in life, when he met his teacher, the latter used his psychic faculties to investigate the record of the past and found that there had existed in that village a very definite witch coven. The actual worship that went on at coven meetings, and that was often held at that tumulus and other such places, was largely a remnant of the old pagan worship, together with the exercise of certain psychic powers. 'These powers,' he added, 'may be used for good or evil purposes, and some of those who were Masters of the covens knew well how to arouse and direct them.' The terror that had seized him as a boy, he felt, was mainly due to the concentrated thought forces that still centred upon the mound in the moor, and could become apparent to anyone who, like himself, had any degree of latent psychic ability.

Nine years old and summoning demons. There haven't been many like him.

An extraordinary addendum to this story comes from Edna Whelan, who has given me kind permission to quote from her as yet unpublished book *Out of the Corner of my Eye*. One particular paragraph caught my own eye not so much in the corner but smack in the centre, in which she describes a visit with three friends to a round barrow, set on the northern edge of the North Yorkshire Moors. While they sunned themselves, unaware of the turmoil within her psyche, she heard a rhythmic chanting from close by, and then a voice inside her brain that said very clearly and plainly, 'Please leave our holy hill.' They left, but while the others forged on ahead she turned to look back at the barrow and commented:

> I was surprised to see numerous tall figures dressed in long creamy white robes and wearing tall head-dresses moving slowly in a circle around the base of the man-made hill in an anti-clockwise direction . . . Immediately as I pondered on these figures, each of them stopped their pacing and turned to face me, raising their arms in an unmistakably peaceful gesture. I was aware of a warm feeling of friendliness and fellowship flowing between us . . .

Her friends called back to ask what she doing and the spell was broken, the figures disappeared.

During the summer of 1986 I was deeply concerned with tracking down fragments of the lost worship that once existed in the valley where we lived, near Bath. For various reasons I felt that the whole area was once devoted to those near-forgotten divinities Beli and Dôn, from whom the major figures in the Ancient British pantheons are descended. I became convinced that the focus of it all lay within a little-known and Silbury-shaped tumulus that was tucked away in the extensive grounds of a large private house, and for a long time this was my own private *axis mundi*, from which I spiralled out to find a whole cosmos of little mysteries in my locality.

On the day I first began trying to learn the magickal secrets of 'Bel's Tump', as I called it, I received an unexpected letter from a complete stranger asking me questions about her own visions involving a hawk, ruby and dragon, while making some passing reference to Merlin also. This type of synchronicity, as we shall see in later chapters, is an integral part of such inner work. You don't need psychic talents or divine inspiration: you just have to make original concerted efforts for things to happen.

Looking back through my diary for the first two weeks in July, I am reminded of myself seeing images of the other sites along the valley, interconnected with lines of light, and then, while trying to link with the inner energies of the mound:

> Had a vision of a broad tree with a whitened bole, and then the Tump itself, a demonic looking creature rising from it. For once, despite the usual *frisson* of fear, I didn't shut it out and demanded, several times, to know its secret.
>
> Then came an extraordinarily long and vivid image of a colossal dragon pouring from the mound, slithering out, vast. Again I felt no fear despite the reality. I knew it was part of me. At my demands to know its secret it crumbled to white powder and bones.

Compared with some of the experiences and insights of the high-grade occultists that we will look at, this is a very modest level of magick indeed, yet more than adequate for my own inner self. But I have to insist that this was more than pictures in the head – hypnagogic or hypnopompic imagery, if you like – but an experience as powerful as if I had wet my fingers and shoved them into an electric socket. There was more to the whole thing than just the dragon: visions of the wheeling cosmos above the Tump – stars, currents in space, and the figure and presence of a king. But these were secondary to that huge outpouring of energy. And, in keeping with the experiences of others, the heavens opened, the thunder roared along the valley, and the torrential rain caused minor floods overnight.

Why the dragon should have crumbled to dust, I just don't know; but I'm reminded that dragons are often used to symbolise the sort of 'Earth Energies' that Underwood attempted to define.

What it all meant, I have no idea. But it lived with me for a long time afterward.

Yet not all occultists *see* things at Silbury Hill, or whatever mound or holy place in their locale becomes central to their inner life. Such places (rather like film stars) attract thoughts, ideas, wishes, longings and all manner of entirely human projections. Sometimes it is difficult to separate the innate energies within a site from that which has been left by the turbulent souls attracted to it, and projecting on to it. Many of the older mystics, for example, are quite repelled by the razzmatazz that has built up around Glastonbury Tor, surrounding it like a psychic cloud, making it difficult at times to get through to the real light within. One who did manage to penetrate that cloud was the American adeptus Marcia Pickands, who commented, 'St Michael's Tower sits on what appears to be a Well of Energy that sort of fountains out of the Tor. Overlaid on that are remnants of consecrated energy patterns that I often see at Holy sites. The Land here has been abused in some ways, but remains very much alive just the same.'

The occultist Murry Hope, never afraid of being controversial, wrote to me of the Tor,

> When it comes to this much publicised (and sadly misused) site I am the heretic par excellence. Give it all the Celtic and Christian significance you like but, to be absolutely frank, it never did nor ever has done anything for me. I would, by nature, tend to be more concerned with sites which carry the stamp of the blueprint for the whole evolutionary cycle of this planet, rather than those which purely emphasise sequences in the hominid religious past!

If, as we said earlier, the psychic Olive Pixley's perception of Silbury is right, that it had indeed been built to disintegrate very evil 'magnetic influences', it would explain why many of the seers are particularly blank about that mound on psychic levels, while still acutely aware that all the mysteries of the area hinge around its slopes.

If nothing else, it is a testimony to the integrity of their powers of vision.

* * *

One story that touches upon these themes, although not directly concerned with sacred hills or megaliths, is from Evan John Jones, one of the early members of the coven known as the Clan of Tubal Cain, and who is now becoming something of the Grand Old Man of the Wiccan movement. While visiting a church in Oxford with the coven's Master, the late Robert Cochrane, he wrote:

> ... it was packed with camera clicking tourists, many of them Japanese. For some reason or other, everyone on the way to the tower stopped and looked in the sunken chapel in the church but didn't go down the half a dozen wooden steps and into the body of the place, which of course made us wonder why. From the doorway it seemed a pleasant enough place, old but not exceptional. Rash souls that we were, we went down the steps and in to it. The atmosphere hit you like a sledgehammer, it was that oppressive. The hair on the back of my neck literally stood up. I looked at Robert, he looked at me, we both looked at Jane then legged it out of there as fast as possible while mentally throwing clouds of golden stars over our shoulders as we went. There was something about the atmosphere that suggested pain, suffering, death and decay and was altogether evil. We didn't scare that easily but in this place we were scared. I'd certainly never felt anything like it in a church before, it was that bad, and was certainly not improved by the few carved effigy tomb slabs propped up against the wall during renovation work. At the time it was suggested that what this place needed was a wedding or two to dispel the atmosphere. Yet a year or two later, I had the chance to visit the place again and felt nothing but peace and tranquillity, the whole atmosphere had changed that much.

So atmospheres can change, and we can change them – for good or ill. On an earlier trip to the Mendips the coven stopped at Silbury itself, and climbed to the top. Cochrane reckoned it was originally a moon-and-water site, but they felt – on that day at least – that the whole place was sterile, probably because: 'Too many people have mucked about with it or climbed all over it, [so] any elemental nature spirit dwelling on the site would be long gone scared off by all the human activity.

You can sometimes actually get this with a working site too. One of ours died when they built a bypass near it. One night it was alive and vibrant, the next, totally dead. You couldn't even raise enough power to fill a triple A battery . . .'

Psychics' responses to places can vary, also, according to their own notions of good and evil. Some are oppressed by the stone circles, others find them liberating. While Grace Cooke may have been horrified by Charles Seymour's vision of human sacrifice at Avebury, his own notions of Willing Sacrifice and Sacred Kingship would have understood it all in a different light. Neither, however, would deny the actual power that each one sensed. He himself may have been unhappy with Grace's perception that the Avebury/Silbury complex was involved in contact with other worlds, but as we shall see there may be different levels of truth involved here.

Ernest Butler's approach to the tumulus on the moor as an old mage (when he had the reputation for being able to deal with awkward, troublesome spirits in a stern, headmasterly sort of way) would have been very different from that as a very young and frightened boy who broke and ran.

Visions are things seen from different angles, with the personality as an imperfect lens. Hills of Vision are themselves often like giant, unpolished crystals: whatever we *see* can be distorted by how the light strikes them.

In the original draft of this book, scribbling my way into an esoteric maze of signs and symbols that seemed writ large upon the ether as well as the Wiltshire countryside, I ventured that the true secrets of the megalithic priesthood would have been concealed within the star lore of the time – secrets that were now lost and irretrievable, except through the merest portion of surviving myth, and hinted at by images of dragons, sacred mountains, goddess webs, lines of light and the stars coming down to the earth . . . As is usually the case when doing such work, however, a book appeared 'as if by magick', which completely refuted my pessimism, and also went some way towards turning these hints into direct statements.

Mark Vidler's important book *The Star Mirror* used

computer analyses of ancient and modern star maps to convincingly analyse the symbolic language encoded in the angles and
alignments of the pyramids on Giza plateau, and extended this
to major sacred sites across the world. This is not one of the
'pyramidiots' using elastic measuring to prophesy on behalf of
the British Empire or the Second Coming in Albion: this is
an inspired visionary using computer science and inescapable
mathematics to draw attention to some irrefutable links. He
summarised: 'What the ancient Egyptian and ancient British
builders achieved was a record for the future, something to be
considered now, an egg that hatches under the light of
Polaris.'[19] As part of this global language and communication
across time he shows that Silbury Hill, at this moment, lies
directly beneath the star Eltanim, which forms one of the eyes
within the constellation of Draco. 'Silbury Hill,' he demon-
strates, 'is a concealed stone pyramid now passing vertically
beneath the brighter eye of the dragon.'[20]

Intriguingly, despite the Reverend Edward Duke's lack of
mysticism, despite a deep if cack-handed scholarship which
drew upon intellect rather than occult insight, and which rather
mocked the ancient mythologies instead of looking at their
hidden meanings, the old vicar was quite firm about the serpentine or draconic nature of the site.

> ... This *compages* of antiquities did represent the Sun and
> Moon (by their temples) traversing the northern portion of the
> Zodiac, designated by the Serpent, and revolving around Silbury
> Hill as denotive of the Earth.[21]

Warming to his own theme, Vidler goes on to insist:

> The Cerne Giant, Glastonbury Tor, Dunkery Beacon,
> Stonehenge, the Peak, Lindisfarne, Peterhead, Silbury Hill, Leith
> Hill and Avebury, all these places are figured on a geometric
> web, and perhaps now as the dragon stars align vertically over
> the high points of Britain, we can more readily recognize the
> conviction driving these ancient builders. They had seen a form
> of God. They had recognized a parallel between the Earth and
> the sky. They made a record for the future, for a time when the

brightest star in history shines over the top of the world, and they moved mountains to communicate this vision.[22]

Another person with a viewpoint similar to this is the psychic surgeon Chris Thomas, who has the ability to see and read energies within the body, the higher self and the planet. He wrote in his brief essay 'Merlin – A Biography' that the ancient sites in Britain and elsewhere were connected with the energy of the planet itself, the ley lines and the energy upwellings. 'This energy,' he wrote, 'could move mountains, could feed us and provide for all our needs. This is real energy, not the pale imitations that we live with today.' With the destruction of Atlantis, Britain became the primary energy feed into the global leyline net. There were energy intake points at (to name just a few) Silbury Hill, Glastonbury and Desborough – 'no longer in use'. Silbury is, he felt, a natural accumulator, or battery, and was actually built as such around 7,000 years ago. He saw it as the primary energy intake point for global energies which came from a source outside of what he termed the 'Orion Gate'.

> The idea was that you followed a sequential route, beginning at Silbury Hill. The 'initiate' was 'bathed' in the Silbury energies to raise their personal energy levels. As they progressed along each stone avenue and circle in sequence they collected the memories programmed into the stones. By the time they arrived at Stonehenge they had a working knowledge of the gateway. The people of this time were able to see and sense energies very easily. At Silbury . . . the energy connected in with the planet's surface structure and created a 'lightening' of the soil's structure. Its visual effect was similar to a lake of water in an open field. More, there were 'energy gates' under the Sphinx, at Teotehuacan, and at Stonehenge, pan-dimensional gateways that were 'designed to assist travel between Earth and the other realms of the universe.'[23]

He learned this by surfing the akashic records as some of us surf the Internet. 'Akashic records' is a term that was largely coined by the early Theosophists to describe an area in the astral plane where everything that has ever happened is stored, and can be viewed. Or not so much viewed, by all accounts, as experienced, so that (for example) William the Bastard's lucky victory in 1066 would be seen, or felt, from his perspective, as if looking out through his eyes.

Echoing Thomas's insights, Tom Graves, through his own work in dowsing the energies of the stones, and from his involvement with magicians who practise their art at or through them, suggested that ' . . . sacred sites are centres which connect up all the earth-fields of a given area, and at the same time connect them with the . . . ley system.' He goes on to warn, however, 'In a personal sense, sacred sites can be mirrors that pick out your flaws, amplify them, and then throw them back at you in a way that forces you to do something about those flaws or go insane.' Even further, he confides: 'magician friends have told me that in their experience both forms of what they call "astral travelling" – projection of the imagination and projection of the entire personality – are made easier by "hitching a ride" on the energy that passes along ley-lines . . .'[24]

One modern would-be shaman, calling himself 'Tellisfree', wrote about touching this network of energy that seemed to be focused upon (he seemed to suggest) Silbury:

> I'd simply built up the image of the hill in my imagination, when I was staying near there one night, with a view to doing some simple path-working or meditation around it. Suddenly I found myself almost ripped out of my body, in full awareness on the astral plane, and to my astonishment found myself being propelled across the landscape, in an absolutely straight line, like a ground-hugging missile, going at enormous speed, although I had no sense of where I was going, except that I felt it was into the past, via another dimension. Eventually I was stopped by a very powerful male figure who told me, by mind to mind contact, that I should not be here, that I was out of place and time. He left me in no doubt that I would be in serious trouble if I tried to go any further.

John Foster Forbes chipped in with the very certain perception that ' . . . all these [ancient sites] were probably interconnected – it seems that the astral bodies could travel while the physical body slept and remember on awaking where they had been.'[25]

Monica Sjöö, the writer and artist who specialises in Goddess-related themes, saw (also while sleeping close to Silbury) a pulsating, light-radiating shape that appeared to her 'organic and moving', which left within her mind an extremely powerful atmosphere that inspired many of her later artworks. She was also one of that historic group that, with Geoffrey Ashe, ritually walked the spiral path from the foot of Glastonbury Tor (another sacred hill) to its summit, while lightning flashed and the heavens made the sound as if great and hidden gates were being dragged open for the first time in aeons – which of course they were.

But, if Chris Thomas's experience touched upon the idea of the 'Outsiders' who were responsible for creating this global network of energy, it also answered the question 'Why?' quite simply: because some of these sacred hills actually did something. They really had, he insists, a practical value for the tribes involved in building them. And one of the figures he felt were very much involved in creating this dormant circuitry was the one he called Merlin.

He was not alone in feeling the presence of this entity when touching on the inner essence of sacred sites: Gareth Knight wrote to me that the odd coincidences he had found when quests and pilgrimages were accompanied by vagaries in the weather all seemed to be ' . . . connected with Merlin or his surrogate as the Lord of Animals . . .'

And Jack Gale devoted a whole chapter to this Otherworld being in his extraordinary book *Goddesses, Guardians and Groves*, which details the research he and his friends have done in the Greenwich area. By this I mean research at all levels, ranging from the archaeological to the psychical, using all faculties from the mundane to the mystical, in order to discover, define and ultimately 'bring through' the indwelling ancient deities of the area. Merlin, whom he initially, and almost coyly (if that's an appropriate word for such a forthright author), called the Man in Black, was experienced as a blunt, no-

49

nonsense, and no-bullshit personality who was intimately involved in the inner life and energies of the 'powerful landscape chakra' known in geographical terms as Greenwich.[26]

And then the synchronicities of this project revealed themselves again with a letter from the shaman-oriented 'Peter Malvern' that landed in my hallway almost at the same moment that I began to tinker with the above paragraphs. He wrote that one of his earliest magickal experiences was in meeting the spirit of Merlin on the Silbury-type barrow in the grounds of Marlborough College, although he declined to go into more detail.

The question of spirits, however, whether they are of King Zel, Merlin or any of the gods or goddesses that spring up like corn, is something that we will look at later on in our journey.

Grace Cooke's statements about the role of the Silbury/Avebury complex in communicating with other planets, written long before Neil Armstrong's small steps and giant leaps, gave me a great sense of unease bordering on scorn when I first read them. In fact, tentative versions of the present book, started several times over many years, always began with a hatchet job on these aspects of her visions, showing her up in a bad light whenever possible. Even after a portrait of her guide White Eagle seemed to apport on to my bed one night when I did a sleep-in at work, I failed to become more charitable or flexible in my attitude. Life on other planets, star people, UFOs, God as an astronaut and all the other extraterrestrial fundamentals of present 'occult' belief have never appealed to me personally because I have never experienced these areas. I was going through one of my rational and probably insufferable phases. Yet it crops up time and again. And mystics that I respect, who have proved their psychic talents over and over, are quite insistent, in differing ways, that we ignore this aspect at our peril.

In fact it was that extraordinary 'paranormalist' Uri Geller who summarised it when he told me that Stonehenge and other sites seem to focus and indeed magnify his own innate (and I believe unquestionable) powers. Powers that he has never been shy to demonstrate again and again, and that he assures us we all have, and can relearn. Yet whether the mechanics for these sites are tied up with the ley lines or geodetic forces in the area, he quietly insisted to me that the true source of their magick is tied up with the stars. That the people who built places like Silbury and Stonehenge were, in some way, using them to link with extraterrestrial energies that we are only just beginning to rediscover.

In fact, hard on the heels of that conversation came a long chat with Ray Bailey, a medium of many years' experience who has always sought to stretch, explore and develop his powers, never let himself be restricted by any dogma, or – much worse in his eyes – become narrowed in his approach by any kind of false religiosity. He is a genial and avuncular man by nature, and I have seen people stunned by demonstrations of his own unique talents, and heard another medium describe him, with a hint of envy, as someone who had 'more spirits around him than anyone I've ever met'. If he talks about chakras and their function, it is because he can see them, and be aware of their function, and not because he has read about them in a book. And, when he gives out hard information that purports to come from some anxious spirit at your shoulder, I have long since learned to listen very carefully to what they have had to say . . .

When I asked him to visit some bowl barrows known as the Bully Hills near his home in Lincolnshire he jotted down his experiences as follows:

We approached from the B153 Louth to Horncastle Road. Where the road rises slightly, and as the 'hills' come into view, momentarily I saw what looked like and felt like light/energy beams from each toward the sky. The whole experience was over in milli-seconds. As we walked toward them (it had rained a few hours previously) I felt a slight tingling through my feet. (I have also had this reaction when dowsing.) Perhaps it could best be described as similar to that which one feels if one touches a low voltage electrical discharge! As we came even closer there was again a feeling of being 'charged'. Much stronger of course at this distance. My impression is that some of these mounds/hills are acting as 'chakras' for the Earth, and may provide a pathway of energy in which the deceased would be carried to the Celestial Gods?

Ray's insight is supported and expanded by that of Tammy Ashcroft-Nowicki, who would have agreed completely with his comment about the 'pathway of energy' rising to the gods – something that we will come back to later, time and again.

Tammy is an acupuncturist who sees her own profession as offering a healthy balance between the scientific and the spiritual, and one that in fact resolves the apparent antipathy between the two. She is also an occultist, with expertise in a wide variety of traditions. Her first experience of Sacred Mounds was when the leader of a Wiccan coven in Dorset (let us call her Melissa) decided to take her to one of the tumuli at Maiden Castle in order to teach her how to 'see' 'one of the live ones', as she termed it. That is, how to recognise a live mound from one that was no longer alive.

Melissa and her husband drove Tammy to the hill just before midnight, as she felt that this was the best time: the land had had a chance to rest, and it was easier to start seeing the energies at night.

'Tell me what you see,' said Melissa, putting Tammy before the tump.

Nothing. Not a thing.

'OK, just carry on; but open your mind and try to look through it. Refocus your eyes as if looking at one of those 3D drawings . . .'

Within minutes things started to happen, and what she saw was 'an intense cobalt-blue light around the mound which sort of undulated, like a huge snake. It was unbelievably bright despite the pitch blackness around.'

'Keep watching,' said Melissa, 'that's only the start.'

'The start of *what*?' cried Tammy.

Then as she watched, astonished, it was as though the mound itself started shifting, as if it had become malleable, no longer a solid lump of heavy earth.

'Then the bloody thing opened up at the top, and blobs of

light, like Roman Candles, seemed to spurt out, while the cobalt-blue light over the top changed into an intense sky-blue while the mound itself became a very bright green.'

'What you're seeing is the ley line,' Melissa explained, touching her shoulder and helping her to close down her psychic faculties for the night. 'That undulating blue light *is* the ley line. They are everywhere. When you see them, you see the life force itself. All life is in it.'

As Tammy came to learn, partly with Melissa's help and partly with her own continuing work with these forces, the ancient peoples used to build their mounds right on a ley. So when they buried their dead in them they were in a place where they could be, as Ray Bailey intuited (using slightly different terms of reference), reborn into the ley itself.

Even more extraordinary, Tammy learned from Melissa how to 'call' the ley. Standing on a height above the Avebury complex she learned how to use her own magnetism to bring the energy towards her: 'It's coming!' said Melissa calmly, and in Tammy's words: 'You could actually see it change course, undulating, like a huge serpent – just as they always said was worshipped here once – and then this brilliant blue light washes over you, this "serpent energy" which is all about Life, and it's a very loving thing, a sense of "Ooh, this is mine, a friend, someone has recognised me!"'

This is powerful imagery: two witches on a sacred height with the rolling hills of Wessex, green as waves, surging before them as they summon the energies of the Great Serpent and watch as it undulates towards them, and they merge with it.

Energies that are both of the earth and of themselves.

Energies that, Tammy insists, we can all learn to work with, starting from our own sacred hills.

I can glimpse my own sacred hill if I lean out of our upstairs window at an unnatural and probably obscene angle. It seems to lurk on the horizon like one of those hares that have figured large within this project, as we shall see. Cley Hill, to give it a name, is one of the most neglected, least known and yet most potent of centres within Britain, whose energies are entirely tuned to what the Christians saw as the Devil, but who is more truly the old Horned God of the West. As a mass, it presents different faces from different angles, ranging from the innocuous to the malign, the beneficent to the purely malevolent. Some of its sides are gently rounded, others are precipitous. At its highest point it is 240 metres (800 feet) above sea level.

Like all sacred hills it is said to be hollow, with secret doors, although these can more truly be found within the psyche of the pilgrim, in that hidden space at the back of the mind wherein we find that the earth's consciousness blends with our own. Local legends offer us keys to get inside, and the most telling is that Cley Hill is the home to the King of the Faeries. His name is still preserved as Bugley (hence the nearby Bugley Barton Farm), which we have already discovered is a variant of Bogle, Buggle, Bwcca, Pwcca, Pook or Puck – and from which we ultimately derive the term Bogey Man. Dr Anne Ross points out in her book about the Druid Prince exhumed from the peat in the Midlands that large horned beasts such as rams are said to guard/haunt places where the Buggle is felt to exist. In fact local tradition has it that a golden ram is buried deep within the hill, which is felt to be filled with a network of tunnels. However, this may well be an overlap from the Templar days, when that order owned property at the foot of Cley Hill, if not the hill itself.

To me, in the true spiritual sense of the word, Cley Hill is royal. It is not greater than other centres, any more than one colour of the spectrum is greater than the others; but sometimes after a surfeit of the present New Agey dogmatism, and suffocatingly impotent virtuosity, it can be refreshing to prick a few bubbles with the battle cry, 'Glastonbury is for cissies!'

There have been times when the hill has called me in a way that I could not resist and somehow made my complicated life suddenly and miraculously clear enough for me to visit. Sometimes it has entered my dreams, or slid in between them and my waking consciousness, so that I found myself there – in some sense – in spirit, and bewildered by it all. Once, after just such impulses, I climbed to the summit, compelled to try to summon up all the souls who seemed to have become earthbound on the top of the hill, and so found myself on a grey November morning leading a procession of these earthbound wretches back down to what I termed the Moon Place, with the injunction being that I must not look back. It was a festival, a delight, I could sense them all behind me – a few dozen perhaps – and hear the babble of a happy crowd, a strangely young crowd, eager to go on a journey. When I got to the curious and adjoining Silbury-like mound known as Little Cley Hill and opened the Gates, it was as though they soared upwards, rushing, but with thanks.

On another time, as I circled the large barrow widdershins (anticlockwise) and invoked Bugley himself by the simplest of means, the crust of the hill seemed to become wafer thin. I had the feeling of being on top of a huge, green, crystal hollowness that could at any moment shatter under my weight. And if I didn't see Bugley, the great Horned God himself, I at least glimpsed his realm, and the green-gold, other-dimensional light of another reality.

Mounds and sacred hills do seem to be able to put the seeker in touch with other realities and realms, whether by means of the indwelling entity/deity, or because they seem to have some other-dimensional function. But it seems that even just thinking about them with intent can trigger off those odd synchronistic experiences.

John Billingsley, the editor of *Northern Earth* (which is now the longest-running magazine devoted to the Earth Mysteries since the demise of the *Ley Hunter*), sent me an email describing what he termed a 'meaningless meaningful experience' connected with a sacred hill that called to him. Oddly enough his vision of the heads arrived when I had just put down a book that I had been reading about the Templars, and the importance of the 'Severed Head' within their Order. I am not saying that the two are in any way connected, at occult levels, but it is certainly symptomatic of the synchronistic events that occurred and keep occurring, throughout the preparation of this manuscript. Events that may, in the last analysis, be 'meaningfully meaningless' but events that can make the hair on the back of your neck stand on end when they take place.

This happened [he wrote] at St Michael's Hill, Montacute, in Somerset. This happens to be where the flint cross known as the Holy Rood was found in the early 11th century, following a man's dream. When loaded on to an oxcart pulled by twelve red and twelve white oxen, it was spontaneously taken by the beasts to Waltham in Essex, thus founding by 'divine revelation' the Abbey there – so it is surely a hill of revelation of some sort.

I felt compelled to climb it one very wet day when climbing hills wasn't the most inviting pastime, and on the field up to it went through an experience which I call 'the veil' – sometimes, I feel like I'm passing through an invisible boundary, and usually after that something odd or inspiring happens. This day, I stepped back and forth through 'the veil' again, and the sensation persisted. I climbed the hill, and at the top there is an old tower. There was no door, so I walked straight in and up the spiral stairs to the top.

Arriving at the top landing, I looked out of one of the windows and in the clouds – above and/or near, I think, the location of Cadbury Castle – a clear image of a man's face appeared, bearded, with jaw-length hair and with a steady gaze looking straight at me. Knowing how easy it is to see faces in clouds, etc., I looked away, unfocused and refocused my eyes, but each time I looked back it was still there. There was no absolutely no message with it – no sense at all of 'clouds part, and I see God!' or anything like that, nor anything of a more mundane feel! It occurred to me that as I'd passed through 'the veil', I'd said a little acknowledgement to the Goddess, but that this was St Michael's Hill and maybe the spirit of the place was a 'male' who would prefer himself to be acknowledged! As soon as that thought came, however, the image in the clouds dissolved away and was replaced by a clearly female face, also looking at me. After a short while, this also dissolved away, and try as I might the refocusing trick, etc., there was no image at all that I could see in those clouds. The experience felt significant, but left me no wiser as to why!

My spontaneous requests for anecdotes or experiences

relating to sacred hills or sites often seemed to coincide with pertinent work being done by the recipients, so that *I* became part of *their* own synchronistic experience.

Thus John's electronic missive about his experience near Montacute (which triggered off that internal mantra of surprise followed by speculation, which sounds something like, 'Oh! Hmmm . . .') was followed by a letter through the terrestrial post, from two magicians who had been drawn to Hamdon Hill, at the same village of Montacute. They had gone there as 'part of a larger project which had originated from a mutual interest in the, seemingly unrelated, mysteries of ancient Egypt'. And, in an odd way that is not really appropriate for, or related to, the present narrative, they did indeed stumble upon Horus, son of Isis.

Was Montacute – or the energies behind the place – trying to tell us something? Was there some Mystery to be unravelled, or magick to be worked involving Egypt, Templars and Head Cults of the ancient past? Or were these clues aimed at someone else who, in reading this, might give a startled cry as they find another signpost on their own quest?

All the people involved in such striking coincidences when researching their own brand of the Earth Mysteries tended to be what I can only call 'respectfully blasé' about the events. None of them felt it had anything to do with any kind of individual 'spiritual superiority', whatever that might mean. But that it was everything to do with touching upon the 'Spirit of Place'. It seems that anyone who sets out to research, visit, experience and learn about the ancient sites by whatever means is appropriate to their needs and capabilities will – always – experience something of this for themselves.

For this project I visited Silbury with Paddy Slade, who lives at the end of a track, atop a steep hill, near a tiny hamlet reckoned to be one of the oldest inhabited places in Somerset. Paddy is one of the hereditary witches. That is to say she was born to the craft, and is far, far removed from those spiritually correct 'dresser-uppers' who blight and curse the New Age movement – those proliferating, self-styled High Priests and

Priestesses who have read a few books, downloaded a few megabytes about the Goddess, and who seem to avoid the hard, lonely and often thankless work of real magick . . .

My first feeling when I met her was one of sheer terror. Not because of any dark psychic energies that she projected on opening the door, but because of the huge, black and wolflike dog that came leaping out of the house at me. You see, I come from a long and proud line of Richardsons who have, over the generations, been frightened witless by canines (however small) and this one had – and still has – a tendency to sniff, lick and nip at whatever I held in my hands. In this case, it was my cupped genitalia, of which I've become exceedingly fond over the years.

'Tell me that he's harmless!' I cried, trying to find shelter behind an old Ford Fiesta 1.8 diesel with cassette radio, optional speed stripes, and disgracefully bald tyres.

'He's harmless,' she said unconvincingly, one eyebrow raised at my funk, and I felt that I had failed my first initiation . . . I muttered something about Cerberus, but she wasn't impressed. 'Come in,' she sighed, shaking her head.

Travelling to Silbury with Paddy was in itself an experience. Something about travelling itself, as the Reverend Duke would have known, can induce a curious state of mind in which the pilgrim is neither here nor there, both going and coming, out of the world yet in it. She told me about curses she had placed, healings she had done, visions she had had, distressed souls that she had dealt with – incarnate and discarnate – badger-baiters that she had attacked, physically, with a quarterstaff, goddesses that she had dealt with and darknesses that she had known. All very matter-of-fact, all very humorous. But I remembered what someone once said about her, that there are two Paddys: the soft, funny, grandmotherly white witch who does the expected sort of white-witchy things at country fairs; and the coven leader who, when working their high magick, is a creature of pure steel. Honestly, I wouldn't cross her.

We walked slowly around Silbury widdershins, as the witches would say, both of us respectfully aware of its formidable mood. Paddy continued to talk: about the land, the spirit of the land, the spirit of the people who live in this land, and it was clear that there were things going on beneath her words, below the surface of the day. Then for a quick moment all the tales I had read about time slips and people disappearing from the Wiltshire countryside shot through my mind when I turned and found that Paddy had completely disappeared. One minute she had been at my shoulder reciting whole chunks from *Puck of Pook's Hill*, by Rudyard Kipling, and the next she was nowhere to be seen. However, it was not so much that she had stumbled through some fourth-dimensional star gate, but that she had gone arse-over-tit on the mud, and was sprawled at my feet like some creature from the primordial depths. She laughed, she swore, she got up – in roughly that order. We continued walking, her silences as expressive in different realms as her words.

Silbury, I realised then, is huge. Not in terms of actual dimensions, but in terms of presence. The sort of presence a mother has in the mind and eye of her toddlers. A presence that is assessed not by yards or metres, but by *what it is*.

'This *is* the pregnant belly of the Great Mother,' said Paddy, referring to Michael Dames's books. 'But it should be visited at night.'

The water that curves around much of its circumference is clearly an integral part of its mystery. Silbury's reflection amid the shallow grass-swirled waters has an odd effect upon the unconscious – just as forgotten names can lurk, maddeningly, beneath the surface of memory, so does the reflection touch upon our ancestors, and the rites they worked. As we viewed the mass from the north, out of sight of the road and sound of the cars, with little to remind us of the twenty-first century, it was hard not to feel touched by a former age.

Thinking about the number of psychics who have admitted to getting nothing from the hill whatsoever, or who felt that there was something about Silbury that actually inhibited psychism, I thought about the sort of pregnant mother who adamantly refuses any prenatal scans, who rejects the seek-and-destroy missions of amniocentesis, and who won't let the mystery within her belly be compromised in any way. The archaeologists may have ripped into Silbury's belly, but they never got anything important out.

'It's no good just coming up to these places and demanding to know all their secrets,' Paddy said. 'They have to trust you first. It can take a long time. And I do wish people wouldn't try to climb the bloody hill. Leave it alone!'

We sat out of the wind and Paddy talked about the English and the Old Ones being, as she thought, Ancient Brits. 'The Celts had not arrived, if they ever did come here, when structures like Silbury were made. And there seems to be some doubt as to their ever coming to the island. New work on Celtic skeletons seems to prove that they didn't cross the channel. Neither Cornish, Welsh nor Scots appear to have any "Celtic" DNA in any of their bones. It would further appear that the Saxons actually had far more of these structures, the "Celts" having gone north in Europe as well as west and south.'

Not exactly the Standard Revised Version of the New Age dogma, in which the presence of Celts is as fundamental as Tibetan Masters are to Theosophists – but Paddy has never been one to toe the line.

I mentioned Olive Pixley's idea that there was something about Silbury that actually inhibited psychism, and Iris Campbell's vision of the dark core, and the malign effect it had upon the populace. Paddy was inclined to let that pass for the time being while she thought about it. Somehow the conversation turned to the Egyptian god Set, Lord of Darkness, and we discussed the idea in Dolores Ashcroft-Nowicki's *Judgement of Osiris* that Set had been taught from birth to represent evil, so that mankind would have the opportunity to choose between good and evil. We spoke of Osiris, and of Nuit and Tiamat, both the latter being Star Goddesses and Grandmothers of the Gods, not to mention Creating Goddesses, and Paddy thought that perhaps the Goddess of Silbury might be another such, an Old One of the Island. At that point she told me she felt a very discontented rumble coming from the inside of the hill.

I asked her what exactly she meant by 'the Island' and she tried to explain how it seemed to her that, when Silbury and the older stone circles, the long barrows and ancient sites were built, the Island was one, complete and indivisible. This was what she was getting from the hill itself, I felt. She evoked pictures in my own head of the sacred sites being found as the hunters had followed the herds north and south with the changes of the seasons, remembering that, when the herds stopped in their migrations, there were always 'special places' – possibly a spring or a natural stone or even a great tree – that marked the place out and later, when the hunters became farmers and settled a bit, were remembered and sought out and revered. Marked by a standing stone or a circle or something that would last. 'There were no separate races then, families and tribes certainly, but one race, not several.'

She got back to the idea of the dark core of Silbury again, as if her mind were touching it directly: 'I think that perhaps this core was the original core of the Goddess. Dark and mysterious. I thought perhaps it had been made from star stuff. If it was underground, then this makes it even more probable that it was for the worship of a goddess rather than a god. Forget the idea of the Goddess always being the kind old granny and think of her more in the nature of a pretty unforgiving deity. If something went wrong, it would have to be paid for. The early religion would have been matriarchal, as would most of the tribes, so this would have been at the core.

'Later generations might be a bit like our own and try to hide from the Dark. It might be too strong and so represented evil, in the same way that new religions always try to vilify old ones. The new ones might even, by that time, have become male dominated.

'So the bright, shining terraces of chalk, built to reflect the new god, the Sun, kept the power of the old core in check. This would probably only work during the day, so perhaps the persecution of the believers of the old religion began then, and its adherents were in some way kept away at night. There was always this fear of the Old Dark Goddess.'

I mentioned as well that there was a place near Marden known as Pookshipton, which means goblins' cattle shed, which caused Paddy's inner antennae to prick up.

'These people,' she added, 'might well have been the smaller, early Brits, who became known as gnomes or the little people. Moon worshippers. It seems that the cattle and the land were rightfully and originally theirs and they had been driven out by the larger incomers, who stole their cattle as well as their land. So they came back at night and stole them right back again, putting the fear of the Goddess into the newcomers. The little people were not afraid of the dark but the newcomers might well have been. This, I believe, accounts for both the fear of the Dark and the necessity for covering the core of the hill with chalk.'

She stared, she brooded, and, as with some of the other seers that I visited sites with later in this project, there was an odd but very real sense in which she wasn't with me at all and was lost, perhaps, amid the energies of the Light and the Dark as expressed by the hill.

'This'll be in my head all night,' she said, pointing to the hill and its reflection. And it was, and its teachings filtered out in different ways throughout the weeks ahead; and, if we want to learn more about the ways it touched us both, then we as pilgrims have to make an easy journey on to the nearby Avebury, and that realm of the stone circles that exists within all of our heads.

CHAPTER

THREE

AVEBURY AND THE STONE CIRCLES OF THE SUN AND MOON

*The stones seemed tuned to the elements and to the
heavens (sun, moon, planets, stars). I believe they
were probably used both practically and spiritually
(provided you can actually separate these two usages)
to make contact with the rhythms of nature and the
energy behind these rhythms in order to guide our
ancestors in their seasonal activities (hunting,
planting, building, etc.). I suspect that if you spent
some time within the stones over the course of
several years you could not only re-establish that
contact but learn how to work with the energy
beneficially even in our present circumstances.*
– Marcia Pickands, *Warden of the Sangreal Sodality*

On a cold January morning in 1649, while engrossed in what
he termed 'The Chase of the Hare', John Aubrey was led in
his pursuit into the stone circles of Avebury. Stunned, he let
the rest of the party and the excited hounds carry on baying
towards Kennet, while he stayed to explore. Expressing himself
'wonderfully surprized at the sight of those vast stones', he
also had to admit that he never knew of their existence despite
having been brought up in Wiltshire, and knowing the rest of
it very well.

And really, it does not take any great talents of imagination
to enter Aubrey's head and see Avebury as he first saw it on
that cold and pure day with the frost on the hills and the
streams frozen, the hounds yelping into the distance, and huge
numbers of immense stones, within a vast henge, standing
mutely in the cool air like a lost race of hunched giants, as if
waiting for something, as if looking at him.

63

But what truly led him there? Was it merely chance? Was it that sacred and secret creature the hare, which was so venerated by the Ancient British and their witch-descendants, who took on its form at various opportunities? Or was it the collective pressure of unborn generations – ourselves – that guided him that day?

Staggered by something that was on his doorstep, yet entirely unknown, he told his friend Dr Walter Charleton of this immense circle of stones which ' . . . as much exceedes Stoneheng in bignesse; as a Cathedrall does, a parish church'.[1] His friend told the King, Charles II, and the King told his brother, the future James II.

So it began.

And we owe it all to the hare.

Avebury impacted on others in different and extremely odd ways, who looked at it through different lights, and with different perceptions of time and space. For example, at some point in September 1937 that was somehow synchronous with a moment in the First Dynasty in Ancient Egypt, a young mother named Joan Grant sat on a couch in a large house at Holmbury St Mary and psychometrised a turquoise-blue scarab amulet which had been put on a card table beside her. Psychometry – the ability to receive psychic impressions through the sense of touch – was her speciality at the time.

Touching the scarab gave her access to the memories of Sekhet-a-ra, who was also a part of herself: a young priestess from the First Dynasty who underwent an initiation in a large building across a lake that was 'like a pyramid, though the sides were not smooth, being built in three great steps, symbolising body, soul and spirit'.[2] From the lake a water channel of stone led to the entrance, where a shaft pierced through to the chamber of initiation, which was shaped like a sarcophagus with a pointed lid. This shaft was closed by three great dropstones during the initiation ceremony itself, sealing it like a tomb, so that it seemed as though the initiate died and was born again with wisdom – if they survived the ordeal. At the top of this structure a beacon fire was kindled for the duration of the rite.

Among many places that Sekhet-a-ra visited while out of the body and out of time was

> ... the White Island, where they know much wisdom. Here there are many who listen, for upon Earth they have teachers who go among the people from a place called A-vey-baru, where priests are trained in the way of Anubis. Their temple is encircled by a great ditch, and the walls are of single stones, unhewn, joined to each other by wood and clay covered with white plaster. With such awe do the people look upon this place that when they sleep they come here to learn those things which it is well for them to know.

Joan Grant wrote up Sekhet-a-ra's experiences in her book *Winged Pharaoh*, which became an international bestseller when first published in 1937. She went on also to become perhaps the very first 'past-life counsellor', setting an increasing trend for later generations, and spent some years living not too far from the Avebury complex itself. Her 'vision within a vision' of Avebury gives us yet another tangential link between the latter and the spirit of Egypt from the earliest dynastic period, and seems to support Grace Cooke's belief that initiates from Egypt were heavily involved in the whole complex, and were responsible for teaching the native British how to work with the earth energies.

Also, her curious comment that the priests of Avebury were 'trained in the way of Anubis' will lead us on, in later chapters, to look at that image of the Black Dog which is so prominent in Wiltshire folklore, for Anubis is the jackal-headed deity linked with magick, dreaming, remembering and time.

In a different sort of way, within our mental map, the Black Dog will prove to be just as important as the Hare at giving us directions, and leading us towards strange places.

To Edward Duke, Avebury represented the sun and moon in perfect harmony as they circled the good earth known as Silbury Hill. And psychologically it makes a perfect kind of

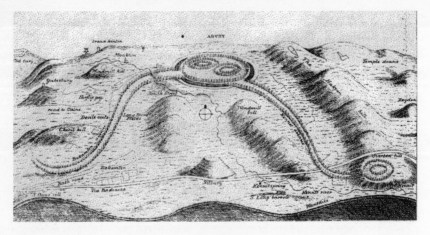

DUKE'S MAP OF AVEBURY

sense to move from the earth centre of Silbury, where we become aware of ourselves as existent beings rising from this primordial mud of unknowing, and start to look inwards at the dualities that shape us: yang and yin; the radiant and reflective; day and the night; positive and negative; the animus and anima ... Or perhaps even, as the practitioners of feng-shui insist, the qualities of *ch'i* and *sha*. The enigmas and mysteries of the stone circles – any stone circles, not just those at Avebury – are of a very different kind from those of the Sacred Mounds, but in various ways they all seem to express these dualities.

Yet although Avebury loomed large in the consciousness of our notional guide, Duke, in terms of public awareness, it is one of the least-known ceremonial monuments in Europe, despite being one of the largest. As impressive in its own way as Stonehenge, and with a completely different kind of atmosphere, there are still people in Britain today who remain, like John Aubrey 350 years ago, largely unaware of its existence.

The psychiatrist Arthur Guirdham, who wrote some influential books on group reincarnation, dualist philosophy and the interplay between the worlds of spirit and matter, felt that the function of Avebury was to absorb into its circle all the dire, malign forces of the area, and transmute them through a kind of spiritual alchemy. As we noted earlier in the context of Silbury, the conspicuous absence of folklore that might be expected to exist around such a powerful site allows us to wonder if he was correct: as if all the hauntings, all the earth-bound spirits and 'place-memories' had been sucked in and sent on . . .

The villagers of Avebury, over the centuries, used the actual megaliths for the raw material of their buildings, so that the houses themselves are almost an integral part of the circle – almost as if the power sought to hide itself through a conjunction of the mystic and mundane. Avebury today has all that we might expect from any modest English village: post office and stores, school, public toilets, two churches, a manor, pub and a high street. Yet the visitor has only to turn a corner to come face to face with the sarsens, and get the sense that one world has given way to another, of very different style and substance.

Sarsens are boulders composed of sand bound by silica cement. Within the Avebury complex some of them weigh up to 50 tons or more and in shape tend to be either tabular, like the flat, polygonal 'B' stones, or more irregular and boulder-like in form. This 'cathedral', as Aubrey thought of it, originally comprised 200 standing stones arranged in an outer and two inner circles, surrounded by a massive bank and ditch. It was approached from the south by a processional way of standing stones now known as the West Kennet Avenue, and another westerly row called the Beckhampton Avenue. These avenues, in Duke's eyes, formed the body of the Great Serpent, and represented the ecliptic, or the apparent path of the sun through the heavens.

The area is surrounded by long barrows, bell and bowl barrows, causewayed camps and countless mysterious fragments of humanity. It has been calculated that the worship within these structures dates from the Neolithic Period of over 4000 BCE, through the Beaker Period, which began about 3000 BCE, on to the Bronze Age starting at around 1700 BCE, and into the Iron Age, beginning a mere 650 BCE. Following that was a long, *long* silence that was eventually broken by the sound of those hounds chasing John Aubrey's hare.

* * *

There is still debate as to the original shape of the main stone circle in Avebury. In the vision of Sekhet-a-ra, who was also Joan Grant, it was a place of white walls, the unhewn stones being 'joined to each other by wood and clay covered with white plaster', which can create a disturbingly evocative image in its own right.

To the Cambridge scholar John Ivimy the name Avebury or Abury is a corruption of Abaris, which he assured us was named by the exiled Egyptian astronomer-priests after the cult centre in their homeland. Avebury, in his vision, was the home of those 'exiles from Khem' who were later responsible for building Stonehenge.[3]

But the popular conception of Avebury was formed by William Stukeley (1687–1765), who recorded and sketched the site during the reign of George II, showing us those interlocking circles of which Edward Duke wrote, ' . . . this *compages* of antiquities did represent the Sun and Moon (by their temples) traversing the northern portion of the Zodiac, designated by the Serpent, and revolving around Silbury Hill as denotive of the Earth.'[4] Although, over the centuries, archaeologists have expressed doubt as to the accuracy of Stukeley's drawings, recent groundwork has invariably proved him to have been extremely accurate.

Mainstream opinion was inclined to suspect that his notions of Avebury as a Serpent Temple so overrode reality that he added the westernmost Beckhampton Avenue to make the ground plan fit his theories. Yet even as I write, in September 1999, new research has vindicated him yet again. There were two avenues. Just as serpentine as he described them.

But what are the stones *for*? What do they *do*? You can almost stamp your feet in frustration when asking that question. Simply using them as means for marking the positions of the sun, moon and certain planets doesn't seem to be enough. There has to be more to it than that. Certain beliefs that an elite class of astronomer-priests used them solely to control the ignorant populace through being able to predict eclipses leaves little more than a dull thud in the mind. People were not that stupid.

The psychometrist Iris Campbell was quite certain about her impressions at Castle Rigg circle near Keswick. This was where kings came to mourn their dead, 'performing their funeral rites by weaving, through sound and invocation, the colour system of the cosmos in order to speed the departure of the passing Soul.'[5] To her this circle served as a bridge between one sphere of consciousness and the next, although she insisted that not all stone circles had the same purpose.

In contrast the Masonic writers Christopher Knight and Robert Lomas, in their book *Uriel's Machine*, argue that the megalithic sites in Britain were actually early-warning systems to detect comets, following major and devastating comet impacts on earth in 7640 BCE, and then 3150 BCE, which were responsible for the global legends of the Flood. Although their ideas connect the megaliths with stellar and planetary alignments, and argue convincingly that many of the sites function as superbly accurate computers, they steer away from any suggestions that the stones may have intrinsic power.

Dowsers, on the other hand (and also entirely orthodox scientists), have found that certain stones are connected with very *un*orthodox but undeniably measurable energies. Briefly: ultrasound detectors have measured repeated pulsings coming from standing stones at dawn and dusk; Geiger counters have shown inexplicable but unquestionable anomalies; magnetometers have found spirals of magnetic intensity; flamelike discharges have been photographed coming from the top of single stones; dowsers have been known to have been thrown backwards by the forces they touched . . .

So it is natural to speculate that the stone circles were created according to a Neolithic alternative science (whose principles still elude us) and were machines that were meant to *do* *something*.

The magus of one overtly magickal group wrote to me of an experience at Arbor Low stone circle which touched upon this:

On one of our visits there, we were rather a large group. There were several who had pendulums and they decided to check if the stones making up the circle were male and female. The consensus of opinion from those there was that they were. We decided to do an experiment with everyone attending. The men standing on the positive stones and the women on the negative ones. Once in place, we began our little experiment. At first very little happened. Then gradually we noticed a whistling noise building in pitch getting stronger and stronger. The whistling developed into a definite loud whooshing sound that seemed to create an umbrella of sound over the top of Arbor Low. At that point we stopped our experiment and everything returned to normal.

Like the bizarre weather phenomena described in the previous chapter, it seems that early attempts to work with the stones often produce results akin to those of children fiddling about with unfamiliar adult technologies. We can get something to happen, but we can't always understand why, or what it's meant for.

But the most usual belief, which is perhaps a reflection of modern tastes for complementary medicine, is that the stones affect the mystic currents of the earth (these are often termed 'telluric' currents) in much the same way as acupuncture needles adjust the flow of energies in the human body – and that the ancient sites are the same as the meridians of the acupuncturist.

The dowser Tom Graves, who is one of the best exponents of such ideas, records a vision of the stones in which he actually saw these energies at work:

But this is not all. The stones themselves glow with light, their colours and intensities changing and pulsing as you watch. The ground itself is glowing, concentric rings of muted colours spreading out from the centre of the circle. Above the ground there is activity too: sparks of coloured light jump from stone to stone, around the circle, travelling along taut wires of light, like messages chattering from stone to stone. Occasionally, all this activity comes to a climax: the top of one stone gleams brightly for a moment as a huge pulse of energy emerges from it and disappears into the distance, like a firework rocket travelling on an almost invisible horizontal wire. A message of some kind, travelling from one site to another – or a pulse in a nerve of the body of the earth itself.[6]

This is echoed to some extent by Wendy Berg's vision of '. . . those two low rounded hills which lie just back from the coast between Land's End and Cape Cornwall', which links these to the recurrent theme of Strangers who created a magickal technology within these isles – whether these be seen as Egyptians from the East, Atlanteans from the West, or denizens of another realm entirely.

> I'm so often aware of these two hills in the back of my mind when I'm walking on Dartmoor. They seem to act as huge lenses which pick up and focus the light from the west and then send it, laser fashion, to Tintagel, broadening out into the full spectrum across Dartmoor and then collecting and pooling at Glastonbury. This is similar to the Michael and Mary ley lines, but I think it's more to do with the continuing influence of the Sun Temple of Atlantis and the Sun Mysteries.

Commenting about such technology in a more specific vein, the resident spirit of the prehistoric tomb – who communicated with the influential writer and musician RJ Stewart – told him that the purpose of the dolmen was precise and scientific: by creating a sealed chamber of massive stones above a specific mass or size, which were then buried beneath earth, certain natural processes could be made to occur that were directly due to the shapes and nature of the structure itself. In other words, *as well as* the womblike symbolism that impacted upon the consciousness of the initiate, some quite specific processes were at work that had more in common with engineering than psychology.

Murry Hope, the founder of the influential group the Atlanteans, which flourished in the 1960s and 70s, once visited the Rollright Stones in Oxfordshire and commented:

> The impression I gained while tuning in to the essences of the stones was that they were programmed to respond to (or resonate with) a specific sonic, which had nothing to do with time as we know it. The original program must have been inserted either by an advanced race from the far past whose knowledge

of sonics far exceeded the bounds of present-day science, or from some extra-terrestrial source. Much as I acknowledge the existence of intelligent life-forms in other parts of the Universe, my gut feeling at the time tended me to favour the former – it was as though for one nano-second, I was 'remembering' a science I had once known and experienced long, long ago.

This harks back to the viewpoint of the psychic surgeon Chris Thomas, mentioned in the previous chapter, who argued that there were 'energy gates' under the Sphinx, at Teotehuacan and at Stonehenge, which were 'designed to assist travel between the worlds'.[7]

Which brings us back again to the 'strangers' that Grace Cooke saw in what might be termed her 'Avebury Cycle' of visions, although stories of such outsiders are not exclusive to that complex. The Callanish stones, for example, were locally believed to have been brought to the island thousands of years ago by a priest-king from a distant land across the sea. This king, who habitually wore a cloak of brightly coloured feathers, was said to have been accompanied by a group of 'black men' who erected the circle under his directions.

In contrast to these essentially magickal insights and visions, there is the approach of the Symbolists, who view such places from a psychological and artistic point of view, and who tend to see everything from the remote past as outer images representing inner realities. Their ideas have gone through a certain vogue in the latter part of the twentieth century, but are in fact no more or less credible than even the most extreme of the visionaries.

If, for example, someone in 5,000 years' time stumbles upon the remains of an automobile from the murky levels of the pre-Catastrophe era, what might they make of it? Would they see it as an expression of the womb – a nurturing protective place? They might guess what the child seats in the rear were for, and hazard at the symbolism of the seat belts. They might decide, from the shape, size and strength of the frame within the remaining shell, that this was probably an initiation chamber relating to the mysteries of women, in the twentieth and twenty-first centuries. The mirrors were clearly for examining the inner self, through some long-forgotten rituals, and the pull-out tray containing ash was almost certainly for the remains of their ancestors. But unless they understand the qualities of that long-since-exhausted substance petrol, and rediscover the principles of internal combustion, they will always be just a little wide of the mark. And, as we shall see, some of the more apparently bizarre insights of the occultists will often prove to be closer to the truth than is comfortable to imagine.

Until we can find out what this Neolithic technology was, and how it worked, we can still go a long way towards experiencing the stones by asking the simple question, 'Why?' This is the question that both vexes us and drives us inwards. It is rather like the moment when the Grail Knights from the Arthurian Romances ask of the maimed Fisher King (and are expected to ask, or their quest fails) what the processions in the Grail Castle actually mean. Once they ask that question the Fisher King is healed and the Wasteland becomes revitalised. The moment *we* ask that of the stones, and link intense curiosity to a numinous pattern such as Avebury, then we become part of its very mystery, and the arid landscape in our souls can burst into a golden flowering.

It was all quite clear to Grace Cooke, who wrote:

> The ritual here at Avebury was linked with the moon. I see a great crowd gathered to perform an elaborate ritual of obeisance to the moon, or to what I can only describe as a goddess of the moon . . . The ritual here was performed under her direction, its object being the actual production of life in form – the bringing into physical manifestation of life itself, coming from the etheric world. You see, in those supremely distant times, life in wholly physical form had hardly come into being. The ancient mother-ritual, which eventually brought about the creation of life in physical form, came from Mu, the Motherland.
>
> This temple of Avebury was the heart and centre of all these ceremonies.
>
> The ritual was designed to invoke the invisible power of the

gods, and then it was concentrated upon the movement of the cells and the building-up of form.[8]

Avebury to her was the place where life was actually brought into being, where order was brought from chaos using rituals linked with powers inherent in the solar system. Long before Neil Armstrong landed on the moon, long before Erich von Däniken turned God into an astronaut with appropriate life-support systems on his back, Grace Cooke was convinced that in the most ancient of days, by rituals 'linked with powers inherent in the solar system itself', people knew how to contact outer space – with their minds – and could have done so at the moon temple of Avebury.

It does not take a great deal of psychism to be aware of the very definite presence that such places can radiate, so that megaliths can feel as alive as flesh and blood, projecting energies comparable to body heat. Psychics do not always find these energies congenial, however. The multitalented medium Ray Bailey wrote to me about an almost punitive visit to Avebury:

> I visited this site many times whilst in Wiltshire, once with my friend George Newton, an excellent dowser. As we approached the first stone George, when attempting to touch it, was thrown back visibly by its energy. I did not get the same reaction, but as we proceeded into the centre area I felt physically sick, and was aware of a definite swirling of energy which produced a slight humming sensation in my ears!

On a more benign note Anne McCourt, a parapsychologist, told me that she felt compelled to lean back against an isolated stone at Arthur's Table, near Penrith, and felt what she insisted was an actual pulse. Not just a random set of vibrations from the nearby A66 but a pulse as definite as anything that could be felt on the wrist – no other word would describe it. A pulse from the heart of the earth itself.

An equally congenial experience came from Rae Beth, whose background is that of a 'hedge witch' or solitary practitioner of the craft. She wrote to me: 'There is no mistaking that special feel of a place where the "veil" is thin between the worlds. In other words, where it is easy to slip from everyday states of mind into a dreamy, poetic or religious mode, where eternal realities or spirit presences can be felt.' She felt that what standing stones can say to us can be simple and yet profound, because we have only the essence left of why they were erected.

The particular set of stones that gave Rae Beth her insights into their nature seems to have had a great influence on a very wide variety of occultists: the Rollright Stones in Oxfordshire. One day while visiting these, she leaned back against a tall stone in the circle and heard the following lines in her head:

> *Minerals and living fire*
> *in my blood and bones*
> *as Earth and stars have*
> *and standing stones*

This led her on to make mythic links which convinced her that stone circles were built to remind us of the connectedness between all beings.

Another person who visited the same set of stones over a long period in the late 1960s and 70s (and came to much the same conclusion) was William Gray, who at regular intervals would get on his old bicycle and heave his 'not-uncorpulent corpus' fourteen miles across the hills to the Rollrights in the middle of the night, determined to fathom their secrets – which he felt had less to do with the channelling of telluric currents than with enabling the builders and their communities to evolve on inner and outer levels – although even he had to admit, as he cycled towards them, that there seemed to be a sort of 'power-perimeter' round the circle approximately a mile from its centre, which enabled him to home in as on a radio beacon.

A chiropodist by profession, Gray lived and worked for much of his life in the faded elegance of Cheltenham. By inclination, however, he was a magician, a formidably psychic man whose books on what he would have termed the inner 'Western traditions' rank among the least bought but most influential in the spiritual genre. It was through his work with the cluster of

standing stones known as the Rollrights that he learned something of the true purpose of such circles throughout the world.

> To each individual member of a Circle, the 'family Stone' or
> 'Old One' had a depth of spiritual significance very hard for us
> to understand now. That particular Stone stood for all they ever
> were or would be . . . The Stone . . . not only offered status in
> this world, *but was the gateway to the spirit world also* [my
> emphasis]. In it lived every ancestor. If an ear was pressed
> closely to the stone when the countryside was fairly silent,
> those Otherworlders might be heard whispering good counsel
> or warnings to their living descendants. No use listening at
> someone else's Stone to learn his secrets. Only family spirits
> spoke to blood-links with Life. That was the Law. Of course,
> there were special Stones which spoke to the people periodically,
> but only those 'in the know', or Wise Old Ones could make
> those talk.[9]

He learned this and spoke with authority because the stones
themselves told him over a long period of time. By a process
akin to psychometry, or sometimes just a simple empathic
leaning back against them (after a quick snort of whisky to
help him recover from the long and knackering bike ride), Gray
learned how the circle was as much a binding, social focus for
the tribal folk who built it, as anything more esoteric. Each
stone, therefore, stood for definite people living in that particular area, together with their relatives alive or dead, and
indicated how those people fitted into the community from a
social standpoint. He insisted that any intelligent man of those
times could take one look round a stone circle and more or
less guess what sort of folk had set it up. Though they had no
alphabets to read, they did have symbols in the shapes and
sorts of stones which stood for certain types of people. One
stone, for instance, may have shown the wealthiest and most
influential people in the place. Another may have stood for a
small family whose speciality was basket making.

No hint here of spiritual technologies, and the interesting
aspect of Gray's visions is how unspectacular many of the
stones' teachings are – as he was the first to admit. Here is one
of the foremost ritualists of our time, a man soaked in High

Magick, who once (some thirty years before the notion became *de rigueur* among New Agers) told me about the demise of civilisation on Mars, who quite simply saw it all from a very human and – almost – mundane angle.

But there was blood and gore too. If Charles Seymour's vision of Avebury was as a place of sacrifice, as described in the first chapter, then William Gray's Rollrights were imbued with similar memories. Just after sunrise at a full moon, when the orbs of the luminaries came level and represented 'both Eyes of Heaven', he saw the victim brought before the King Stone, where he stood with his arms spread out something like a crucified man, and was then swiftly speared from the front up into the ribcage, straight into the heart. 'Sometimes his body was cooked and shared out as a sacred meal, but often his flesh was eaten raw in small morsels, his blood being drunk by the chosen few, and the remainder sprinkled over the assembly as a token of a spirit shared among everyones' he added.[10]

One thing both Gray and Seymour agreed upon was that the sacrifice was a willing one: the King or the Priestess respectively had agreed to die in time-honoured fashion, with a view to guiding the people thenceforth from the inner planes, through the help of those shamanic tribal mediums that both realised were the origins of the modern witch. This was not a savage act of ritual murder, they felt, but an accepted spiritual practice among people who regarded death quite differently from ourselves.

Another person who has linked with the energies of the Rollright Stones is a nurse from the Midlands who uses the witch-name 'Rowan Greenwood'. Irritated by what she felt were the calumnies of a fiction writer who described the stones as sinister, and evil, she made a special visit to see for herself. In her vision the tone of the activities was essentially as Gray perceived it:

> There was food and drink, and people dancing around the Circle (deosil) and singing. The dance I recognised as a Spiral Dance which a lot of Covens still use, with alternate man and

woman holding hands and dancing inwards to the centre of the Circle then doubling back and dancing back out. As I've always witnessed this, it was complete mayhem, with everyone ending up falling over! This was not a Coven of thirteen people but seemed to be most of a village, men, women and children all joining in. After the dancing they sat just within the Circle and sang songs. At the height of the singing one woman stood and made a blessing over a loaf of bread and a metal cup which I assumed held either wine or ale. This was then set upon the King Stone as an offering. The women then stood and one by one, threw corn dollies into the fire. (This solved the date problem – it was probably Lughnasadh.) After this the merriment died down and people started to leave. . . . This, then, was the use of the Stones . . .[11]

If we can accept such analyses of the magick behind the Rollrights, then we have to assume that similar would hold true for all circles everywhere, including mighty Avebury. Thus, to use a modern analogy, while there may be huge differences in scale and prestige between the financial institutions of the City of London and those found in the business district of a small provincial town, the principles and motivations are the same. So as far as Gray and Seymour were concerned, individual stones are inextricably linked with individual people, both living and dead, and with their past and future. The circles are to do with whole communities, and their continuing survival and growth. They are links between the worlds, where life and death conjoin like the two stone circles that Duke saw from the top of Silbury Hill as representing the sun and moon.

Jack Green spent a lot of time visiting a standing stone which he felt had once been in a long ceremonial avenue, but was now an integral part of a series of dry-stone walls near his village. 'To be honest,' he wrote, 'I set out with the intention of making this my stone. Whether it had any mysterious radiating power was always going to be beyond my own perceptions. But I felt that if I adopted it, so to speak, and treated it as I would a dignified and solitary person, that something might develop.' It became, in fact, what he encouraged his children to call the family 'Wishing Stone': a focus for their worries and fears; an encouragement for their hopes; a protector on inner levels and subtle ways. 'We never did (or do) anything bizarre around it. I mean, there was no naked prancing, or chanting, or burying crystals at its base, or any bollocks like that. But it was always important to touch the stone, and try to empathise with it, and over a period of time it really did give off a sense of having its own character, and presence. To me at least it has become an important part of my family in its own right, and in quiet ways I can't easily explain it does seem to teach me things . . .'

Edna Whelan, whose innate psychism came to the fore only comparatively late in life, had a very similar experience with a cup-marked stone set on a sloping hillside near Skipton in Yorkshire. After a lot of work dowsing its energies, and finding all the geodetic lines described by Guy Underwood, she came to feel an increasing attachment to the site in general and the stone in particular, and even 'saw' the energy rising from it like a kind of bulging bubble which rose into the air and fell again without bursting. One evening she actually felt a message from the stone within her head, asking her not to leave. It was not, she insisted, imagination. Later, she began to wonder if there was something else hidden beneath the stone's accompanying cairn-like boulder-strewn slope: ' . . . a burial chamber connected with the nearby Iron Age settlement – perhaps a skeleton curled up in the foetal position, a ceremonial polished stone axe beside it, a circlet of small faience beads on its head and the remains of wild flowers at its feet?' She quoted Rupert Sheldrake's opinion that our definition of 'living' may have to be expanded to include such apparently inanimate things as rock.[12]

The stone communed with her. It touched her. And, as Joan Grant saw it through the astral vision of Sekhet-a-ra, Avebury and its stones were once a pre-eminent 'college' whose teachings radiated out through the people and touched their dreams. And as Paul Devereux and Jack Green found out, certain places – stones, hills – assumed the power of being able to teach them in subtle and unexpected ways. So perhaps the 'sacred colleges' still function, still have their own curricula and can still initiate us into their quiet traditions.

In Duke's scheme the twin circles representing the sun and moon immediately link us with the archetypes (and sometimes stereotypes) of God and Goddess, Great Father and Great Mother, Man and Woman. Thus bringing sex into the equation.

The populist idea is that our neolithic ancestors used the major festivals as excuses for mass rutting within the stones. Seething naked mobs, without shame or awkwardness, procreating like beasts. Yet neither William Gray nor Rowan Greenwood had any glimpse of this, and felt that there was a very high degree of discretion and privacy involved. 'What coupling did take place,' wrote Gray, 'was conducted with surprising reticence ... couples went off by themselves and performed in private.'[13] He added that, because fairly strict taboos on unsuitable mating were coming into force at that time, and because disobedience to established rulings meant a dishonourable death, there was less sexual laxity then than now. While Rowan Greenwood commented:

> Nothing sinister, no orgies or sacrificing of unbaptised babies, just a group of people celebrating life in the Old Way. If it was Lughnassadh then they were giving thanks for the Harvest and asking to live through the cold of oncoming Winter, and the only sacrifice mentioned would have been that of the God of the Harvest, giving his life that the people could live, as represented by the loaf and the corn dollies. [14]

To Terence Meaden, however, sex was pre-eminent within the stones. Witnessed by everyone. An awesome and cosmic act ensuring that the stars, sun and moon, and all things receiving their light, continued to exist. But it was not a prodigious sexual act between any mortal king or queen, priest or priestess. It was the sacred marriage of the Sky Father and the Earth Mother.

Now of all those who have studied the megaliths using the disciplines of the pure scientist, it is Wiltshire-born Terence Meaden who has managed to strike an almost visionary note without losing touch with those thought processes that gained him his doctorate in solid-state physics.

Using hard work to back up his (scientifically based) intuitions, Meaden has convincingly demonstrated that at certain times throughout the year the sunrise would create a phallic shadow from a particular 'male' stone in both Avebury and Stonehenge, which would thrust itself into the clefts found on the appropriate 'female' stones, which he termed Womb Stones. Which calls to mind the old folklore that said that the circles were maidens or wedding guests transformed into stone, and which at night were said to dance, speak or go to a stream to drink or bathe. More, he asserted that at the moment of this mating the Womb Stone would become, in the minds of the people watching, filled with the spirit of the Earth Mother. This was more than just a large stone receiving light and shadow. During the moment of coition the Womb Stone would be perceived as the Great Goddess. As he summed it up in *The Stonehenge Solution*:

> What happened at the Goddess Stone was received as a manifestation of the divine before the worshipping populace. On account of its position at the heart of the temple, this splendid stone – a transmutation of the Goddess who on the day appeared in her guise as the Womb Stone and was impregnated in parallel with similar events at Stonehenge no more than thirty kilometres [18½ miles] to the south – must have been the most important stone at Avebury.[15]

The idea, belief and sheer experience that stones can be imbued with spirit is universal. Arthur Guirdham, whose books on group reincarnation helped bring dualism back into the New Age movement, was fond of quoting the lines, 'God sleeps in the stone, dreams in the plant, wakes in the animal, and lives in Man . . .' To animists the consciousness is already there. It is not a case of individuals or groups projecting it. Stones can be filled with divine consciousness just as humans can.

In Ancient Egypt the ritual known as the 'Opening of the Mouth' involved imbuing the statue of the deceased pharaoh with the latter's soul, for moments of semipublic communion.

Which may be why the eyes on many such statues were made from precious or semiprecious stones. The experience of statues 'coming alive', or apparently becoming suffused with life, is common to every religion, and is not something that should be dismissed as mere mass hysteria. This is not a question of lumps of shaped rock clumping around the fields or up and down the aisles, but of stone becoming imbued with soul.

Although I have visited Stonehenge and driven past it many times it has not always come alive, no matter how intense my inner entreaties. There are moments when it has seemed to thrum, like a generator, and others when it has been entirely flat, no more than a collection of lifeless chunks, pleasingly arranged. It felt like that recently, as I drove slowly past it with Monique Michaud and Caroline Hancock, and found myself gawping as much at the hordes of tourists as the stones themselves. It was only when I was almost out of their orbit that a very powerful sense of consciousness was transmitted to me, that I can best symbolise as someone looking at me out of the corner of their eye, but with a cunning glint. The nearest parallel I can think of to describe this very strong but allusive contact is with Muhammad Ali's rope-a-dope trick, when he feigned defeat and exhaustion, while waiting for his own moment to come out fighting. It seemed to me that that was what the stones were doing just then.

So even if psychics feel nothing from them, stone circles are not necessarily 'dead'. They may be just waiting.

Of which more in due course.

Meaden, however, became aware of something else within the Avebury circle.

The faces. Unmistakable features that had been carved into the stones by those who were responsible for them. Discounting the obvious suggestion that these faces were no more than the result of his projecting his ideas on to 'accidental ambiguous shapes', he insisted:

> When studied closely from particular angles, regardless of the
> time of day, some of the stones reveal profiles of human heads

or faces, or more rarely animal heads. But when the sun is out and shining at critical angles and at certain times of the day, many more heads can be seen, usually one side only, and always with an eye.[16]

Even if, as his critics argue, the faces are merely caused by felicitous weathering, it is already too late. Buttons have been pressed, new perceptions come into play. Once pointed out, it becomes hard not to see the Avebury faces, and near impossible not to go looking for similar in other stones, in other circles. Then it becomes harder still not to feel the consciousness within the stones once they have been personalised. Difficult not to feel that they *are* watching you with those newly discovered eyes.

Even though Meaden himself would probably be unhappy with this purely magickal stance, what he has caused is a change to occur in the consciousness of everyone remotely interested in the topic. This in itself is the purest definition of magick: 'the art of causing changes to occur in consciousness'. Even the Reverend Edward Duke might feel some validation in the fact that here, in what he saw as a Temple of the Sun and Moon, in a place of light and reflected light, where the Great Mother was mated with the Sky Father, life was brought into the stones.

These faces, as identified in Meaden's lucid and beautifully illustrated *The Secrets of the Avebury Stones*, seem to have personalities that might be defined as sombre, austere, thoughtful; passive, dour, venerable; brooding, watchful, jocular . . . a whole tribal range of personalities, in fact, which almost cajole us into using one of those traditional magickal techniques involving the creation of 'telesmatic images'.

This term was probably first used in print by WE Butler, who as that ten-year-old boy had attempted to raise the Devil on a Yorkshire moor, and who later became an initiate of Dion Fortune's Fraternity of the Inner Light, as well as the founder of the Servants of Light – magickal organisations ultimately descended from the Hermetic Order of the Golden Dawn. Basically it involves the creation of images within the imagination which, in effect, send out signals to the inner worlds. With due quality of effort these images can become ensouled by evolved and specialised entities. The images are thus seen as points of contact between this and the other world, and are used by the entities in question as vehicles for the duration of the magick. Anyone who has ever used this technique can testify to the peculiar thrill of the moment when these created images no longer dance to the tune of the individual's imagination because they have suddenly become real, with independent knowledge and consciousness, and a very marked sense of presence. No need to quote Jung on this technique, and claim it as his. Magicians were using this when he was still a young man 'Freudened' by ghosts.

Imbuing the Avebury stones with faces can be used in just this way. And although there are many pitfalls along the way when using this technique, and many mistakes that can be made, even the briefest sense of the stones coming alive and watching you, and seeming willing to communicate with you in their own, slow, stone way, can be a deeply moving moment.

In 1998, at dawn on 1 May, which is the old pagan festival of Beltane, two dowsers named Hamish Miller and Paul Broadhurst followed the old processional route along the West Kennet stone avenue. They were following what they had discerned as a Serpent Current, part of a huge ley line running from St Michael's Mount in Cornwall, up through Glastonbury, Avebury, Royston and Bury St Edmunds – a current of terrestrial energy that they felt could transform human perceptions. To them the energies amid the circle behaved in such a way that the results were unequivocal. William Stukeley had been right. Avebury *was* a Serpent Temple. They were aware, too, of the male and female nature of the stones within the avenue, and had the impression of 'petrified sexual balance that was evidently an important feature in the ethos of the megalith builders'.[17]

Two modern magicians whose experience at Avebury almost encapsulates much of the foregoing are John and Elizabeth Fox, founders of the group Sirius. Real magicians, who have been quietly and effectively practising magick for a good many years, they belong to that old and diligent school which understood why magick was always referred to as the Work.

In the mid-1980s they stumbled upon Avebury as John Aubrey did. That is to say, by 'accident'. After spending some time exploring the village and taking photographs, they began to feel the interconnectedness of the whole area. Eventually they drove up to the end of the avenue and parked the car, collected their cameras and went between the lines of stones.

> The sheep were still there in their hundreds and didn't seem to object to our presence. We walked about getting the feel of the place, the sheep moving to one side to let us pass. I noticed that the stones that Keiller had placed on one side of the Avenue matched up to those on the opposite side and created a male–female line the length of the Avenue. I took a place against one of the Keiller stones (male) on the left hand side of the Avenue looking up to where the Avenue of stones disappeared over the rise and out of sight. By coincidence Elizabeth leant against one of the large lozenge (female) stones on the opposite side of the Avenue to me. Then the whole flock of sheep became animated and began running up the hill as if they had dogs chasing them. Some began to jump in the air as if electric prodders were being used on their rear ends. Within a couple of minutes all the sheep had disappeared out of sight. We now had the Avenue to ourselves. During this time Elizabeth or myself had remained by our respective stones.

As the last of the sheep went over the rise they 'saw' the procession approach from the direction of the Sanctuary and West Kennet. It was made up of about fifty couples, with the men being from the Sanctuary, the women from West Kennet. 'They were dressed like ancient Egyptians, the ladies were bare breasted and wore long ankle length skirts. The men wore a short kilt.' In John's narrative he 'was told' by his inner sources that these couples were heading to the Main Circle for mating, 'as it was the mating time'. That when they arrived in the circle each couple would conjoin – make love – and that the ceremony would take place during what we today call Beltane. The couples, he noted, seemed to be very happy and looking forward to the ceremony. He concluded with the comment, 'The whole period lasted seconds but it left a strong impression on me.'

Elizabeth's own vision, written separately, supported his in all the salient details, and within this one brief experience we have the themes of: serendipity, which took them into the circle and Avenue in the first place; the notion of the male and female stones, which the patron Alexander Keiller identified, and which Meaden later expanded upon; the sense of 'sacred mating', either on the human or astronomical level, or both; and yet again this persistent theme of Egypt. This from two people who before that moment had no particular interest in Egypt at all.*

In contrast, one anonymous woman ordained as a priestess in the Fellowship of Isis, who has a life-long passion for all things Egyptian, felt nothing of the latter within the Avebury circles during the visits she has made, usually at the time of Samhain, or 1 November, which is traditionally the time of the Ancestors. Celts she felt in abundance, but Egyptians? No. She was, however, acutely aware of a 'Crone Goddess' standing next to the largest of the stones, cloaked and hooded, plain and black, watching very carefully and with an air of bittersweet melancholy wisdom that edged towards pure sadness.

I think we can all feel that at the ancient sites: a yearning for that which has gone, that which has been lost. Perhaps it's the Ancestors we feel at our shoulders as we stroll around, wondering . . .

Wendy Berg is one of the seniors in the Avalon Group, which describes itself as a 'magickal fraternity which works within the Western Mystery Tradition and seeks to serve the folk soul

---

* However, on seeing the manuscript in progress, John later commented 'What folks "see" is what they think are Egyptian but they are not Egyptian. They look Egyptian because of the costumes they wear. Checking into the period we think it is – post the last Ice Age – they could be Phoenician or Minoan. Because the ladies wear no covering on their chests and the lads wear only kilts, could well mean that they are a very hardy race and if Phoenician they could be seasoned seafarers and not notice the cold like we do today. I know that this will not go down well with those Egyptian freaks who swear that everything of value came from there. I don't think so.'

of these islands'. It is another group that is ultimately derived from those majestic, swirling currents of the Hermetic Order of the Golden Dawn – a tradition that, I have to admit, is my own first love. When I asked her to tell me of her own experiences at any site she singled out Scorhill stone circle on those bleak realms of the Dartmoor she has come to love. At Scorhill she got the impression that:

> . . . the stones are not so important for themselves and although one may touch them and dowse them and feel etheric energy around them, to concentrate on this is to miss out on the 'higher' levels. The stones act as storage points, as the earthing pole of the battery, as one half of the polarity. The other half, which is the inner beings who still use the site, I have seen as tall, shining, hardly human figures, neither separate from the stones nor merged with them. It's as if they can bring their energy down when necessary to resonate at the same frequency as the quartz within the granite. These beings appear sometimes to be carrying some sort of metallic shield and I am reminded of the popular depictions of faery warriors who carry similar weaponry. But it seems to me that these are not for protection (protection against what?) but are part of the tuning, resonating process. The shields are not always of recognisably earthly metals although some appear to be like copper, or mercury. I've also seen them carry 'weapons' which I can only describe as a sort of astral tuning fork. I get the impression that these beings are tuning in to various planetary or stellar bodies so that the stone circle can be set to vibrate at different frequencies and receive the various celestial influxes according to how it has been tuned. Rather like, for instance, the great receptive radio dishes at 'Goonhilly Earth Station' in Cornwall.
>
> I believe that because of this 'purity' of Dartmoor it's more possible here than almost anywhere in Britain to pick up, through the land, a feeling of Atlantis. The feeling seems to disappear once you've passed Exeter, but west of Exeter I'm often mindful that the land is attuned to Atlantis, that it's looking West to its inner source . . .

Berg's perceptions were, unknown to her, anticipated almost exactly by the Highlander second sight of John Foster Forbes. Writing and broadcasting on the radio in the late 1930s, he insisted that the megalith builders came from this sunken land of Atlantis that Wendy sensed lurking beyond the horizon. Survivors of some cataclysm, these elite scientist-priests used the circles to control the weather, as we touched upon in the previous chapter, and to link with spiritual energies from the stars. They were in fact 'receiving stations', he stated, 'for direct influences from heavenly constellations' – though this was decades before the radio dishes of Goonhilly Down were able to provide Berg with her own analogy. More, the quartz rocks that (in the belief of almost all the occultists I spoke to) are an important aspect of many stone circles responded to what might now be termed the 'telluric' currents of the earth, and the power generated was stored in places such as the Dartmoor tors. Or Silbury Hill, perhaps? His psychometrist friend, Iris Campbell, wrote in *Giants, Myths and Megaliths* that survivors of the Atlantean cataclysm 'erected magnetic centres and constructed pits which were to become vortices of power which they induced by their rituals and their knowledge of the stars', the ultimate aim being to create spiritual power centres 'for the purification of the earth's own magnetic streams and atmospheres, so that when the time was ripe the true spiritual powers should gain in volume and impetus.'[18]

When it comes to another stone circle, in Cumberland, one couple in particular not only 'saw' the female spirits within the stones, but actually communed with them as clearly as if they were living flesh-and-blood women – although with the unusual insights and attitudes that come from another age.

Ray and Cass are two experienced magicians who choose not to use their last names, to avoid any scorn they might get in their respective workplaces. Cass is an Australian writer and Ray an aeronautical engineer from the Midlands. Together they have visited almost every major circle in Britain, but the one that holds the greatest appeal – for Ray in particular – is that of Long Meg and her Daughters in Cumberland.

This is the fifth largest of the stone circles in Britain and Ireland, and is, according to medieval tradition, believed to be composed of petrified witches. Some say this was done by the magician Michael Scott, who was annoyed by the dancing hags; others say they were simply girls who were punished for dancing on the Sabbath.

In short, yet another example of women being turned into stone. Or else the stones themselves being profoundly linked with the consciousness of women.

To Ray, the stone known as Long Meg is almost an entity in itself. He speaks of 'Meg' appearing at unlikely times, and communing with him as readily as if it had been a woman spirit of that name.

This in itself, I must add, is nothing unusual. Almost all of the people I spoke to, or corresponded with, had the experience of stones being able to 'stay with' them, on inner levels, long after an actual visit. Silbury, as I have said, had this effect on me, though it is not the only place.

Ray started by telling me of his feeling that there is a sort of 'invisibility spell' over the place, which causes newcomers to wander about, lost, quite unable to find the circle no matter how hard they try. As we see in later chapters this is quite common for some sites, and I can vouch for the truth of this in respect to Long Meg. When I was nineteen and doing my first teaching practice, I lived within a modest stone's throw of the circle for three months, yet never once got there, or even glimpsed it, despite constantly being pointed in the right direction by locals.

To Ray, using computer terminology, Long Meg and her Daughters was a kind of 'backup' circle to the programming of the main sites at Avebury, Stonehenge, Callanish and others. As with others, he regarded the circles as interlinking parts of a national, and probably international, magickal technology that we are only just beginning to rediscover. Now Ray had never heard of John Foster Forbes or his psychometrist friend 'Miss Campbell', but it is worthwhile looking at what the latter wrote about Long Meg in the late 1930s, using the most up-to-date analogies that she could think of:

> This is a central receiving-station used for tuning in to all other stations throughout the country. As we now use wireless

transmitting for communications, so in that past age the earth was used in the same way to transmit messages by tapping.[19]

The content of the messages between distant circles was received by ordinary psychometry, the palms being held against the stones to pick up information. All such stones were once tuned in to Long Meg. This circle was, to use her analogy, akin to a national control room.

Ray told me of one incident during their first visit, when Cass was touching Long Meg, her forehead against the stone, and two Tornados from the Italian Air Force, on a training exercise, thundered over. To his inner eye it was almost as if the two of them – stone and woman – flinched, and huddled against each other for comfort as two children might.

Ray, communing with this very marked but very unhuman consciousness he thought of simply as Meg, then took time to explain to her what these creatures, these 'dragons', really were. The response from the stone was that no one had taken the trouble to do that before, and Ray – again using the computer terminology with which he is most at ease – then had the sense of Meg downloading this information and effectively reprogramming the whole circle to take it into account.

Cass herself added that Meg was able, at the next fly-past, '... to utilise/convert the energy of the sound and transfer it into the circle. I/we believe that the circles were originally "powered up" by song, dance, drumming, sexual activity, etc on the part of – for want of a better word – the congregation, with the energy raised being channelled and directed by the priest and priestess of the circle.'

Ray also experienced something similar at Avebury, much later, when he was walking along the line of white concrete posts that mark the position of the original stones.

'I was suddenly aware of Meg looming behind me, and asking what these odd posts were. I told her what they were for, and that they were made of concrete – which I also explained, for she was quite unfamiliar with the substance. Then again I had the sense of Meg connecting with this post and downloading information into it. You know what it looks like on a computer screen when this sort of thing goes on, with huge masses of information being transferred in seconds, to create a new program? It was like that with Meg and this concrete post, so that by the time she had finished this humble lump of concrete had been programmed to act as the original stone was meant to do!'

Cass in her turn describes herself both as a Wagnerian Valkyrie who has temporarily lost her shield and sword, and also as 'psychic as a brick' – to the extent that when something does come through it has to be pretty important, or powerful. She believes that many if not all of the secrets of the stones can be unlocked by music. 'You can find the pitch of a stone by harmonic overtone chanting, and you can actually feel the stone vibrate to the touch when the correct pitch is reached.' Among the many things that Long Meg taught her was that, as mentioned, not only were the stones originally energised by song, dance, drumming – something with which Murry Hope (no mean musician herself) would agree – but that they also appreciate actual conversation, as opposed to people just coming along to bless or dress them in the most patronising manner. To the best of my knowledge they have never met, or communicated, yet Murry's earlier comment that the stones were ' . . . programmed to respond to (or resonate with) a specific sonic, which had nothing to do with time as we know it' matches Cass's perception exactly.

Long Meg and her Daughters was actually 'closed down' as an active unit, she felt, when the Romans in the area massacred within the stones' perimeter every man, woman and child they could capture. This spilling of blood was not in keeping with the ancient tradition of the sort of 'willing sacrifice' envisioned by Charles Seymour in a previous chapter, but was just pure murder. In fact this may well have been what Anne McCourt was sensing when she described the air of sadness which seemed to suffuse that same circle on her visit.

So some of Cass's work involved cleansing the stones with the help of water from the Chalice Well in Glastonbury, and singing them back into wakefulness. This was aided in part by someone who simply wanted to be known as David the Harper, another Australian, who created a 'Song of the Stones' that was a response to their own consciousness. David also found that, by letting the wind itself play the strings, Long Meg – and all other circles – had their own peculiar songs.

One person who tried to 'awaken' some stones by the same techniques of sound and dance but had quite a different (and less benign) experience was Mike Harris, in his early days of stumbling into wisdom. There is a Bronze Age trackway located above his home along which are standing stones, burial mounds and one particular row of five standing stones. He wrote of these:

> Many years ago a group member and I went to this stone row with what may best be described as 'ritual intent', hoping to wake up the powers of the place! The best way of stirring up the powers seemed to be for one of us to dance through the stones in a figure of eight pattern whilst the other chanted, beating out the time of the dance. Things soon hotted up, the sonics and dance patterns hit the right frequency and I looked up to see my co-worker totally 'gone' dancing like a maniac with a procession of Faery beings in his wake. 'This is good' I thought 'great stuff' then something nudged me inwardly to say no it *wasn't* good. My friend was fading somewhat, being utterly drawn in. I stopped chanting, stood up and shouted 'Cease!' My friend collapsed in a heap and the Faery folk vanished.

It should be noted that the 'faery spirits' of our ancestors had nothing to do with bluebells and snowdrops, with crystals, tree-hugging or that smiling, cloying brand of infinite 'niceness' which many adherents of the New Age imagine is akin to spirituality. As we shall see later they were – are – creatures of another, nonhuman, dimension. They can be wild, ecstatic, immensely attractive – and quite capable of destroying us if we fail to relate to them properly.

Having survived this encounter Harris later felt that the sensible way to have gone about this would have been for them to have gone there, meditated and received some procedural guidance, then taken this with some token from the place

('Though one shouldn't of course encourage archaeological pilfering!'), left a token in exchange and gone home and sorted it out in a ritual there.

Another person who associates the stones with a kind of inner music is Dusty Miller (of whom more later), who wrote:

> But what the others don't know is that ... we hear the 'Faerie Music' which we refer to as 'singing', hence the term 'Singing-Stones'. To me, it sounds something like 'Gregorian Chant or Plainsong' heard indistinctly through an Abbey wall. It can have the effect of making you want to dance in harmony with this enchanting, unearthly sort of music. Maybe it is the 'Fairy Music' that 'Thomas the Rhymer' heard in the famous poem. Just what this 'music' is I don't know, but I suspect it is the radiating vibrations emanating from a 'Programmed Thought-form' left in the stone ... to guide travellers.

In the same context, talking about a visit that his group made to a local cromlech called 'The Chestnuts', he added:

> It was proposed that it might be nice to show appreciation to the Stones by singing 'tones' to them. The atmosphere of the place certainly seemed to get better and better, and then to our astonishment, two rabbits came to see what we were up to. Unfortunately, one of the children found them rather exciting and frightened them off.

Of course, not all the circles are concerned with awesome levels of energy. One person who was heavily involved in Wicca spoke to me of a small group of stones near Soissons Wood, which is near Postbridge/Bellever on Dartmoor.

> It's a circle of low stones, not particularly remarkable in appearance. When we found it, the day was warm and sunny, and the stones as comfortable as an armchair to lean against.
>
> When I approach a circle, it's with an open mind – literally. Hold an inner stillness, and the stones will tell you what they need. This circle wanted to be told stories – who we were, where we'd come from, what the land thereabouts was like, what grew there ... My partner says it was also a teaching circle – teaching through storytelling, whether of hunting or harvest or the ways of the seasons. When we gave water and

grain to the stones, as is our custom, he reminded me that the two outliers (guard stones) were asking if there would be enough for them as well.

It is our general custom to give grain and water as an offering to the stones – often muesli because it's inconspicuous to carry and combines grain, fruit and honey. The water is usually from Chalice Well (in England, at least – Welsh sites may get water from Winefred's Well at Holywell). My partner calls it 'paying the rent'.

This is the same approach that Jack Green took with his family 'Wishing Stone': simple conversation rather than strenuous invocation. Which in its turn results in simple but effective communication between two very different types of consciousness.

And it is this notion of different – and differing – types of consciousness that can help us break free of the orbit of Avebury rather like a spaceship using the slingshot technique, and head towards a place where our minds can impinge upon those of *very* different entities indeed.

CHAPTER

FOUR

WALKER'S HILL, THE INNER ORBIT OF
MERCURY AND THE SPIRITS OF THE BLISSFUL
DEAD

*'When I stand,' said Wang Xiang Zhai, 'the earth
is in my hands and the universe is in my mind.'*
Liongate *magazine*

Our notional guide, the Reverend Edward Duke, made his
stately way towards the next orbit on his scheme that he
described grandly as being the site of the Temple of the
Mercury, although it was known to the locals simply as
Walker's Hill. He located the place by a combination of map
reading, line-of-sight and the felicitous logic of his visionary
scheme. Quite simply, if Silbury was the earth and Stonehenge
was Saturn, and if all the other planets fell at the appropriate
intervals on his meridian, then whatever site lay upon the
intersection of orbit and meridian *had* to be the Temple of
Mercury. Even if it did appear to the mortal eye as an unexceptional, sheep-scattered place.

The hill itself can be reached easily enough. Just cross the
London Road and wend along some pleasant side roads. A
ramble rather than a hike. Before too long Walker's Hill itself
can be seen, a few miles south of the Avebury/Silbury complex,
and clearly crowned by a huge long barrow known as Adam's
Grave, or sometimes Adam's Peak. Unless we prefer the etymology of 'Atum's Grave', then this is a clear case of Christians
usurping and renaming a pagan site.

In Edward Duke's time this barrow, which is visible from a
great distance, was known as 'Old Adam', while the standing
stone at its base was 'Little Eve'. During the Saxon era its name
was recorded as 'Wodensbeorg', or 'Woden's barrow', sacred
to their own sacrificed god. Traditionally this god, or giant,

95

could be raised simply by running seven times around the grave. In fact, a similar technique is suggested for the round barrow on top of Cley Hill, and other barrows throughout Wiltshire; usually the 'giant' within also has to have his name called three times. Hardly the most demanding of rituals, but then, as all the correspondents have insisted, it has never been a case of what you do at these sites, but how you do it.

Likewise, although our guide drove to the hill by coach and horses, he (and we) could as easily have taken Wang Xiang Zhai's approach and turned inwards – and get there just the same. Just as quantum theory suggests that the experimenter plays a role in the experiment, occult theory seems to insist that the energies of the megaliths are inseparable from the personal energies within those who link with them.

At one level, this is the place where we meet the spirits and their symbols, for you cannot go far through any kind of solar system, or philosophy, without touching on them. Whether it is the Spirit of Place, Spirit of the Age, Spirit of the Stones, earthbound spirits, guides, gods or guardians, or simply the all-pervasive spirits of Ancestors, you can hardly avoid them as you travel through that savage and beautiful country of the psyche towards your own personal equivalent of Walker's Hill. Sometimes, according to the seers of all traditions, you can find them speaking to you through symbolism. Sometimes, as with shooting stars, you can actually glimpse them flaring briefly in that last nanosecond before burn-out. Other times, they can smash into the atmosphere of your mind like a comet, creating global havoc.

And the old Stone-King is one of these . . .

When someone in the twenty-first century comes to write the inner history of all those spiritual movements and impulses from the preceding two centuries, they will surely identify one spirit in particular as having had an impact that will be realised only in retrospect. The entity in question called himself the 'Earth-man' or 'Stone-King', and he had been the leader of his tribe thousands of years before. He seemed old, very brown, with curly hair and black beard, and spiral cheek tattoos. His

eyes were like large black stones, owing to the visual effect of
tattooing or colouring around the deep eye sockets, and he
wore clothing made of skins: a tight tunic and trousers tied
around with sinews. And when he came to the mouth of the
chambered tomb at Les Monts Grantez, in Jersey, in 1978, and
communed with RJ 'Bob' Stewart – a musician and writer
specialising in mythological and magickal topics – he turned
the whole of the modern magickal movement on its head, and
showed the generations that followed that there may be a little
more to the business of Earth Magick than hugging trees and
embracing stones.

This 'Earth-man' or 'Stone-King' had been a tribal leader, a
local king, in prehistoric times. According to his ideas he had
'merged with the environment' and finally emerged 'on the
other side of it' as an entity whose role it was to communicate
'Earth-peace' to his people, and link and mediate through
various stages of human and nonhuman evolution. The inner
chamber of this womblike tomb (like the chamber described
by Joan Grant in her life as Sekhet-a-ra) was thus used for
consultation with the resident entity and initiation. Although
the spiritual contact was made at the tomb on Jersey, it continued in Stewart's flat in Bath where the King began to offer
several 'obscure intimations' which Stewart found difficult at
the time to translate, but which he felt were:

1. The King is now part of the solar system . . . linked through
the stones and the special structure of the dolmen and mound,
which become an Earth-power gate or amplifier for his awareness, a focus by which his differing viewpoint may be translated
into one which is accessible to physical humans still on the
planet.
    The curious and difficult point about this concept is the
accompanying awareness that (to the King) the solar system is
inside the structure of the stones and in the very bones of the
Earth itself and is in no way external or removed from it. . . .
2. The purpose of the dolmen or passage grave is extremely
precise and 'scientific'. A sealed chamber of massive stones,
which have to be over a certain mass or size, is buried beneath
a mound of earth. This causes certain natural processes to occur,

directly due to the shapes and nature of the structure itself. This
is usually aided by the knowledge and co-operation of the being
or beings buried alive within it. . . .
3. The aim, as the King expressed it, was to achieve integration
with the Earth environment, moving through it to other states
of awareness. 'These are *in the Earth*, according to the King,
or more strictly speaking, the Earth is *outside the stars*, and is
the gateway to them. The actual physical structure is womblike,
and was identified as a returning to the Mother.'[1]

Stewart's experience with this spirit from the depths of the
tomb is an extremely powerful and moving one. The difficult
insights that he sought to express in modern terms are so far
removed from the tree-hugging, happy-clappy, let-everyone-be-
nice practices that pass as modern paganism that it is hard not
to be influenced by what this tough, uncompromising Stone-
King tries to say. Linking the Earth and the people, the bones
and the stones, the underworld and inner world, with those
stars above which are really beneath . . . Then ending with the
sort of words that you only occasionally find, but that you
know hold the true secrets of magick, somehow, even if your
conscious mind cannot quite grasp them as yet:

On attempting to convey the meaning of the flow of time,
the response from the King was the equivalent of 'there is
no line of such a shape. There is only turning until you are
inside the Earth. From the little turning to the great turning
that is inside the little turning. Inside the great turning is Earth-
peace.'[2]

But, if we are to learn from entities like the above, we have
to do so in those areas of the psyche that might be termed the
Temple of Mercury. There is nothing very esoteric about this:
we go there whenever neurons fire in the brain, whenever we
use our minds to try to make sense of things. This is the area
of Edward Duke's brain that helped him link his vision, his
scholarship and his geography in a way that took him to the
top of Walker's Hill.

In astrological terms the planet Mercury's role is to establish
communication through any means – to interpret and analyse

information and experience. It is connected with the intellect and all the reasoning processes.

In classical mythology (with which our guide the Reverend Edward Duke was dauntingly familiar) Mercury was the messenger god with wings on his ankles and carrying the caduceus. To the Greeks this was Hermes, from whom we get the term 'hermetic', referring to those mysteries that sought to fathom the secrets of the universe using the powers of the mind and appropriate rituals.

Many of the people involved in the present book have described themselves as involved in the Hermetic Path. Mercury/Hermes, in various aspects, is the patron of travellers as well as being guide to the dead, for he was a god who 'walked between the worlds' carrying messages from one dimension to another. He represents those qualities of the mind that help us make sense of where we are and why we are here. He helps us forge links between outer circumstance and inner event, and enables us to create our own myths through which to evolve. On other levels the planet Mercury is connected with the intellectual qualities of wit and humour, puns and puzzles, cryptograms and cyphers, as well as with all those dramatic ritual techniques that require pageantry and ceremony.

'Trickster' is the name given to a Native America deity whose role is exactly that: to bring people to wisdom and understanding through means of practical jokes, tricks, bizarre escapades and adventures – some of which bring about wry, painful smiles rather than uproarious belly laughs. As we shall see in a later chapter, almost every person connected with exploring the Earth Mysteries eventually uses the term 'Trickster' to describe the bewildering events that happen alongside their own quests.

So in the punning, tricksterish manner appropriate to this planet there is a certain rightness in linking Mercury, the Walker Between the Worlds, to the geographical reality of Walker's Hill, even if the name did simply derive from the landowner Clement Walker, who inherited the property in 1801.

Jack Green wrote:

When I first became obsessed with [the sites of Northumberland] and somehow stumbled into their energies, I suppose I went through a kind of madness. Belting around all over the bleak countryside. I was convinced that the sites were situated in a series of concentric circles, like the cup and ring markings, with the centre at the Three Kings just south of the Catscleugh Reservoir, and the easternmost limit falling on the ancient cairn known as Glitteringstone, on the hills above Rothbury. I found what I was looking for, I think, but my map-reading and measuring has always been so shoddy that I could probably have imposed any pattern on the maps and found old stones to match.

More importantly, Green felt that the outer circumstances of his life were being affected by the inner energies – the spirits, if you like – of the once-sacred places. He found himself in the centre of synchronistic chains of events whereby people, places, images, symbols all seemed to impinge upon him in daily life as if carrying a secret coded message – all quite in keeping with these energies of Mercury. It all seemed to be spiralling around in a huge circle of bizarre coincidence until it reached a point where it seemed as if, as he described it, ' . . . just one more little revelation and all would be explained – something in the nature of a cosmic secret which the stones and their places would reveal, and which would make sense of *everything . . .*'

And then it all stopped. Dead. And went in the opposite direction – rather like one of those inward-spiralling cup-and-ring marks that he had spent so long trying to find, with the straight line leaving the centre for directions new. Imminent revelation gave way to denouement, seeming to confirm the medium Ena Twigg's 'law of frustration', which asserts that, when all loose ends are tied up and a definite pattern is seen, something happens that undoes the pattern completely.

Green came to feel that although the stones had awakened something quite profound within him, they necessarily tended to manifest their energies in terms relevant to him at that time, while leaving enough mystery to ensure their potency in later years.

In fact he came to use this spiral design as his own personal mandala, which is strongly reminiscent of the right-hand spirals that Underwood could dowse into awareness. It became his key to that which that lay behind the sites.

> I actually spent some time wondering if there was some symbol, or device, that I could put on my 'door' to the innerworld and inner Earth Mysteries. Something that could key me in, or help me unlock the door when necessary. Then it was like a voice said 'You've already found it, you arsehole!' And I realised it meant that spiral with the centre line, which up until then I'd been thinking of in a generalised sense. Mind, I'm not sure everyone could use it to unlock Mysteries of that area, but it seems to work for me. I'm sure if I belonged to a group – which god forbid I never will – I think it would help them open the doors too.

Michael Everest, one of the pioneers of research into 'sacred geometry', and a man who pushes his intellectualism into near-mystical levels of perception, is another who became as obsessed as Green was, and whose experiences at sites in the South of England left him with, in one 24-hour period, visions of spirals, Maltese or Templar-type crosses, Celtic crosses and mandala-like figures which seemed to have encoded information for him.

His insights are attuned to James Lovelock's notion of Gaia, which holds that the entire earth is a self-regulating entity which acts almost as a single, holistic organism. Although we will look more closely at some of his insights from this angle later, the point is that such inner events are more common than people realise, and could be said to represent Mercury/Hermes at his enigmatic best.

In looking at the concept of the Sacred Hill in an earlier chapter we mentioned Arthur O'Neil's experience at the top of Cley Hill, where he touched upon the spirit of Arianrhod, perhaps. Before that, however, his days were dogged by the recurrent image of the crescent, which appeared time and again in striking but unexpected ways, and always as though powers were trying to tell him something. It seems that such patterns, symbols, images – working themselves into the consciousness on all sorts of levels, including the physical and intellectual – are invariably an integral part of the experience when the seeker first connects to a site.

So although it does not – in any way – denigrate or diminish the essential genius behind his vision, Duke was always going to find that his orbital pattern linked with revealing sites in an area that is, even today, reeking with prehistory. Walker's Hill, therefore, was a lucky place to find the orbit of Mercury, and seemed to be confirmed by the name origins of the neighbouring Knap Hill. 'I am no visionary,' he wrote, 'and utterly unwilling to stretch etymology beyond its due bounds, but I must explain myself. Kneph or Cneph... was, as well as Thoth, the Egyptian or Phoenician name for Mercury.'[3]

In fact Kneph was a self-begotten divinity rather more akin to Robin Hood than Mercury, for he was the commoners' hero who favoured neither high nor low, and who was given the role of 'vizier of the poor'. Duke picked the wrong one there, alas.

But, even so, 'to stretch etymology beyond its due bounds' is part and parcel of working the Earth Mysteries, akin to followers of ley lines extending them to see where they might lead, or imposing an intuitive pattern on the land as Jack Green did, and seeing what he might find. Although the experiences may seem at first to lead to nothing and nowhere in many cases, the travelling alone is often wondrous enough. Playing with word and name origins is all part of Mercury's realm. It is a matter of making rhymes between insights of imagery and the rhythms of experience. It is a question of pulling order from chaos. The moment that we ask of the ancient stones, 'What are they for? why were they built?', we actually touch upon this 'orbit of Mercury', and come near the spirits.

Spirits, of course, may be said to exist beyond time. As we shall see again and again within this narrative the Mysteries of Time – or rather how we try to fathom them – are fundamental to just about everyone's experience of the sites, no matter what

102

tradition they come from. It seems you cannot touch upon the concepts of time without the attendant spirits.

In fact time slips are another curious aspect of this actual geographical area along the neolithic route known as the Ridgeway. Not merely seeing into the past but actually stepping back into it and observing the (often silent) people there. The stories are standard: people out walking their dogs, or hurrying home, stumbling upon cottages they had never noticed before, inhabited by oddly dressed people. Then later learning that said cottages had been destroyed centuries before. This is not to denigrate the experience. The experience is astounding. For example, when Edna Hedges was in her teens, in the early 1930s, she was forced to take shelter from a storm while cycling along a bleak and lonely stretch. She saw an isolated thatched cottage, plucked up her nerve, and knocked on the door. It opened noiselessly and an old man stood there – tall with broad shoulders, long grisly hair and beard, wearing a dark green waistcoat with metal buttons. On hearing her plight he removed an old-fashioned pipe from his mouth and beckoned her inside.

The room was dark and low-ceilinged, with a bright fire in an old-fashioned grate. There was no sound in the cottage at all, even when the storm was at it height. And although the old man stood and smiled benignly enough, at no time did he speak. She had no recollection of leaving the cottage, but found herself on her way when the storm abated.

Again, when talking it over with friends and family, and checking out all possible local records, she found that the cottage had been derelict for years.

Had she stepped into the past? And how would she have seemed to the old gentleman? As some oddly garbed spirit being – an elemental come out of the storm? Nothing else happened. Nothing came of it. Yet the delicious eeriness of the scene – the young girl out of time completely, sitting in the silent room while the heavens raged – has an impact in its own right.

Are there places in our landscape that act as gates into the past? Or, if not the past as such, parallel but subtly different worlds? There are experiences from visionaries that indicate that both possibilities exist, and that certain neolithic sites were actually built to take advantage of this.

One of the common denominators for all stone circles, however, and most sites, is the belief that magick was worked in them. Not simply arm waving with attitude, or examples of mass hypnosis among the unsophisticated tribes, but actual techniques that could manipulate the energies that the sacred places were meant to radiate. We simply need a half-decent imagination to conjure up for ourselves images of priests and priestesses – initiates of ancient wisdoms – doing long-forgotten things. Things that actually worked, and could be *seen* to work. And there is the feeling that if we could just, once, glimpse them working their magick, then we might get to touch upon the true inner purpose.

Margaret Lumley-Brown, who was the formidable 'pythoness' within the Society of the Inner Light, had a powerful vision of a 'quite small hill in north east Cornwall', next to which were priests performing a ritual dance. They were white-robed and black-bearded, and one of the movements within the dance consisted of each priest turning round, slowly, and lifting one arm over his head while he leaped two or three times in the air. 'Not unlike the Highland sword-dance!' she added brightly. The spot they were on, she felt, was connected with a temple to Astarte-Ashtoreth, and had been consecrated by Phoenician tin workers in this country.[4]

Are these gods and goddesses that constantly crop up actual independent entities? Are they images expressive of the 'spirit of place'? Are they simply projections from the unconscious of the pilgrim? It seems that how you answer that one determines what sort of traveller you are.

In a similar sort of vision, when Jack Gale led a group meditation at Maidenstone Hill, near Blackheath, which he felt had links with the megalithic culture and the Goddess, several independent people described 'seeing' a ritual dance of grey-robed pagan priests which involved complex steps and angular body shapes highly reminiscent of runes. The dance was joined by Herne the Hunter, an aspect of the Horned God, as well as the site's guardian, described as a tall, gaunt, elderly man in a brown robe who stepped out of the gnarled ash tree that was one of the site's foci.

According to all the people I spoke to – magicians, mystics, mediums, Christian and pagan – this interaction with the energies behind the sites and stones had, understandably, profound effects upon the psyches of the individuals involved. And thus (according to Jungian theory at least) upon the collective unconscious of whole nations, eventually.

One priestess who had a powerful vision of the people who worked magick in the sites, and who were/are still connected to them across time, was Dolores Ashcroft-Nowicki, the director of the magickal organisation known as the Servants of Light, or SOL for short. A hereditary psychic and a born magician, as are all in her family, she is difficult to pin down with any label. She could answer to witch, kabbalist, shaman, High Priestess of Khem or any one of half a dozen other occult disciplines, and could do the business – and effectively – in each one. She has power, and probably more knowledge than anyone I've met – and she makes me laugh.

On this occasion in 1997 she was visiting Newgrange, in the Boyne Valley, with what she termed a gaggle of magicians: Anna Branche (Shakmah Windrum), a powerful Solomonic magician, and her priestesses Lyrata and Avizan, all of whom had arrived from Philadelphia. In company also with Herbie Brennan (author of *Astral Doorways* and *Time Travel*), his wife Jackie and a few more like-minded friends, they visited Newgrange on one of its 'closed' days and, like so many children on an outing, they ran wild over this beautiful and powerful location. Newgrange itself is regarded as a real palace of the underworld, and said to be the home of the Dagda, chief of the Tuatha de Dannan, or his son Oengus, those pre-human ancestors who dominate the Irish traditions. In many ways Newgrange makes all other megalithic sites look soft. Described as a passage tomb, it was built nearly 1,000 years before the pyramids. It was built using over a quarter of a million tons of stone, and its hemispherical eastern section is faced with white-crystal quartz on top of a ring of dressed granite stones. In more ways than one, Newgrange shines like nothing else in the megalithic world ever did. Dolores's trance work here involved communing with the entities who could be reached within it:

After the first flush of enthusiasm Herbie called us together for one of his 'experiments'. This usually means trancework, a headache, and strange dreams for the rest of the week in my case. We penetrated the stone lined corridor and came to the centre with its small chambers. In one of these was a curious shallow bowl beautifully shaped and holding what I can only describe as a shimmer of power.

Herbie's idea was that each of the psychics would, one at a time, go into trance and suss out whatever was hanging around. The others would wait outside so that no interference or mind to mind contact could be made, it would be just one person's impression.

I have worked with Herbie for almost twenty years now and where trance work is concerned he is the one I can trust absolutely. If he says, 'Dolores I want you to do this . . .' I may grizzle a bit but I'll do it knowing I am in safe hands.

I tried out one of the small chambers first, but there seemed to be little beyond a sense of movement and intense purpose. I then moved to the central point around which the chambers were grouped and lay down. Immediately there was a different feel. The intricate spiral pattern of the roof hit me in the solar plexus and went straight through . . . to a similar spiral below me. Without even having had time to draw breath I was entranced and floating free, held between worlds by some sort of power thread that ran through the solar plexus. I remember thinking that this was how a butterfly pinned to a board must feel.

Abruptly I was somewhere else but also in the same place, just the time was different. I could still feel my physical body though faintly and knew that its heart beat had increased, but my mind was in a different space. I could not see at first, but then things cleared and I became aware of people, tall and mostly with red-gold hair and fair complexioned. Even the women were six foot and over. Alongside them another kind of people smaller and dark haired. They seemed to know I was

106

there but ignored me. I was still horizontal and like a bead on
a thread but everyone moved through me without comment. It
lasted for just a few moments, barely a minute I would think.

Then the second phase began. The tall people had gone, the
smaller ones were building what would be Newgrange. They
built from the middle outwards. As each chamber was finished
earth was packed around it to keep it all in place. Finally when
the centre was finished they began on the stone walls. Again
they set the stones in place, packed earth around them and then
built the next lot. Then the roofing, and all covered with earth
packed tight. Then and only then did they dig away the internal
earth leaving the stone lined corridors in place. I seemed to be
there for years, but it was only a few minutes. Then the darkness
came down again and I became aware of an Axe far below me
deep in the earth. Beautifully chased with spiraling designs it
was used only once, then buried deep.

Strangely when our day was over and we had written down
our findings, all of us had had similar visions and feelings. But
the strangest thing for me was the discovery of a sacrificial axe
on the site. Not in Newgrange, but buried beneath one of the
smaller mounds nearby. I'd like to go back and see what I
would get a second time around.

Dolores presented the vision as it stood, and made no
attempt to analyse or comment on it, the essence of which was
shared by several others at the same time. But it seems to me
that what she experienced was strangely contemporary – not
so much to Newgrange in its various phases, but to ourselves
today. As if the chambers were still, in some sense, inhabited
and utilised by people who – in terms of linear history – existed
thousands of years ago.

Similarly, on one of his trips to the Rollrights (whether on his
old Raleigh bicycle or on the wings of spirit from his bed in
Bennington Street, Cheltenham), William Gray saw the old
crone who, at one phase in the Rollrights' usage, channelled
through the powers of the Otherworld, and acted as one of
these guides between the living and the dead. As he 'saw' it,
the Counsellor Stones, when new, formed a central chamber
of quite a sizeable pyriform structure, mostly composed of

smaller stones and turfs laid like bricks. The way into this chamber was along a narrow little tunnel just big enough for a smallish person to crawl, while at the top, under the capstone, was a small ventilating shaft communicating with the outer air. This, he was sure, was the Holy of Holies, where the tribal deity manifested its presence to mortals. On sacred occasions the human medium, usually an elderly female, would be sent inside the chamber where she went into a semitrance condition, and called out whatever came to her inspirationally.

It seems that if the inside of the pyramid was warmed up previously by a turf fire for a day or so, the heat and smoke-smell greatly encouraged the wise woman or shamaness to 'go off' into volubility for quite a while before she passed out into unconsciousness or even death ... When such a demise occurred, which was not a terribly rare event, the body was given honourable burial, and later the bones were lifted, cleaned, and put with others of the same class usually in a skin bag kept in a side-cyst of the main pyramid. In that way, the spirits of the ancestors were supposed to keep in touch with their living descendants. It was probably a commencement of the custom of storing saintly bones in sacred shrines.[5]

The ageing priestess that Gray saw going into the darkness of her artificial cave was skin-clad with an amulet necklace and carried a skull rattle. She seemed at first to be small, ill-nourished and frail, but he was aware of how sinewy and tough her stringy muscles were.

Her age is difficult to estimate, though she looks incredibly ancient with her white hair bound back and her almost toothless gums receding in a hollowed and wind-wrinkled face. Yet her eyes seem bright and almost supernaturally sharp though their focus is obviously not with this world any longer. She has the strangest sort of smile as she sinks to her knees before the short tunnel entrance and begins her crawl into the interior.[6]

In front of the structure, facing a forecourt marked out with small stones and staves, burns a fire which flickers and sends up smoke columns, like spirits. The fire is tended by another devotee, a male, with 'a well developed sense of showmanship,

108

plus a shrewd insight into average human affairs'. His job is to act as an intermediary between the people and the Oracle.

The entity that the Midlands witch Rowan Greenwood linked with at the same stones was given the name Bethan, who appeared to her inner sight as a 'tall young woman with long blonde hair ... She is not, however, the Guardian of the Stones but appears to be either someone who worshipped at the site or maybe a "composite" of those who did.'[7] With Bethan's help she was able to tune in to the site, and understand something of its purpose.

Although there are differences between the visions of Gray and Greenwood, and the former made no mention of the latter's spirit helper and guide, we must make allowances for the fact that here are two individuals tuning in to a site that was in use for several thousand years. Rather akin to someone from the far future tuning in to St Paul's Cathedral and seeing it at different times in its history: the gleaming new stone and the packed congregations when first built; the marked divisions between the working- and upper-class worshippers; that dreadful moment when women entered without hats; the empty pews of the late 1980s; the chaotic hordes of schoolchildren; the bewildering multifaith congress; the Japanese tourists ... Yet, when we look more closely at the essence of individual visions, what is stunning is how much they actually dovetail into each other.

This again is one of the qualities of Mercury: the ability to make links, and understand. This was what Edward Duke did when, panting, he climbed to the top of Walker's Hill and looked back at where he had been, and then forward to where he must end up.

One anonymous correspondent felt that the name of the Walker's Hill barrow was less to do with Woden, however, than the ' ... native Wildman spirit once known as the Wood-wose, or even Woodhouse – a huge, rough and fearsome elemental being from another dimension. A Green Man sort of entity, of the sort once commonly experienced by the rural folk.' Rather akin to what Carlos Castaneda might have termed a 'power-ally', perhaps. The correspondent believed that the 'giant graves' and giant legends throughout Britain were related to this particular kind of being. 'It scared me f****** witless when mine appeared,' he wrote, although it was not clear whether he was referring to the entity of Adam's Grave or another closer to his Cotswold home. 'But he taught me a lot over the years.' However, this giant indwelling spirit seems to be of a different nature to the tomb guardians that will be discussed in a later chapter.

Another of this ilk, perhaps, is the huge spirit that Paddy senses at Waylands Smithy, in Oxfordshire – Wayland himself, or perhaps the deity known to the ancient British as Govannon, the Smith-god. Visiting the site early in the morning she is particularly aware of this massive presence, and an inner-world sound that is very like a great hammer smashing down on a giant anvil.

John Crabtree, editor of the magazine *Liongate*, made a striking inner contact at the stone circle in Auchgallon, on the Isle of Arran, where he effectively 'summoned up' the spirit of a Bronze Age seer connected with the site. On being asked who he was the answer came that he was one who had 'split the stone'. Crabtree then had a vision of a stone being split in two, with a feeling that the inner sides had eyes. 'I had the sense and impression that he was a figure who walked the worlds and had Knowledge – a seer . . . I asked his name – he said it was Eland. There was also a sense of oracular experience . . . a beautiful compassionate feeling.'

In practical terms, those individuals in the circle-building communities who were responsible for fashioning the stones, creating them according to the 'geodetic' energies and requirements, would have been regarded as specialists of a particular breed. The claim that he was one who had 'split the stone' is a declaration of high status.

Although this was not Crabtree's first visit to Arran, nor his first inner contact, his encounter with Eland was a deeply touching one whose impact is still being worked through.

We do not have to be great magicians, however, to link with

such entities. Sometimes we stumble upon them. Some areas seem more conducive to this than others. The environs of the adjoining Walker's Hill and Tan Hill (which would fall on the same orbital path) seem to heave with these inner-world contacts, who retrace ritual steps, make themselves known even to the least sensitive souls, and leave echoes that can be heard generations afterwards.

In 1904, for example, the Methodist lay preacher Alfred Fielding was driving home late in his horse-drawn trap when a tremendous storm came on. Through the pouring rain he saw the figure of a woman in white coming towards them along the road, and the horse stopped dead. As she came up level with the lights on the trap they saw a young woman with a beautiful angelic face and with auburn hair – who promptly vanished. The same figure has been seen many times since, in different circumstances, but always around the base of Tan Hill. Some have felt that she was the same entity as the woman with golden, glowing hair, 'pulsating with light', who has been linked with Glastonbury Tor in Somerset. In other words, Queen Guinevere.

Oddly enough the same figure's 'funeral cortège' has been seen atop Tan Hill on more than one occasion. In 1940, two shepherds, George Tasker and Tod Beake, were watching their flock of 300 sheep there when they heard the unusual sounds as of men and horses coming towards them. When the moon came out from behind a cloud they could see a party of men carrying torches and walking behind a wagon drawn by black horses. On the wagon was strapped a coffin, on top of which lay a crown, or circle of gold. When the cortège drew level with them it vanished into thin air. 'Me fustian cap rose right off me head,' George Tasker told his family.

The last two stories, interesting in themselves, are made more intriguing by the fact that they were collected by the late Kathleen Wiltshire, who presented them to Women's Institutes across the county. Wiltshire wrote three small books: *Wiltshire Folklore, Ghosts and Legends of the Wiltshire Countryside* and *More Ghosts and Legends of the Wiltshire Countryside*. The last one is little more than a collection of jottings – the bits and pieces that did not fit easily into the first two. But the first book in particular showed that Wiltshire had either dug into some very accessible and very rich seams of folklore or was speaking from first-hand experience as a witch of no small experience. Although she died before I could meet her, several people told me they had been invited by her to attend coven meetings 'on Salisbury Plain'. Exasperatingly, none of them went.

Kathleen Wiltshire was writing before the present glut of books on witchcraft with their spells, recipes, lotions and potions for every eventuality; and throughout the best of her writing she gave the impression that she knew more than she was saying – often that she was pushing us in certain directions by anecdotes such as those relating to Tan Hill. At one point she even mentioned the spirit of a man with a red hat who had been seen 'by many people' in her own little village of All Cannings, near the foot of Tan Hill.

> It has been suggested that this 'little man in a red hat' may have originated with the 'outliers', pastoral horsebreeders said to have lived on the downs. The 'Peaked Red One' was one of the gods in Dr. Ann Ross's *Pagan Celtic Britain*. He is described as being accompanied by a trout and a stag, and to carry a black-bird on his right shoulder. He is said to give half a nut (hazel?) to the blackbird and to eat half himself. He also carries an apple in a bronze vessel, half of which he gives to the stag; the other half he eats himself. He sips the water, and then all three, trout, stag and blackbird, drink from his vessel.[8]

There are times within her writing when a mask drops. She ceases to be the jolly old lady who regales her audience and their cucumber sandwiches with arch tales of rural spookery and becomes someone who knows a very great deal about magick. There is often a sense that she is saying subliminally: 'Remember this . . . It is not trivial.'

'I have heard,' she wrote coyly, 'that a coven called "Moon-rakers" a few years ago still gathered at Gorse Hill near Swindon and at the Devil's Den, not far from Avebury.'

Indeed. Was she herself a witch? By witch, I do not mean

those who merely dress up as such, for there is a profound difference between witches and those who merely practise witchcraft. Evan John Jones, who might be expected to know about such things, said:

> ... there is only one way of finding a Witch: judge them by their works and by their silence – unless there is a need to speak out. If one who claims to be a Witch can perform the tasks of Witchcraft, i.e. summon the spirits and they come, can divine with rod, fingers and birds. If they can also claim the right to the omens and have them; have the power to call, heal and curse and above all, can tell the maze and cross the Lethe, then you have a witch.[9]

Did Kathleen Wiltshire have any of these powers? Did she make an 'inner contact' with the 'Peaked Red One' and the young priestess with luminous hair, both linked with the witch-soaked atmosphere of Tan Hill, which looms over her village like her own sacred mountain?

To her the craft of the witch had been handed down by the descendants of the druids.

> Traditionally the traits of the Druid were control of the body (hypnosis, telepathy, auto-suggestion, detached consciousness), control over animals, and a knack with herbs. All these were traits of the witch. It was said that with bare feet, loose hair, and robes tucked up round their waists, the Druids gathered herbs in the light of the new moon, and from the north side of the hedge, and they gathered and distilled using the left hand. Trees, groves, springs, crossroads, and river boundaries were all their holy places and also where the sarsen stones lay. This, too, applied to a witch.[10]

And what of Tan Hill itself? The fact that the highest point was once marked on the old maps as 'Devil's Church' says something.

The name is possibly a contraction of St Anne's Hill, but there is also the idea that 'Tan Hoel' is Celtic for 'Fire of the Sun', and that it was either a prehistoric centre of fire worship, or else a natural place for beacon fires used for various religious and practical reasons. This is a common theme in all the analyses of the name.

Oddly enough, one person who waxed almost lyrical about the peculiarly pagan atmosphere and antecedents of the hill was our own Reverend Edward Duke. While he could understand the common folk getting confused between Tan and St Anne, he was quite certain that the origins lay within the goddess name of Diana. 'I cannot divest my mind,' he wrote, 'of the notion (but I do not propound it as a fact) that, in the days of the Romans, the shrine of the chaste Diana held her sway over the hill, now indeed rendered sacred by the aid of the modern St. Anne, the mother of the Holy Virgin.'[11] He went on to speculate that the *feriae*, or festival of the goddess, was superseded by the fair of the saint. Giving full rein to his Latin and Greek, he evokes a sensual picture of the worship on this hill, of the beautiful Diana weaving the mystic dance, followed by her lightly clad nymphs, on those bare heights overlooking what was once the lush wooded vale of Pewsey, where the wild boar and red deer once roamed.

The old dog... I've had those dreams too. A man of the cloth and a gentleman he may have been, but something within that ancient site touched upon the dreams of his flesh, even if they were given a scholar's garb to stop him walking naked. I mentioned this about fairs to Paddy Slade, who commented that *feriae*, a holiday, was related to *festum* – a feast, and added:

> I wondered if this could also have something to do with iron – ferrum, and ferio – to strike, knock, smite (smith) or to kill, slay. The hills of Somerset were exploited for their easily mined iron, lead, copper and silver. The newcomers were probably workers in iron and the Little people regarded it with hatred.

Tan Hill Fair, however, was essentially remembered as one where the Gypsies would gather on the fringes to buy and sell horses, and farmers would trade their (now rarely seen) long-horned sheep; Tan Hill was once *the* place to go for the sort of general merrymaking that later gave Silbury such a bad name. Roundabouts were set up on that bleak hilltop, and all manner of stalls, and when the farmers and the dealers left, then the common folk enjoyed themselves as only they could. It had such a reputation for debauchery that decent girls in the area were gated on the day.

Yet the censure it attracted from the authorities was less to do with fears that the lower classes might be indulging in riotous pagan pastimes than that they might be capable of finding deep enjoyment outside the jurisdiction of the Church, and out of the watchful eye of their masters in the upper classes. In truth, despite the ringing words from the pulpits or in the local newspapers, the 'goings on' on Tan Hill and other places were entirely in the spirit of the Glastonbury Festivals of the present day. They were hardly as lusty as the average hunt ball, and considerably less violent than the regimental dinner. Even so there were persistent rumours that underneath the fun something else was afoot, and that black cocks were secretly and sacredly burned, and the ashes saved as they would have been saved of old.

Held on 6 August near the old Celtic festival of Lughnasad, the fair was in such an odd place that, in the forgotten past, something, some public rite or ceremony of immense importance, must have drawn the people there as it had done throughout recorded history. There were far more convenient sites on the low ground – to which it was eventually transferred in modern times. The Reverend WL Bowles, writing in 1828 and deeply concerned with the ultimate precedents of such fairs, mentioned a British trackway which led from Marden, which was one of the principal 'orbits' on Duke's scheme, and ran in a straight line to Tan Hill, and so to Avebury. He suggested that the whole assembly, headed by the priests, may have proceeded along this and that the Tan Hill Fair was the remains of this annual assembly. [12]

Did John Fox's vision of the men and women walking down the ceremonial avenue into Avebury represent the final stage of the procession from Tan Hill?

Lost below the hill, between it and Rybury Camp, is a miniature stone circle of nine upright sarsen stones over a metre

(3¼ feet) in height, in the centre of which lies a prostrate stone, about the length of a man. From this circle a pathway leads up to one of the many lost chalk figures of Wiltshire, the partly visible 'Donkey', as the shepherds called it, for lack of a better description. This large-headed beast, which was once about 22 metres (72 feet) from nose to tail, is one of those enigmatic figures that hint at very odd mysteries indeed.

Old John Green told Kathleen Wiltshire that one night in 1940, when the white horse on the hill heard All Cannings church clock strike midnight, it came down to the dewpond above Cannings Cross to drink. This was not the first time this had happened. Other worthies of the village claim the horse is sometimes seen at the top end of the village still. 'Maybe,' she suggests, 'it accompanies "the little man in the red hat" on his perambulations?'[13]

It is hard, when reading the folklore about these hill carvings, not to be reminded of the 'Something' that came to the stones at Callanish at the sound of the first cuckoo. Modern authorities are quite certain that a number of the relatively modern hill carvings (dating only to the last century) were actually scoured over far older originals. Modern magicians are equally sure that a number of these are gates to inner worlds. Or else, if not gates, then expressions of the indwelling totem – the spirit being that guided and protected the tribe.

Murry Hope had a bizarre experience when passing the White Horse carved into the hillside at Cherhill, near Silbury Hill. Although the present figure was cut into the hillside around 1780 by 'Mad Doctor Alsop', who was obsessed by white horses, she wondered whether a genuinely old Horse had existed there centuries earlier, which he simply renewed. She wondered this because of an experience she had in company with four others when passing the present Cherhill Horse one dark and stormy night. 'Just as we were passing the Horse, which was to our right, a strange apparition of a giant bird of pterodactyl-like proportions seemed to emerge from the very hill itself, fly across our path and vanish into the darkness to the left of us . . .'[14]

This might be written off as a visionary quirk, a glimpse of the Jurassic past, or just a piece of astral junk which should have decayed a million years ago, if it had not been for a long tradition of similar sightings. Again, Kathleen Wiltshire draws our attention to the 'White Birds of Salisbury Plain', which are said to be seen whenever a bishop of Salisbury is dying. These are large birds, huge birds, with dazzlingly white wings which do not move as they fly. They were clearly seen in 1885 by Miss Moberly, the bishop's daughter, who saw them rise from the ground in the palace garden and sail away towards the west just before her father died.[15]

There is also the tradition of the Great White Bird of Market Lavington, which had been seen by many to – again – rise from the ground at midnight, nearly at the top of Clyffe Hall Hill.

So Murry Hope was not alone in seeing her avian. On its own it might have seemed a trivial encounter of questionable importance. But its value is confirmed by many similar sightings over the past few hundred years. In most of the examples the crucial aspect is of these extremely large creatures rising from the ground, thus showing themselves to be of the same ilk as the 'Donkey' of Tan Hill, as well as the 'Something' of Callanish and several other hill carvings, and countless individual standing stones which are said to come alive and seek water at certain times.

Guy Underwood, as he himself often strove to explain, was involved in more than just dowsing. His concern was in touching upon, working with and seeking to understand those energies within the earth that found outer expression. In relation to the hill figures he commented, 'As had already become clear to me, the location and shape of all prehistoric structures are determined by geodetic lines . . .'[16] Thus the ancient White Horses, the Cerne Giant, the Long Man of Wilmington and many others were all cut to express the indwelling 'geodetic' currents that ancient man and modern dowsers could clearly define. Even the apparent quirks of many medieval churches and cathedrals were more a case of the masons making their buildings respond to the forces within the land than mere bad architectural planning. This is another example

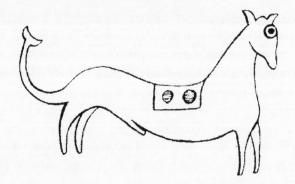

THE ORIGINAL HORSE OF WESTBURY C1770

of inner energies working their way to outer levels, and making themselves known to the rational mind via symbols.

With some of the White Horses themselves, Underwood felt that the geodesic lines revealed original shapes, long since forgotten or obliterated, that were more dragon-like than equine – dragons, of course, being primal symbols of earth energies. The Westbury White Horse today, for example, presents an unexceptional eastward-looking steed that was scoured into its present form in the eighteenth century. But the original was a beak-nosed, short-legged, westward-facing beast with a marked crescent on the tip of its serpent-like tail, moons and crescents on its saddlecloth and a single cyclopean eye. Locals called it affectionately the moon stallion.

Although the White Horses of Wiltshire were undoubtedly linked with the horse cults among the tribes who lived there, it may well be that something else was involved also. Of course, it is not always wise to look for neat explanations of things that find expression on magickal levels. Sometimes it is best to let mystery prevail. One common exclamation among occultists is that, if they had wanted to make their experiences up, they would have described events that were far more explicable than those that had so bewildered them.

The writer JH 'Herbie' Brennan was greatly taken with the energies behind Longstone Rath, in the grounds of Furness House, Co. Kildare, in southern Ireland. This rath is a great earthen ring work surrounding an inverted saucer enclosure, with a huge granite pillarstone at the centre. When excavated in 1912 the cist grave was found to date from the early Bronze Age, or Beaker period. It included the bones of a woman and a wolfhound. It was the site of several psychical experiments described in his very first book, *Astral Doorways*, and the area generally is credited with many reports of leprechaun and wood-nymph sitings. On an evening of bright moonlight and scudding clouds, near midnight on Hallowe'en, Brennan and two friends visited the site, walked over the fence, and stood looking up at the giant stone.

They began to feel uneasy, as if hidden eyes were watching them. Nape hairs began to prickle. Disturbed by the unwelcoming atmosphere, they turned to leave. As they did so a herd of about 25 tiny, pure-white horses, 'none larger than a spaniel dog', appeared at the top of the earthwork, galloped a distance of about 25 metres (82 feet), then disappeared down the slope at the far side. Needless to say, when they went to check, there was no sign of the horses anywhere, no hoofprints or marks of any sort, nor any cattle or sheep grazing anywhere in the vicinity.

But, as they discovered the next day, there were persistent legends of 'fairy' or 'ghost' horses associated with certain prehistoric sites in the area – legends insisting that such beasts were white, much smaller than ordinary horses and left no traces on the ground when they galloped. His story is therefore firmly in keeping with those many legends of the White Horses coming alive at certain times, to the astonishment of their observers.

So were the Wiltshire hill carvings outer expressions of inner realities that we do not quite understand? Did the tribes people who inhabited Bratton Camp above the Westbury Horse and those who lived at Rybury Camp next to the Tan Hill 'Donkey' see them as stylised representations of – perhaps – their spirit 'allies'?

The Uffington White Horse is one of the most famous examples of hill carvings, and its lines are enigmatic enough to attract more than one interpretation. As said, there are those who insist that it is more dragon-like than equine, although

the scientist John North argued in his book, *Stonehenge –
Neolithic Man and the Cosmos*, that it is more likely to be
linked with the cult of the bull than the horse, and what people
take to be its rear leg is actually the bull's penis, the whole
outline being astronomically aligned to Taurus, and the Pleiades. He even suggested that some of its outlines were used by
the tribes as viewing galleries, which was actually something
'seen' by the magickal adept Christine Hartley many years
earlier, as mentioned in her important book *The Western
Mystery Tradition*. To her the White Horse was the seat of a
mystery school of immense antiquity:

> The teaching in this Mystery School took place literally upon
> the horse, the initiates being grouped along the body, the neo-
> phytes at the tail and the more senior members of the
> brotherhood towards the head. The priest instructor sat at
> the nostril and gave his teaching from there, so instituting the
> familiar saying 'Straight from the horse's mouth' as something
> which must be indisputable.[17]

Murry Hope's feeling, when she climbed on to the Horse,
was quite different. To her it was not a horse as such, but a
feline entity of panther-like proportions that had been appro-
priated later by the conquering Celts. 'My mind strayed to the
old Atlantean protective deity, Akhantuih, who . . . was always
depicted as a black panther. I felt that the geographical posi-
tioning of the eyes carried sacred geometrical implications with
"multiples of seven". Now there's a little conundrum for those
of "sacred geometrical inclination", who strive to connect the
far past with the approaching future, to get their teeth into.'

Douglas Chaundy was quoted at length in Arthur Shuttlewood's classic *More UFOs Over Warminster*. He demonstrated
that the White Horses of Wiltshire actually formed a very
intricate pattern that he felt was tied in with known landing
sites for extraterrestrial craft.

Teresa Mooney, whose approach is out-and-out pagan, told
of an ecstatic occasion when she felt compelled to walk bare-
foot on the Horse – which she felt was actually more serpentine
than anything else, with its long body and small head. As she

looked at the hills billowing into the horizon and felt the wind sweeping the hair from her shoulders, she became aware of:

> ... something else, something surging, heaving and rolling, a great tide of power gushing from the north through the landscape and through me as it cascaded inexorably onwards. It was like the coils of a serpent looping vertically as it moved over the hills, it was like the beat of a huge heart, pounding an unseen flow through the earth and through me, for I was part of this exultant tide.
>
> From the north I turned through east, south, west and back to the north, conjuring the four elements of Earth, Air, Fire and Water in turn. Now within my Temple of the Winds I was even more powerfully aware of the energy current. It filled me with joy, it seemed to dissolve the boundaries of my being so I could participate fully in this great, unending belly-laugh of the hills. With starlight vision I saw the inexpressible – it seemed as if strands of my hair trailed into the Milky Way. I wanted to dance, jump and call out, but instead I lay down on the ground, legs towards the north and rode on the current for a while. Then I stood up and placed my palms on the horse's eye. The sun lanced down through my hands into the eye and I felt a surge of personal energy. I knew my experience was complete. Slowly I circled through north, east, south and west, and emerged, walking gently from the horse's head, as I had come ...[18]

Intriguingly, her description, 'It was like the coils of a serpent looping vertically as it moved over the hills' echoes Tammy Ashcroft-Nowicki's experience of the serpent-like ley energies that she learned to summon, as described in the chapter on Silbury. As she told me, Tammy saw the energy as ' ... undulating, like a huge serpent ... and then this brilliant blue light washes over you, this "serpent energy" which is all about life, and it's a very loving thing, a sense of "Ooh this is mine, a friend, someone has recognised me!" '

Both pagans, but with no contact or knowledge of each other, yet they show through their vision of serpents what seems to be a commonality of experience. This is not simply a case of individuals having ecstatic reactions that are essentially expressions of their own emotional natures. It is more a case of tangible and definable energies causing a wide range of individuals to respond in remarkably similar ways.

Although Jack Green had no such moments of *sartori* in connection with the hill carvings, he opined that they were in fact means of access to the inner worlds rather like his own spiral device. Keys that might help unlock the gate to the psyche of the individual *and* the indwelling spirit of the land around.

Ray Bailey, who lived most of his life within sight of the Westbury White Horse, felt that early barefooted man could sense the geodesic currents naturally. In fact, returning to the theme of dowsing again, he felt that our legs are the most perfectly adapted dowsing rods, our bare feet sensing the energies beneath or within the soil. Everything else would follow on from that.

Chris Thomas, commenting on the ithyphallic Cerne Abbas giant, felt that walking around the figure in a meditative way, stamping at intervals, would imprint the energy of the symbol into the chalk; while J Havelock Fidler, approaching it all from a dowser's point of view, found that certain stones could be energised by striking them – rather like the school experiment of magnetising an iron nail by striking it at a certain angle.

All of which might be summed up by the ideas of effort, thought and action: the more work you do at a sacred site (however that might be expressed), the more does it respond to you, in a kind of synergistic reaction. The more you think about the ancient deities, the more they think about you.

Looking at people's experiences so far, it does seem that these sacred places, these mysterious stones and mounds and circles, were built to do something. It does seem that they were expressions of a kind of magickal technology that relied upon something within the mind of the individual to make it work. Something that mankind has, over the millennia, lost touch with, and that is intimately connected with time and other-dimensional awareness.

It is up to your own mercurial powers of wit and intelligence to make the initial links.

FIVE

THE INNER ORBIT OF VENUS, THE GODDESSES AND THE MYSTERIES OF WOMAN

*It was also very easy to pick up the contact with
the female 'guardian', the abiding presence of the
site, who seemed quite happy to call herself Hetty
Pegler. I asked her who she was, which was
unusual for me; this abrupt kind of question is not
always the best place to start, but she answered
immediately that she was me. That is to say that
she was anyone and everyone who asks, because
anyone who comes to her house and asks that
question in sincerity has come there to find their
true Self.*
– Wendy Berg, *co-Magus of the Avalon Group*

Edward Duke placed the next orbit, that of Venus, where his meridian struck the circle of stones at Winterbourne Basset. When Stukeley first noted them in 1743, they comprised a double circle set on elevated ground in a field northwest of the church, and were still prominent in Duke's day. But now only a handful remain, and they lie prone and easily missed, and sunk below the surface. Whatever powers they once had to enchant and entrance are long since faded. Whatever may have taken place in the circles of Winterbourne Basset is hard to determine today, for sacred places – like lovers – can get exhausted and lose their energies. The magick can go as lovers cease to love, and move on.

As with humans so with stones, it seems.

Any trace of Venus near the short meridian linking it with Avebury, six kilometres (3¾ miles) away, is perhaps best found by following the Winterbourne stream to glimpse the *sheila-na-gig* engraved on the twelfth-century font of the church in

Winterbourne Monkton. A *sheela-na-gig* is the term given to figures that once appeared in, or on, a surprising number of churches, and show naked women, legs apart, exposing themselves to the onlooker in the most unchristian of ways. As Terence Meaden describes this particular figure, ' . . . the lady vaunts a big belly and open vulva from which emerges spring vegetation. This would seem to be the Earth Goddess giving seasonal birth to abundant plantlife.'[1]

This would also seem to be the local mason, drawing on pre-Christian traditions, using the imagery of the vulva and plantlife to give perennial and semi-secret birth to the Earth Goddess's memory, in the eyes of those who knew how and where to look.

So, although the circle at Winterbourne Basset may no longer express the energies that were once fundamental to its existence, other circles still can and do – at least in part.

When Elizabeth Anderton visited the complex of stones at Stanton Drew near Bath she felt that, although the large circle itself had long since 'gone to sleep', the adjoining cluster known as 'the Cove' (a small enclosed area which is said to have once had two standing stones with a third forming a trilithon) was a *very* different proposition:

> As soon as I entered the area of these stones I felt a very powerful feeling of the sacredness of the place. It felt as if it was dedicated to the Goddess and had been served by Priestesses over the centuries. The words and actions of the ceremony were running through my head (which I can no longer remember). It was a very powerful spiritual experience.

Strangely enough it is John Aubrey (again) who is regarded as having been the first to observe the stones of Stanton Drew for what they were, as for centuries these had lain in the fields neglected, disregarded, and maltreated by the rural owners. It was William Stukeley (again) who imposed his own notions upon them, and decided that here was a Temple of the Sun, with representations of the five planets near it. While hard on his heels came the Freemason responsible for some of the

124

greatest architecture in Bath, John Wood, who insisted that the Cove was nothing less than an altar of Venus.

More than that, he ventured that Stanton Drew was the university of the druids, and Wookey Hole their initiation centre. The university, meanwhile, had four outlying colleges: Harptree, where the bards and poets studied; the megaliths of Exmoor, where the druids made human sacrifices to obtain prophecies; Stonehenge, where spirits were raised from the infernal depths; and Avebury, where the philosophers studied.[2]

It is interesting that he regarded the Cove, where Elizabeth Anderton had her vision of priestesses, as this altar of Venus. She herself was completely unaware of Wood's comments. So conversely, we have to wonder whether the latter's oft-criticised romantic imagination is actually drawing upon psychic perceptions of a very high level. And it was through the modern mediumship of Iris Scott that I began to think that this was so . . .

I first met Iris many years ago in a 'Psychic Fayre' at the Royal York Hotel in Bath. I had never heard of such a thing before. Intrigued, I walked in off the street, then waited my turn in the small queue at her table, trying to adopt the sort of louche but interesting air that would mark me out as one of the god-kings of the Limpley Stoke Valley. Surely she would look at me, pause, then see through to the *real* me beneath the duffel coat, at which she would then summon me to the front and say something like, '*You* should be doing this for *me*!' and I would look modestly to the floor. But she didn't look twice. In fact she didn't look at all. Even when I eventually sat down and gave her a trinket of mine to hold, she still hardly looked at me. But I spent the next half-hour being stunned by the accuracy of what she picked up, without clues: hard, specific details about my chequered past, my dear departed, my immediate present, and my possible future. There was nothing vague here, nothing speculative; no trying to tease me out and reveal clues. It was direct, decisive and accurate. Straight into my psyche and my secret trivia, and told in an almost uninterested manner, as if she would rather be anywhere else but doing another 'psychic fayre' to pay the rent. When I first began to get the idea for the present project, Iris was always going to be involved if I had any say in it . . .

We visited Stanton Drew on a bright day with a bitter wind, and as we drove there we talked about anything but stone circles and ancient sites. 'Don't tell me anything about this place beforehand, Alan,' she insisted, and I agreed. She says much the same thing when doing readings for people seeking guidance, contact with the other world, or needing glimpses of the future. The only time she has ever been really fazed was when someone phoned and asked her, in all seriousness, if she could use her psychic powers to find the remote control for the television.

We parked next to the Cove and climbed the steps into the little fenced area which contains the stones. Two are still standing, one (originally the backstone) is recumbent. They are traditionally known as the Parson, the Bride and the Bridegroom. The three pieces originally came from a single block, and they were possibly planned to face towards the major midsummer moonrise, according to Aubrey Burl, author of *Great Stone Circles*. He also felt that it was probably built before the nearby stone circles, and was originally a funerary shrine for a particular family, rather than a focus for clan gatherings, as provided by the circles.

Iris immediately folded her arms over her solar plexus in an unconscious gesture for protection, and seemed to take some comfort from the jackdaw that perched on a post and watched everything she did. Although I never felt anything myself, there have been moments in the past when, usually in the presence of highly psychic individuals, I have felt energy almost pouring out of the same place, shivered from an intense inner cold, and found myself covering my solar plexus in the same way.

To her, this was an area that had very intense overtones of sacrifice, though perhaps at a much later period than the time when the stones were built. There was tremendous energy there, she felt, and got the sense that this little complex was originally connected with a specific and very powerful individual. She was also constantly drawn to what once lay over

126

the wall, in what is now the graveyard of the adjoining church. She got the theme of water, and also saw masses of what seemed like vines, which could have been related to the Roman period.

I said nothing, just watched. But it struck me again that when I've watched women do this sort of work there is a curious vulnerability about them, as if they drop their tough mortal defences against the mundane world and let their spirit come through. And, as she walked about the stones with the hood of her dark blue woollen top pulled up against the cold, I was aware that the priestesses of ancient times are still among us today, often functioning as mediums like Iris, and if there is any deep secret to the stones it is to be found through the women with whom they were once inextricably linked.

Once Iris had attuned herself to the unexpected energies, however, she relaxed, unfolded her arms, and asked that we go on to the main complex of circles, which lay on the other side of the adjoining church. On the way past I did point out that ancient sites of goddess worship were often 'redeemed', as the Christians saw it, by building churches dedicated to St Mary the Virgin, as this one was, heavily reinforced with gargoyles to ward off the adjoining evils. We made a quick visit inside but found the place curiously bland, lacking in atmosphere of any kind.

As we walked past the farm, and put our money in the English Heritage honesty box, Iris stopped and stared at the nondescript outbuildings, which she had seen, days earlier, in a dream. Just next to that, in the field, we saw the three stone circles. The Great Circle is one of the largest in the country; the other two, known simply as the North East and South West Circles, are smaller. Both the Great Circle and the North East Circle were once approached from the northeast by short avenues of standing stones. One of the avenues stopped at the river, and was aligned to a single stone on the other side known as Hauteville's Quoit, which was probably even earlier than the Cove.

'I get a picture of a bridge,' said Iris, who didn't even know there was a river nearby, and who was starting to get tuned

in. Now Burl reckoned that the Quoit and the Cove may have
been linked by a prehistoric road: if so, a simple bridge would
have been an important focus for the travellers. 'And water
again – I see some of the stones in water, or connected with
water,' which may be a glimpse of the nearby River Chew's
flooding. But these were just mutterings to herself that I doubt
if she even remembered, as she worked herself towards the
spirit of the place.

According to Stukeley in his *Itinerarium Curiosum II*, the
stones of the circles looked like 'a paste of flints, shells, crystals,
and . . . like solid corpuscles crowded together and cemented,
but infallibly by Nature's artifice'. They are certainly very
beautiful, varying from salmon-pink to rose, overlaid with all
the colours that lichen and weathering can provide, and looking
for all the world, on that bitter day of our visit, like huge
chunks of coral from a warm sea. In fact the job of the medium
must often be like this: floating through the ocean of the collective unconscious, pushed and pulled by unseen currents, all
senses altered by the strange element through which they
plunge, all manner of things floating past.

'I get different times,' said Iris, whose psyche was floating
up and down through the currents of time, and was seeking
some sort of ballast. 'There was a time when the worship here
was forbidden, and the people resorted to caves, somewhere,
and what seems like tunnels, to carry on the worship that once
went on here.'

Could this have been Wookey Hole, whose caves and tunnels
John Wood had identified as an initiation centre? I don't know.
Neither did I say anything in reply.

'I've got a link with a white-robed figure. I wouldn't say he
was a druid, but he is definitely connected with this place. He
seems to look after it in some way. He's not hostile, but he
definitely wants to know why we're here and what we want. I
can't get a name.'

'Call him the Guardian,' I said, eager to give a label but not
wanting to reveal too much of an area of magickal tradition
and 'psychic archaeology' about which Iris knew nothing.

'Yes, I suppose that's what he is . . .' she answered, her voice tailing off as she floated off into deeper waters than I could manage.

The Guardian came to occupy her psyche more than the stones themselves. Although we will look closely at such entities in the next chapter, this being was a very cautious one – though not actually antagonistic. Slowly, almost hesitantly, he allowed Iris just a little insight into what had happened here.

'There is almost a university aspect to this place. People coming to learn. Some of them are marking things on what seem to be slabs. Not writing as such, but similar. The number ten seemed to be important within the circle, but I can't get what he means. There was some healing here too, but this seemed secondary to the teaching.'

She drifted off. The Guardian would come back to her later, in her sleep, and at unexpected times during the day, which seems to be an almost universal experience among sensitives. As Mike Harris pointed out, once you have made some sort of link with such sites, at whatever level, you don't actually have to be there in the flesh to work with their energies.

We walked around the other stones. She saw – at a much later period in the stones' history – someone being slain on one, then burned, but this was more a vengeful, ritual murder than any kind of neolithic Willing Sacrifice. And best of all, in terms of her own vision, was her awareness of the faces in the stones, exactly as Meaden had pointed out in relation to Avebury, although she was unaware of this. She saw them, or had her attention drawn to them, by the Guardian figure, clear as day. Once she had pointed them out I saw them too. 'I'm sure that the faces in the stones depicted different qualities. One was for wisdom, one was for sorrow – that sort of thing. And the people or the students went to them accordingly. Does that make sense?'

It did. It does.

Now on psychic levels I can't say that I felt anything much at Stanton Drew myself, but that means nothing. For me, psychism comes unexpectedly, when the places themselves have a pressing need to say something. Usually I just have feelings of the most general kind. Stonehenge, for example, feels to me like an area of hard, clustered and attractively dark energies which sometimes crackle; Avebury a more openly benign and 'fluffier' place, bright like clouds. These are not the sorts of perceptions that could glimpse spirits in the vasty deep, admittedly, but might be accurate enough in relation to Stanton Drew. In comparison with the other circles, this was just . . . well, pleasant – gorgeous colours beneath a pure sky – but the real magick was being found through this glimpse of a modern priestess like Iris Scott walking and working among them. Perhaps the late Iris Campbell, agreeing over the decades with Elizabeth Anderton, summed it up when she wrote of *her* visit there:

> . . . there is little left of the old magnetic content in the stones and I only felt that once a great concourse of people had gathered there for religious ritual, but the stones are now mostly displaced and the circle destroyed. I have always found that when this happens, the earth's magnetic power has shifted away from the site, otherwise the stones would not have been removed.[3]

As we have noted before, through the perceptions of different kinds of seers, some sites can seem asleep, some waiting and some dead entirely. Evan John Jones, who was instrumental in bringing about the post-WW2 Wiccan revival, mentioned a site that had died almost overnight, like a battery going flat, when a road was driven past it. The author Tom Graves, who in part linked the energies of stone circles with underlying streams, commented that the circle at Dinnever Hill in north Cornwall is now completely dead 'both below ground and above, because all the water in the immediate area has been drained away into the vast china-clay works that starts a mere fifty yards [46 metres] away.'[4] Now pagans have never accepted the miracle of raising from the dead as part of their mythos, even if it is stones we are talking about, rather than humans. But some of them at least, and one in particular, are quite certain that if they are merely waiting, or asleep, then something very definitely can be done . . .

* * *

In terms of Venus, the Mysteries of Women, and the equally bewildering if apparently dormant stones, Paddy Slade had some fascinating insights, which began in the early 1950s.

For some time I had heard references to Carreg Inc. (*carreg* being the Welsh for 'stone'), which was a semi-whimsical name given to a very serious project undertaken by the group of witches that Paddy gathered together in 1975 for a very specific purpose. The aim of the project, or rite, was to undo certain Women's Magick which had taken place 1,200 years before, after that crucial Synod of Whitby, which started the death knell both for Celtic Christianity and the equality of women in this country. It was a rite that was based upon the perception that the bulk of the stones and sacred sites of Britain were, until then, sleeping. What Paddy felt that she and her witch-workers *had* to do was wake them again.

It was not her idea that she should do this, but the injunction of 'one of the best warlocks it has ever been my privilege to work with'. On a 48-hour pass from his RAF station at the time, he reminded her, 'You told me when we first began to work together that the stones had been put to sleep at the time of the Synod of Whitby, by women who had been born for that purpose.'

As Paddy described it, the Synod was a gathering of churchmen whose aim was to take away the power of the old Culdee Church, which was supposed to have stemmed from the time of Joseph of Arimathea, and which had been an integral part of native spirituality since before Augustine had brought Roman Christianity to the land. As she felt, all this innate power was to be taken by the Roman Church, and the wise women of the time decided that this was *not* a good idea.

She explained further:

> The Culdees and the Old Religion had lived together, side by side, for over four centuries and they, the Women, naturally feared that the Stones and the Circles would be drained by this new power, the concentration of psychic power destroyed, and probably the circles themselves broken. In order that the new administration should find no power within the circles, they

131

thought that by sending them to sleep they would pose no threat to the regime.

And so they did. Women, who were naturally in touch with the divine anyway, linked with the power network behind the circles and put them into a kind of standby. Something akin to the scorched-earth policies that retreating armies use on their own land and equipment in wartime, to prevent the invader gaining advantage from them.

'Now is the time to wake them up,' the warlock told her. 'This is what you were sent here for . . .'

It took me a long time to coax this story from Paddy, but I was determined to have it because there is something powerful and poignant about the idea of the women, whether the Culdees or the Old Ones, being so involved with these strange energies that they could make them dormant. And it reminded me and my generation of the fact that, until the mid-1970s, you could visit Stonehenge and other sites at the height of the tourist season and still have the places to yourself. There was interest, yes. There were the beginnings of populist books on the topic of Earth Energies, and the vague general knowledge that the sun could be seen to rise over the Hele Stone on the longest day, certainly. But the masses were more interested in yoga, or the chakras, or the secret mantras of the latest Indian guru; and even I, who had been more or less brought up with magick and who had read almost everything ever written on New Age topics, could not have told you much about these enigmatic circles, while almost none of my heroes in the Order of the Golden Dawn and its many offshoots said very much at all.

Did Paddy wake the stones themselves? Or did she wake *us*? I offered her my right testicle if she would tell me more.

'I had to go to London,' she told me, 'and as I came home I spent the journey studying an Ordnance Survey map of Ancient Britain, which shows all the standing stones, camps and barrows. This map has now been superseded by a newer and to my mind not better one. The train from Paddington runs east–

An ancient Druidical ceremony depicted (Mary Evans Picture Library)

restoration of the great stone circle of Avebury, Wiltshire, with the smaller circles within it, and two ceremonial stone avenues leading to it (Mary Evans Picture Library)

Left A child is sacrificed to
the Druid deity (Mary
Evans Picture Library)

Right Lunar ceremony
(Mary Evans Picture
Library)

Below The Wicker Man in
which people were burnt as
sacrifices to their deities
(Mary Evans Picture
Library)

Above Old engraving of Silbury Hill (Fortean Picture Library)

Left Televised press conference at Silbury, 1967 featuring left to right, Professor Richard Atkinson Paul Johnstone, (BBC producer), and Magnus Magnusson (Wiltshire Newspapers)

Below Silbury today (Kerri Sharp)

above left and right
the stones at Avebury
(Kerri Sharp)

right Rollright Stones,
Oxfordshire (Janet and
Colin Bord/Fortean
Picture Library)

below Callanish Standing
Stones, Isle of Lewis,
Western Isles at midsummer
sunrise (Gerald Ponting/
Fortean Picture Library)

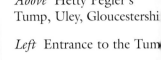

Above Hetty Pegler's Tump, Uley, Gloucestershi

Left Entrance to the Tum

Below Interior of the Tum (Kerri Sharp)

above Belas Knap long
barrow near Winchcombe,
Gloucestershire (Janet and
Colin Bord/Fortean
Picture Library)

right Feeling the energy
of the Minchinghampton
long stone, Gloucestershire
(Kerri Sharp)

Four major contributors to *Spirits of the Stones*

Mike Harris, psychic archeologist

Wendy Berg, visionary

Paddy Slade, hereditary witch

Ray Bailey, psychic and medium

west and as we passed along I visualised each circle to the north–south, trying to call upon them to be ready to wake at the appointed time. At that time I thought this would be at the next moon with the solstice. As I went further across England I began to try to consciously get in touch with the spirits of the Four Quarters. And I also thought that not only the stone circles and rows, but all the camps and barrows, the woods, streams and rivers, all the land, grass and trees should all be concerned in this, because it affects the whole island.'

She was helped in her enterprise by the spirit of a djinn whom she had summoned, and communed with by lighting a fire under the stars and putting some of her carefully hoarded driftwood on to the flames. A djinn is a fire elemental, and this one in particular had promised her that when the time came she would be helped. But she added, 'It is all very well for a djinn to promise impending knowledge, but he is a fire being and can be tricky. I was still bothered about working against the tides.'

It was then she realised the solution to the timing of the rite, which had been worrying her, because she thought at first it would simply be a matter of working through to the next moon of the solstice. But:

> From the Summer Solstice to the Vernal Equinox is nine months . . . A seed planted in the womb comes to fruition in nine months, and an idea planted in the Earth might work in the same way. The tide of Earth, ebbing fast, the sap falling back into the root, Moon in the last quarter, might take the idea down, and down and down, to the roots of the Stones, and perhaps, with luck to the roots of the ideas behind the Stones, and take hold . . . It would go back to the time of the Dark Lady who at Arbor Low had told us that that was time she should be thought about deeply.

She felt, from communing with the Dark Lady, that, after 1,200 years asleep, it would take a full twelve months for the circles to awaken, during which regular magick had to be performed to help them return through the layers of sleep, bringing them out of it like someone out of deep hypnosis. But

– and this was the most important part of the inner message –
the stones will respond only to those they trust. This came
through to her with enormous emphasis.

So at the crucial time, before dawn, she went into the sunken
garden at West Down House, placed the Symbols of the
Elements round the circle she formed, then 'danced a maze
over the lawn', while summoning the Old Ones, before greeting
the moon and the coming sun, and tuning in to the rest of the
coven, who were working at the same moment in different
locations.

Meeting and then travelling together in spirit, they found
themselves entering the West Kennet Long Barrow, and came
to the centre.

There were many people in that Temple, including Dryads, giant
green and shining, and a great figure from the Stones, and many
many Old Ones ... The Lady came too, looking serene and
lovely, and Herne, tall and great eyed, his antlers gleaming.
Hounds too, dignified and quiet. We were all greeted by the
Lord and Lady who told of the reason for this calling together.
She called a Stone forward, asking him if he and his brethren
were ready to wake. He made an obeisance and said that they
would all soon be ready to take their part in the protection of
the Island. The light and energy were pulsing. I was asked to
explain my reasons for the awakening, the timing, and Carreg
Inc. The Stone had been watching me steadily all the while I
spoke ... He explained that some circles were more deeply
asleep than others; that those whose stones had been destroyed
or dispersed would need more time to collect themselves. He
said sadly that as they stirred in their deep sleep, their energy
had sometimes been used for the wrong purposes ...

We left the Temple in procession and the whole plain was
alive with people, many towering beings near Silbury. We went
along the processional way to Avebury. There in that great
concourse we sang the hymn to the Lord of Life as the Sun
rose.

The power, light and music reached a pitch as the paean of
sound closed and the whole land sparkled with energy and
pulsed with power, the great circles sending out the message
along the ley lines ...

It faded. She returned to her body, saluted the Elements, unwound the maze, collected her things and went back to bed.

Did Paddy Slade, making witch magick under the stars from a garden in Somerset, help wake the circles that had been dormant for centuries? Having seen the effectiveness of her talents first hand, I believe she did.

But it was the occultist Dion Fortune who once wrote that changes in consciousness in the psyche of just one individual will, eventually, affect us all by opening gates in what Jung termed the collective unconscious. Those who feel uneasy with the whole magickal scenario might find it easier to accept that, because one witch became aware of and awakened the stones within herself, she made it easier for the generations that have followed her to do the same – but by the coachload.

Whether it was the stones awakening, or our attitudes towards them, is a matter for personal conjecture; but certainly, the years following Paddy's rite saw the beginning of the explosion of popular interest in the stones and their energies.

Yet if we are to understand these energies and the way they can change, and try to regenerate their mysteries within ourselves, then we must first come to understand Venus itself, and learn how it was the women who seemed to hold the links between the Earth and the stars they served.

It is humiliating that we have to depend upon specialists to tell us that which our ancestors once knew as a matter of course through everyday (or rather everynight) experience. Everyone – simply everyone – in the tribe once knew that Venus was the brightest object in the sky. So bright that it could cast a shadow and make you squint when you stared at it; so striking and quickening to the spirit that it felt like a living entity which pinned you against the night, poking you like a finger. Everyone knew that, like the moon, it would rise and set at different points on the horizon; that it would be visible before sunrise or after sunset (but not both) and was never too far from the sun, which it seemed to serve. As a morning star, the sun would rise before it set; as an evening star, the sun would appear before it rose. When viewed against the backdrop of fixed stars

135

known as the zodiac, Venus appears to move in the form of a five-pointed star (so beloved of the witches!) with the sun at its centre. People *knew* Venus. It had a marked character. It was part of their lives.

Technology, which has increased longevity and made our lives easier, has also made us lazy and ignorant, despite those information superhighways that crisscross the planet like ley lines. It has also diminished the darkness, the night, and made the stars into mere incidentals which lurk above the neon. Stars, to most of us now, are patterns within lavishly illustrated books, or cute arrangements on multimedia CD-ROMs. Few of us have made the trip into the darkness, away from the towns and into our heads, and seen the stars so bright and potent and majestic that you can feel the light against your skin, almost hear them singing, and know that they have consciousness and characters as tangible as that of our partners.

So listen, for this is perhaps one of the real secrets of the stones – they are inseparable from the stars they served. And what we have to do today is rediscover or re-create the links. What we have to do is use the powers and consciousness symbolised by the planet Mercury to make sense of that which is expressed by Venus.

We do not know what name the Neolithic tribes gave to this planet. But the Greeks called it Phosphorus, the Romans Lucifer – both of which mean 'Lightbearer' – and the Hebrews called it Nogah, 'the Shiner'. It is significant that in the Judaeo-Christian traditions all of these names became euphemisms for the Rebellious Angel who fell from Heaven, and whose secret role it was to 'test' mankind – particularly in the areas of sex. Put in terms of medieval Christianity, places where the spirit of Venus lurked were also places of the Devil and all his hordes.

We have already seen how the Church censured those ancient fairs and festivals which were held on or next to places such as Silbury and Tan Hill, where priestesses would once have worked their rituals; and how it did its best to link the image of the Devil with the whole experience.

Astronomically the very motion of Venus precludes it from being the planet of straight lines and linear thinking. Astrologically it is universally known as the planet of co-operation and unity; of the Mysteries of Women; of love, sex and marriage; of greed, lust and selfishness – and most of the seven deadly sins.

According to Duke's scheme the small stone circle at Winterbourne Basset, to the north of Avebury, was – logically – the perfect place to find Venus. But so little of the circle remains today, in such an unpromising spot, that we should really look elsewhere, and use the orbital curve upon the landscape as more valid for our present scheme then the rigid meridian. In fact Duke himself was not beyond 'bending' his meridian to make it fit the overall scheme: the felicitously named Marden, on the next orbit, lay a little way off the line, but because it was so appropriately named he made due allowance. So we can do similarly with this orbit of Venus, because a short distance to the east of Winterbourne Basset, but still on the requisite orbit, lies a whole complex of mysteries in which standing stones, trackways, sacred ponds and tumuli jostle with ancient spirits, underworld centres, devilish atmospheres, modern hauntings, mysterious suicides, faery underworlds and Knights Templar . . .

Hackpen Hill, when viewed from the circles at Avebury, is where the sun emerges from on Midsummer's Day, and is skirted on its western edge by the Ridgeway, that ancient hilltop trackway across the high and dry ground of the downs which has been called the oldest road in England. Its route stretches from Norfolk to Wiltshire at least, but there is evidence to suggest that it may have gone as far as the Dorset coast. Here, it is hard *not* to feel the presence of the folk who once walked it, and smell the long-horned sheep they drove, or feel the thud of the even longer-horned cattle as they made their way towards or past the places of the Horned Gods and Goddesses. And you cannot help but be reminded that the mysterious tumuli, stones and remains that litter the landscape were intimately connected with the common people who walked this route, and that their mysteries were not – and are not – the sole preserve of some withdrawn magickal elite serving their own ends. When elitism, class or politics involve themselves in the sacred places, then (in an inversion of the true purpose) the talents of the masses are coerced into meeting the personal needs of the few, and the inner links are weakened or broken. Then what we are left with is folklore, and the fragments of those traditions that all commoners would once have worked with and understood.

Which may be why there was once a large prehistoric temple with what William Stukeley described as a mortuary enclosure and standing stones collapsed on it, on Hackpen Hill, near the place called 'Glory Ann'. Stukeley sketched this place in 1723 and referred to it as the 'Old Chapel'. He and a clutch of Lords studied it in 1723, and felt that this was the place of internment of an Archdruid, at very least, and described its formidable structure as:

> ... a large square entrenched, one hundred and ten Druid cubits by one hundred and thirty, like a little Roman camp, with one entrance on the south-west towards Abury, for it is posited with accuracy, as all these works are from north-east to south-west. The situation of the place is high, and has a descent quite round three of its sides, the verge of the descent inclosing it like a horse-shoe. The entrance is on the side next Abury ... on the shortest side of the square, the south-west. It is made of a vallum and ditch; beyond that a row of flat stones set quite round, and pretty close to one another, like a wall; beyond that another lesser ditch: there are stones too set on each side of the entrance: on the north-west side is a large long barrow, fifty cubits in length, with two great stone-works upon it; one on the end next the great stone place we have been describing, another stone-work towards the other end, which seems to have been a semi-circular cove ... consisting of five great stones; a Stonehenge cell in miniature, but now in ruins. The barrow likewise has been set quite round with great stones. In the second stone-work, one stone lies flat on the ground, along the middle line of the barrow. On each side a flat stone stands upright, at right angles, as wings to them; upon them I suppose other stones were piled ... here probably lies the body of the interred. The stones are generally very large, about ten feet long.[5]

In its pristine state this 'Old Chapel' could well have rivalled the barrows at East and West Kennet – long barrows 'entering the earth', and taking us back where we belong. Stukely also draws attention to another 'singular excavation' next to it, a 'pyriform concavity, set with stones on the inside' and known locally as Balmore pond, aligned exactly to the Old Chapel entrance, and supposed to have a secret vault beneath it. He speculated that the pond was a place of executions.

Set amid a rock-strewn landscape littered with sarsens, the whole area around the former 'Old Chapel' is in fact soaked with a brooding, watchful atmosphere, as though the ancestors who worked their rites four thousand years ago have still not come to entirely trust the generations of today. Although the Old Chapel itself is long since gone, annihilated by time and the heavy plough, we can almost use its image as a kind of Virtual Long Barrow – an archetypal structure that we can place within our imaginations to explore as we will, because on this Orbit of Venus as it exists within our psyches, there are some *very* curious insights to be had.

For a start, this may also be why Terence Meaden found on the same hill, on this exact orbit, and in direct line with the magickal sunrise, an oddly shaped five-sided stone (perhaps representative of Venus?), which is marked with a deep and exquisitely distinct blood-coloured cleft, naturally stained by fungi, creating an unmistakable vulva that helped confirm his own theories relating to the Goddess and the Stones.

In this respect, one thing that mystics, symbolists and main-stream archaeologists tend to agree upon is the essential womblike nature of the chambered tomb, and one intimately connected with the concepts and experience of time. Paul Devereux described how the artist and researcher of ancient sites, John Palmer, slept in one of the side chambers of the West Kennet Long Barrow. During the night he was woken by a light moving about in the central passageway, but when he went to investigate he found nothing. As he went to the entrance and looked out to the moon-bright landscape beyond, he was astonished to find that it was not the same one he had left when he had entered the barrow at dusk. Fully awake, fully bewildered, he wisely went back to his sleeping bag and made no attempt to explore the new world he found himself in, waking in the morning to the familiar scenery.[6]

However, we will come back to the 'Womb of Time' concept in the chapter on Stonehenge.

Christopher Knight and Robert Lomas showed, in *Uriel's Machine*, how the chambered long barrow of Newgrange (and others) had intrinsic alignments towards the planet Venus. More, the overall pattern is uterine in shape, while the triple-spiral motif cut into the imposing stone at its entrance was convincingly argued to represent three periods of three months – or the length of human gestation. Weaving their astronomical, astrological, geological, mythological and Masonic research together, they evoke a poignant image of the pregnant women gathering silently within the tomb to receive the light of Venus's transit, and take its blessing for their unborn children. Knight suggested that perhaps women were impregnated at festivals held at certain times of the year that reflected the status of the potential offspring, whether royalty, priesthood, mason or commoner. He felt that:

> The heavily pregnant women of high-status individuals, such as the priesthood, may have been taken into the chamber with the remains of the recent dead to await the coming of the light of Venus, whose ghostly light would have been deemed to reincarnate the spirits of the dead to the birthing infant; minutes later the warm glow of the life-giving sun would celebrate the resurrection of the deceased person in their new form as a child.[7]

But compare the above notions with what Elizabeth Anderton Fox experienced within the chambers of West Kennet: a vision that entirely supports the above, although it happened (and was written up in her own personal diary) ten years or so before *Uriel's Machine* was published.

> As we walked up the path towards the West Kennet Barrow there were some people walking back down. When we reached the site it was deserted, we had it to ourselves for about an

hour, nobody came near until we ourselves were walking back down the path to the road. It felt a bit like being in a 'time bubble.' John [her partner] had gone ahead of me into the chamber, as I approached the entrance, where there is a very large vertical stone, I looked up and the sun was shining directly from the centre of the top surface of the stone above me. I felt this had been a very deliberate orientation and had significance of a sacred nature to those who erected the stone.

I joined John inside the chamber. While we were in the farthest 'room' looking back towards the entrance we had the impression of people who had used this place in the far past. They were tall, not white skinned but not dark either, more Mediterranean in appearance. They wore short kilt like garments and had a somewhat military look about them.

Then I went into the small chamber to the left of the entrance, facing into the barrow. There are some stones in the floor of this chamber which form a kind of rough natural seat. I sat down and had a very strong impression that this was a birthing chamber where very important babies were born. I leaned backwards until I was lying down, immediately my head started to spin, I felt as if I was dropping backwards into deep dark space. I felt that if I stayed in that position I would very soon lose consciousness and sat up rather quickly. I do not faint!

These images of the pregnant women in the tomb that is also a womb are extraordinarily poignant. Roman travellers, thousands of years after the time in question, noted that Celtic women believed pregnancy occurred when they were touched by the light of the moon. Although the Romans would have completely misunderstood what they heard, or misheard, or even failed to realise that they were the butt of Celtic women's humour, it hearkens back to a time when it was felt that light from the stars carried the consciousness of the ancestors, and the souls of kings. It hearkens back to Ray Bailey's perception in a previous chapter that the barrows, with their radiating light energies, were built to 'provide a pathway of energy in which the deceased would be carried to the Celestial Gods'. Similarly, Chris Thomas's viewing of the akashic records saw West Kennet Long Barrow as the site of the most powerful upwelling of planetary energies anywhere on the planet, and that it had been built by a local chieftain who wished to be buried within those energy upwellings which linked to the stars.

And it draws attention also to the bones that were often found in connection with such chambered tombs – rarely full skeletons, more usually selected bits which were obviously interred for a reason.

The artist and visionary Judith Page had an experience at the West Kennet Long Barrow which touched upon this, and also hearkened back to that troubling anecdote from the first chapter, about the unquiet spirit of the 'old woman' from the bowl barrow at Manton.

Entering the long barrow is almost like Jonah entering the whale, but instead of the smell of digestive juices, it was the aroma of the earth itself. The innermost structure of seemingly fossilised bone, which although once held the remains of the long dead and sacrificed to the great mother, did not signal a cold heartedness, but a warmth and glowing of an inner sun.

The mound held no threat to me or my fellow pilgrims, who lingered and chatted quietly amongst themselves as if they were coming home, or visiting their long lost ones out of respect. Each occupying a space in time.

Leaving the Inner Sanctum, I made my way to the outside and sat on the north face of the barrow. It had been a truly lovely Spring Day, and I was pleasantly surprised to find myself being joined by a small herd of cows who curiously chose this particular face instead of the warmth of the south eastern one. Nevertheless, it was good company, and as I watched them shredding the grass, my fingers did their own raking into the earth which gave up strangely shaped long whiteish stones. Well, everyone loves a souvenir, so I pocketed them.

Later that evening back in London, I met up with some friends and related the events of the day, and showed off my prized stones. One of the company being a vet, exclaimed that they were not stones, but petrified human bones, one an adolescent child. On closer inspection, he noticed that the bones were in various stages of arthritis, and the individuals would undoubtedly have suffered a degree of pain.

I retrieved the remains of our past ancestors, and went home. My dreams that night were disturbed to say the least. I had flashes of the barrow, and three visitors invading my space. A man and a woman, accompanied by a child. All were very gaunt looking and had a strange pallor about them. They were crying, and I assumed they were all in pain, but it transpired that they were distressed due to the fact that part of their remains had been disturbed. I woke up, and couldn't get back to sleep through sheer guilt. I was indeed a grave robber.

It was not until Whitsun that she was able to get back down to the long barrow to make good what she now felt was her witless action. She duly went back to the spot on the north face where the bones had been uprooted, and, scooping the top soil away, redeposited these ancient folk back into the womb of their mother.

Judith's experience, however, is almost exactly matched by that of Tammy Ashcroft-Nowicki, whose insights into the tumps on Maiden Castle we described in an earlier chapter. In the early days of 'opening up' psychically, Tammy visited West Kennet with her husband, Roy, and found that the place was not so much weird as 'wyrd', for lack of a better term. The veil there was definitely very thin. After doing the usual touristy thing in the barrow, and avoiding a number of bulls on the way back to their car, they eventually arrived home, went to bed and went to sleep. It was then that the magick of the barrow started to make itself felt to Tammy:

> I awoke suddenly, and sat bolt upright in bed, knowing that there was something or someone in the room with us. In fact something was holding my neck, my throat, so fiercely I had to pinch myself to make sure that this was not a lucid dream, but it wasn't. The room was full of shadows, particularly in one corner, all weird shapes, half-seen faces, beings . . . I couldn't get Roy to wake up, and I began to get more and more frightened. It was like an old 'B' film. Still in the early days of my magical expertise, I tried using all the techniques I had been taught: banishing pentagrams, protective light, the lot. But nothing worked. Finally I called on the goddess Sekhmet to whom I had been dedicated when I was 13, and then everything went, and the room was empty again.

Despite her fear, Tammy was aware that there was no inherent evil involved here, but more a kind of anger, of someone trying to say something to her or through her. In discussing it with her mother and Paddy Slade, she decided that – in her psychically nascent state – the beings whose remains were once buried in the long barrow were expressing their outrage at being removed, at their burial site being desecrated. 'These were anguished inhabitants who were really quite pissed off about it all.' She went back next weekend, as she felt that these beings were still lingering around her during the days that followed. While sitting in one of the chambers she lit a candle and apologised for the abuse of their tomb and womb, explaining that, despite what had happened, their remains were still honoured.

And then they went from her psyche, and back to their rest.

Wonderful, confirmative stories – but did anyone, quietly and without any fuss, do similarly for the poor wretch at Manton? Did the removal of her bones interrupt her sojourn in the stars? Did anyone at least light a candle for her cold and cast-out spirit?

If our ancestors linked the notions of womb and tomb, and saw them both as a means of dwelling inward in order to go Beyond, in a manner of speaking, it highlights the extent to which they saw life and death as just different points on the circle of birth and rebirth.

And women, it seems, have far more dramatic responses to long barrows than men. When Paddy Slade made her way up to West Kennet with one of her sons, Pete, they passed a group of sniggering young men coming down. When they entered the hallowed chambers, and Pete strolled away to investigate by himself, Paddy was appalled to find that mindless graffiti had been scrawled on one of the walls. In a spontaneous outcry of pure rage, uttering a wide range of verbal obscenities, she struck the inner stones with her clenched fist.

'Whatever energies my anger had summoned up seemed to whirl around the passage and chambers like a tornado, before shooting outside. Pete came staggering towards me, white-faced and shaken, muttering, "I don't know what you've done, but . . ." And he was unable to finish the sentence. I did my best to clean off the graffiti and we went back down towards Avebury. On the way we saw the morons who had despoiled the barrow, sprawled in their crashed car, with ambulances attending them. The energy which had shot out of the chamber had hit its target after all. Bloody good job!'

It also takes us on to that star lore that is as fundamental to the sites as the lore of Venus.

Gilbert and Bauval convincingly showed in their book *The Orion Mystery* that the original myth of the battle between Horus and Set for the Earth god's crown was a symbolic and highly accurate depiction of astronomical precession. That is, the apparent movement of the stars as viewed from the religio-political centres in Upper and Lower Egypt was told in terms of gods in contention. Similarly, the magician Mike Harris's important book *Awen . . . the Quest of the Celtic Mysteries*, which is the fruit of many years' magickal work in the field, shows how planetary and stellar forces found expression through human Mystery Dramas acted out in the landscapes of his native Wales – landscapes that in themselves mirror certain constellations, thus echoing the later discoveries of Mark Vidler in his bestselling *The Star Mirror*.

It seems that all of the megalithic 'Earth Mysteries' were connected – directly or indirectly – not just with the primaries of the sun, moon and Venus, but with the stars above. The interconnectedness of the people and their sacred landscape was such that there was no question of the stars being seen as distant objects. They were thought to be aggregates of consciousness, collections of souls, leading to other dimensions that could be reached by turning inwards.

Magicians and mystics of all traditions have been saying this for many years. And it is a notion that is now supported by John North, a professor of the history of philosophy and the exact sciences, in his formidable book *Stonehenge – Neolithic Man and the Cosmos*. In this he seems to have written the ultimate and definitive book on the solar, lunar and stellar alignments of the major British sites, confirming, correcting, rejecting or refuting the apparently irrefutable measurements of Norman Lockyer, Gerald Hawkins and Alexander Thom, but inadvertently confirming what the unscientific, entirely mystical 'irrationalists' have always maintained.

The essence of his conclusions is that certain sites were deliberately aligned to certain stars. Although he eschews anything in the way of occult speculation, he does express the feeling that 'in different territories there were allegiances to different stars'. For example, he found that the West Kennet Long Barrow had primary alignments at the autumnal equinox and winter solstice to Arcturus, Rigel, Sirius and Vega, which he felt were 'four spectacularly well-chosen stars of a character that might be interpreted as somehow relating to the spirits of the dead.'[8]

I am not in any way denigrating his superb level of research when I say that North's meticulous work might be seen in the eyes of all the correspondents and contacts of the present book as an act of confirmation rather than discovery. A confirmation also of the allusive truth offered by Bob Stewart's experience in the womblike chambered tomb with the Stone-King, who told him that 'the stars are within the earth'.

In a sense, the humblest of lovers know the truth of all this intuitively when, hearts melting, they gaze at the stars and choose one for themselves, swearing that even when they are far apart yet they will still be in touch, simply by sharing its light. Such a romantic impulse among star-crossed, moon-blessed lovers everywhere is a memory of the oldest magick on the planet. The magick that held that the stars were the dwelling places of the dead.

How we can actually experience this for ourselves is something that we will discuss in a later chapter.

Sometimes, in reading such anecdotes, then letting their ideas and images sink into your head before sleep, you can get the idea that – somewhere at the back of your mind – some of these things you can half remember yourself. Rather like siblings coming together in middle age and swapping memories of growing up together. Pictures, feelings, moods that your conscious mind has pushed aside come creeping back in. Paddy's image of the Culdee women sending the circles to sleep can have that effect, touching upon the collective memory banks, perhaps.

When I visited the Stoney Littleton Long Barrow with my old and fey friend Annie Tod the feeling was rather like that: something slumbering – but only lightly. As if keeping one eye open for the right visitors. *Venus Observ'd* was the title that kept coming into my mind, for no real reason. There were indications of very low-grade attempts to work magick. A yin–yang scrawled in the concrete that seals off the chambers. A long sharpened pole that someone had probably used as a wand, then discarded. English Heritage, which owns the site, had put up a board telling what was known of its history, and included what at first glance was a lurid picture of its use: the funeral bier, the priest wearing the bull's head, the rough worshippers. On looking at it, however, and soaking up the feel of the site, we both agreed that the artist, Ivan Lapper, was probably truer than he knew.

The world turned around us. There was a series of bonfires alight on the distant ridge, doing strange things to the fabric between the worlds. Crows sent their cryptic messages. As Elizabeth Fox felt at the West Kennet Long Barrow, we were in something of a time bubble also. Nothing and nowhere else existed. The barrow may have been a sealed and sleepy womb but it was certainly not dead. And somewhere within it, down the long spiralling labyrinth of time, lay the horned ones.

As is usual the sense of the place stayed with me long after we had left, and the image of the bull-headed shaman amid the fires tended to hover on the edge of my mind, at the edge of sleep, and I wondered how I might find an objective confirmation of this to justify including it.

In fact it came from Australia, via email, and was sent by Tom Graves whose book *Needles of Stone* is known to say as much between the lines about magick as it does about dowsing. And it concerned the very same place and the very same imagery.

About fifteen years back I was with my then-partner Jan exploring the Stoney Littleton Long Barrow (the current locked gate wasn't there then): I sat in the cell at the far end, and meditated for a short while, with the intention of sensing or experiencing whatever was there, whilst Jan wandered in and out of the low tunnels and side-chambers. I felt nothing unusual, but at some point Jan stopped suddenly at the crossing, went down the exit passage quite quickly, and then called from the entrance, 'Tom, would you come here for a minute?'. She sounded a bit worried, so I got up, and crouched my way out through the exit passage. When I got there, she said, 'Thank heavens, it *is* you: it definitely wasn't when I looked at you from the crossing. You had horns growing out of your head, for a start . . .'

So one of the primary images relating to these times, these energies, and this planet is that of Taurus the Bull. And there is evidence that many of the long barrows like the 'Old Chapel' were – originally – specifically aligned towards Taurus or its ruling planet Venus at certain crucial times of the year.

In Britain and Ireland today we are so taken with the cult of the horse, and so keen to project it back on to our ancestors, that we ignore the Cults of the Bull. Agrarian cultures could manage without the horse. But the Bull and its Cow were life itself.

Robert Briffault pointed this out forcibly in his influential book *The Mothers*:

> But although the bull is a natural emblem of fertilising power, it appears, I think conclusively, that the primary ground for the equation and for the widespread identification of gods with bulls was the assimilation of the horned animal to the moon. In the great religions in which bull-gods are most prominent, the divine bull is either expressly identified with the moon, or is specially associated with those gods who are most unequivocally regarded as moon gods. The horns of cattle and the lunar crescent are interchangeable.[9]

When I was working out the impulses behind *Inner Celtia*, co-written with the slightly satanic poet David Annwn, the bull became a primary image for energies that seemed to lie behind an inner contact that we called Lleuadd. We defined her as a moon priestess from the end of the Bronze Age, heavily tattooed and heavily pregnant, and as the 'guardian of the Bull-dream, and all the lore of the Bards of the Bull-enclosures . . .'[10] Lleuadd started off as a manufactured image, for literary purposes, but quickly took on such a life and vitality of her own that we had to accept her as an independent entity. And one who was inseparably linked to the Bull Cult of pre-Celtic Britain.

The vigour, vitality and sheer strength of this animal made it the cornerstone of the agricultural and trading communities. In continuation of traditions that were vital to the tribes long before the Celts arrived, we find a great prone bull on the famed Gundestrup cauldron, and bull motifs common throughout Celtic art and artefacts. Pliny spoke of the druids sacrificing two white bulls after mistletoe-gathering ceremonies. In Ireland the seers used bull broth as a source of divination to protect new kings, while the 'bull vision' was induced by wrapping the specially trained shaman in the hide of a freshly slain bull. There is also evidence to suggest that the druids' enclosures on the hill forts were known as the 'Bull-pens of the Bards'.

Then again, on the very crude but very telling levels of those who worked the land, few other creatures had a penis to match that of the bull, and the emergence of its massive and serpent-like organ to search for the cow's vagina would have created links in the mind between bulls and serpents that would energise their poetry, magick and dirty jokes.

As we insisted then in a slightly different, historically later, but still relevant context, 'Bulls and Cows, Moons and Suns, Serpents and Caves were not sharply separate energies which came together from time to time in various kinds of union, but different aspects of the same thing.' And as John North pointed out, 'Fertility is the complement of death; fertility and the Moon go together in many ways, and the Moon and oxen likewise.'[11]

Quite simply, our ancestors were not like us. Often their ideas and thought processes would have seemed – by our standards – nonlogical, or at best allusive. Preliterate and agrarian,

149

matriarchal and shamanistic, their lives ruled by seasonal considerations of daylight, moonlight and weather, they saw how things fitted together quite differently from us. They were aware of colour, texture, sound and shape to a far greater degree than we are today. For example, the images of snails, moons, crows and bulls were as obviously connected to them as, say, steel, petrol, wheels and road are to us.

A number of psychics, touching upon the minds of the old 'bull-headed ones' at such sites, have actually blacked out, or come away feeling that the worship in question was very dark indeed, when the real problem is more to do with our own lack of insight. Some glimpsed spirits at the tombs that they felt were part-human, part-animal, but fled before learning whether these were in fact glimpses of the priests wearing the horned headpieces of their cult.

Some of long barrows then, when opened, were shown to contain the skulls of oxen still attached to skin and hooves, and apparently once hanging from posts in the rear. These were not the skulls of the modern breeds of domestic cattle but of the *Bos taurii*, those huge creatures no longer seen in our fields, but which once broke the ground when harnessed to the plough, and gave the common ploughman and farm worker the secretly respectful title 'Brother to the Ox'. These were the skulls that would have been worn by the shamans of each tribe as they sought to link with the ancestors in the stars, and bring wisdom back to the earth. And the people who listened to them, and sought to become wise, were the same people who – thousands of years later – still made their way to the ancient hilltop fairs that they knew echoed to the Old Ones, and the bull-headed seers who mediated them.

In fact the very shape of the great stones forming the entrance to a number of long barrows – the West Kennet in particular – is reminiscent of the old cults that would have seen the dawn or evening rising of stars within the Taurean cluster as heralding the spring or autumn respectively, and adjusted their lives in the appropriate way.

One woman who was troubled by similar beasts in a similar manner to that experience by Annwn and myself was Margaret

THE BULL-SCHEME OF THE WEST KENNET CHAMBERS

Lumley-Brown, the 'pythoness' mentioned in the previous chapter. She had been given a vision of a certain spot in Cornwall: 'of wild aurochs indicating a certain spot on a moor which it pawed with one of its hooves till a well of water began to bubble up from the ground. Later, as we were on the moor outside Callington wondering if this very wild and remote place would be the spot . . . all I felt was a vast battle of Celtic or pre-Celtic days in which *women* as well as men were fighting in chariots of bronze (greenish) or iron-work ornamented with gold. The woman I especially noticed was standing upright in her chariot, spear in hand and with fierce eyes; on her bronze helmet was a great golden bird – perhaps a swan – with out-spread wings.'[12]

Later on, she was led into a separate vision at Kit's Hill by a glimpse of 'wild aurochs standing on the heights and of a strong fire force as well as earth power; water spirits were also present.' There were great tumuli and boulders all over the district, she noted. A great sense of joyousness as well as power came from the whole area.

Bulls and beasts apart, how can we possibly make links with

such people, given the vast differences between their time and ours, and their thought processes and ours?

The late, great and curmudgeonly mage Bill Gray had no doubt about the answer: love is the link. He himself was often seen as a dark, somewhat frightening and vindictive individual, but perhaps, like those ancient souls who served the Horned Gods, he was misunderstood. As he wrote:

> ... there is no use merely touching our foreheads indifferently against the surface of any stone, feeling round it with our fingertips and expecting all sorts of information to come pouring out in vividly pictorial or other fashion. What we want we must go in and get for ourselves. There is no other real way of obtaining anything worth while. Until we learn how to do this in a spirit of love for the Life-forces connected with the stones or other materials in question, they will remain uncommunicative or merely misleading. Nothing but this one factor will really open them up.[13]

This hearkens back to Paddy Slade's perception of the stones when she felt that they needed the right amount of time and empathy before they would awaken. It touches on Murry Hope's 'pan-animism', which regards everything, no matter how small, as having inherent life and consciousness.

The light Bill Gray shed with his personality was often hard and acid, but his words can glow differently: 'Love,' he insisted, 'opens the gates of life everywhere, and when it is properly applied in its right degree, it will even let us into the secrets hidden by the humblest stones.'

Touch upon this energy in connection with the stones and sacred sites, however briefly, and we cannot help but become their champions, concerned for what they were, are, and will be.

The Knights Templar had nothing to do with the megaliths, of course. Historically they did not appear until thousands of years after the first stone was hewn and erected. Yet at Avebury and Cley Hill they can appear, like guard dogs, not actually barking and snarling but with enough watchfulness and menace to make the nape hairs prickle. Although the story of the Templars is far removed from the present theme we cannot help but be aware of them. It was as if their order recognised the importance of these two sites at least, and settled there as if to keep an eye on them. There is an argument that holds that the Templars are the inheritors of the old druidic wisdom, sharing the same passion for the head cult, and the same white robes. Although the druids did not build the megaliths, they certainly took them over, and used them. It would be natural, then, for the Templars to hover around the primary sites of druidic and pre-druidic worship. And to return yet again to an old theme, Keith Laidler argues in his brilliantly researched book *The Head of God* that the Templars – ultimately – are derived from the court of Thutmose III.

At Avebury, the Templar presence is found on Hackpen Hill, next to the Ridgeway, where they once had a receptory near the eerie waters of Glory Ann Pond, and where the 'mortuary enclosure' known as the Old Chapel once lay, and which William Stukeley the Freemason made a point of sketching. The farm at the top is still known as Temple Bottom. Next to it is Man's Head, which hints at the Templar cult of severed heads. The valley stretching down from there towards Rockley and Fyfield was once known for its hauntings, its suicides and its brooding atmosphere generally.

At Cley Hill, which is reputedly hollow and said to contain a golden ram, they were based at the nearby village of Temple. During a time when I was obsessed with the mysteries that lay within the hill the Templars themselves often seemed to float around and follow me, but their ambience was never easy, and not one that I wanted to indulge in.

It may seem that a link between the Order of the Temple and the planet Venus would be somewhat tenuous, but Lynn Picknett and Clive Prince make a persuasive case, showing that the inner order of the Templars was in fact fundamentally concerned with the Mysteries of Venus. More, their adepts were involved in tantric practices which hearkened back, through the sacred whoredom of Mary Magdalen, to the Egyptian Mysteries of Isis and Osiris.[14]

If, as folklore insists and Terence Meaden has confirmed, the Avebury circles expressed the mating of the Goddess and her God, then what better place for such an order to be than perched, watching, on the hill from which the generative powers arose?

In terms of such female power, Paddy referred to the Dark Lady in her account of the Carreg Inc. working. This related to an experience when she visited Arbor Low circle in Derbyshire. As she listened to another witch tell some students about the triple-faced goddess of Maiden, Mother and Crone, she felt herself pulled into the centre of the circle and was suddenly aware of a very potent entity telling her not to forget that there is, in fact, a fourth face, a dark face: that of the Dark Goddess, who looks forward and back, rather like Janus. This goddess, she was 'told', was the true keeper of those secrets of death and darkness that are all too often lumped on to the image of the Crone.

It was not so much a goddess that sprang to mind when I visited Hetty Pegler's Tump in Gloucestershire, but an often jolly though always formidable, mature but still fertile Mother. Not a Dark Mother or a Great Mother or a Cosmic Mother existing in the elevated realms of archetypes, but a very local one. In plan, the tump is reminiscent of those figurines found in connection with caves in Europe, such as the Venus of Willendorf in Lower Austria, or the Venus of Lespugue, from the Haute Garonne region of France: emphasised breasts and bellies, full in their curves. I was reminded of what Dusty Miller told me once, which I stole for one of my books: 'By what name did the ancient ones call the Great Mother? That's easy . . . they called her Mum.'

Hetty Pegler's Tump is a neolithic long barrow above the village of Uley, perched on the edge of a very steep escarpment and presumably aligned towards the midsummer sunrise. The sort of hill from which you could have launched hang-gliders if it hadn't been for the winter-bare and blackened ash trees. I went there in company with Mike Harris and Wendy Berg, whom I met in the village pub, the Old Crown, for the first time, although we had spoken on the phone and corresponded for some months beforehand. Wendy had led me to believe that Mike was a hideously warped, dwarfish figure but the reality was very different, for he proved to be a tall, solid and powerful man with a dry sense of humour and that curious but deliberately restrained magnetism that all real magicians have. And he was very kind: he let me pay for everything. Being of the same age, we spent some time chatting about afghan coats, platform shoes, flared trousers, Easy Riders, hippie beads and flowers, magick, Aleister Crowley, and the strange toxins that our generation once punished itself with. Wendy listened gracefully, a sybilline but comforting presence, tilting her head from time to time as if aware of levels of communication behind or beneath ours. I'm sure she found me fascinating.

It was Wendy who had suggested that we visit this long barrow, whose name had long been familiar to me, although I could not have drawn on any previous knowledge of history or myth in connection with it. I have always believed that places can call us, for reasons that are not necessarily apparent at the time, so I was more than happy to rendezvous with them in this compact little region of narrow valleys and steep hills, which seem far higher than they are.

It was a very cold day in mid-January. The wind turbine spun hard in the northerly breeze and the nearby microwave tower seemed to radiate sinister forces; but gulls soared and swooped upon the ploughed fields between the barrow and the road, and the distant passing traffic on the B4066 made a noise like the sea, and we had the place to ourselves.

We were all naturally but not pompously quiet as we approached the site: the last thing they would have wanted was my crass banter as they sought to attune themselves. In due course we crawled into the tomb and took turns to sit in the three remaining chambers. For myself, going through some fierce and personal emotional turmoil just then, I felt safe and calmer within this obvious womb than I had done in a long time. The cold wind didn't reach. Nothing could get me there.

Despite the dripping damp, the cramped conditions, I think I could have stayed all night.

Neither Wendy nor Mike spoke. They matter-of-factly moved about and tuned into whatever they felt was there. It was only as I left first, and looked back inside, that I caught a glimpse of Wendy at the end of the passageway, apparently illumined from the waist down as she squatted with her back against the wall. Likewise, when they had finished within the chambers and emerged into the daylight, they deliberately said very little about their experiences, promising to write them up quite separately and without collusion. Wendy's report was as follows:

> I walked about on the top of the tump for a while before going in and felt the approachability of the site – there is a friendly 'ease' about it. It was also very easy to pick up the contact with the female 'guardian', the abiding presence of the site, who seemed quite happy to call herself Hetty Pegler. I asked her who she was, which was unusual for me; this abrupt kind of question is not always the best place to start, but she answered immediately that she was me. That is to say that she was anyone and everyone who asks, because anyone who comes to her house and asks that question in sincerity has come there to find their true Self. There was something comforting, reassuring and completely matter of fact in the way this was said. It was not threatening or severe, but with an understanding that the process would without question go well and reach a happy and perfect outcome. I think this was in itself quite remarkable. Places like this – of any age or time – which have for thousands of years been connected with the passing of souls from this world to the next can easily attract or accumulate unbalanced energies or unhappy souls.
>
> There was no sense of any pomp and ceremony, just of a quiet and loving acceptance back into the Earth, probably for very ordinary people who lived nearby rather than kings or chieftains.
>
> The impression I received of 'Hetty Pegler' was of a figure something like the Washer at the Ford – a Celtic or pre-Celtic figure – who received those who had lost their lives in service to the land, or who had been otherwise fatally wounded by life.

She stood between the worlds and washed the stains from their clothes, figuratively speaking, in what amounted to a pre-Christian act of redemption.

Her report then went on to analyse the functions of the five chambers:

The function of the passage and chambers inside the barrow seemed to carry out five stages of passing from this world to the next. Two chambers have collapsed and are blocked up, but you can get a good impression of what lies behind by squatting with your back to the wall for a time. There seemed to be a certain order of progression which I didn't follow – but it didn't seem to matter in the general 'all will be well' atmosphere. To my mind the sequence in which the ritual of passing to the underworld took place was as shown, and I've written my impressions in that order:
1. This seemed to be where there was a gathering of the immediate family, who could come this far and no further, and where contact was made with the spirits of the ancestors who had come to assist in the process. A picking up of the threads of the greater family. There was no feeling of sadness, only of connectedness and joy.
2. This was the 'heaviest', and I experienced a slight breathlessness as if something was weighted on my collar-bone. Nothing untoward, but my impression was that this was in a milder way the equivalent of the 'weighing in the balance' – a searching look at what the soul had really achieved in that life-time and how this balanced up with the measure of ability and opportunity which had been given at birth into the world.
3. There was a curious sensation in here as if the flesh was somehow melting or dissolving into light. I don't know if the body actually rested here for a while or at what point the physical body decayed, but my impression was of becoming 'whiter than snow', of the heaviness and toxicity of the flesh being made pure and whole.
4. This seemed to be the heart chamber. As if the essential loving heart was all that was left of the body and it was this which would safely propel the soul on to the next world.
5. This was very stellar. I had a brief impression that all that remained of my physical body was the circle formed by the

sacrum (which I believe is the last bone to decay) and that this formed a sort of vortex through which the soul rushed through to the stars. There was a powerful feeling of being drawn back and upwards at great speed into the star-filled sky.

'Altogether it was a lovely experience,' she concluded, 'and coming out of the tump into the Winter sunshine I felt happy and wanting to laugh with joy. I've actually felt very content and balanced since this visit.'

I found the report oddly moving. Perhaps because it touched dormant ancestral memories? Or because its images gave shape to the mush of feelings I had about the visit from my own largely nonpsychic viewpoint? And, if nothing else, the long barrow being perched where it is on the edge of a substantial drop, with the land falling sharply away towards the distant River Severn, it is easy to imagine the soul taking flight from that point and rising (as the people hoped) to its true home in the stars.

Mike's impressions of the same place at the same time segue neatly into those of Wendy, and were written without collusion:

It's almost impossible not to take preconceptions to a well known and documented site. I was aware that the Uley tomb incorporated, for example, the five fold construction found in many Neolithic tombs. This was later copied in the geometry, ritual and mythology of a number of Bronze Age structures associated with the sacrificial 'rites of Hercules'. A temptation therefore exists to impose such theories *en bloc* to sites which appear to share the same constructional symbolism. This was especially so in this instance, because as I approached the site, I felt psychically 'neutral', without the inner tension which attends many site visits. I can only describe this by saying that the site, or any discarnate souls there, 'weren't expecting me' and that I hadn't felt (as is sometimes the case) that this visit was inwardly contrived. There were no bound souls seeking release, no guardians to be encountered, no sacred kings to interview. Only the memories of the place to observe, report and, as far as possible, interpret. In such circumstances it is too easy to fill any psychic vacuum from an informed imagination. But when we actually came to the site, the place memories were

158

unique and vivid enough to read, and perhaps even in this one does a service to the prehistoric dead.

Two of the five chambers are now, being unsafe, blocked off, but the tomb and its covering mound fulfil all the conventions of the type. The entrance was interesting. As with most burial mounds it is found between two 'thighs' of earth that extend from the pregnant belly of the main mound, which contain the tomb/womb of mother earth. Most tombs of this type have in their entrances something of a stylised vagina. In this instance however I had to almost go down on my stomach to get inside. There was therefore the feeling of having to crawl like a baby to get back into this womb-like structure and if the gynaecological symbolism is pursued, it's rather like passing beneath the pubic bone before entering the vagina-like passage beyond.

Inside it was quite 'motherly' and comfortable. There was a warm 'homespun' feeling about the people who had used the tomb. It was no Neolithic sorcerer's lair with dark rites of ritual slaughter or complex stellar magick. One got the impression that those who 'returned to the Mother' there were content to do so. There was a feeling of 'being cherished' in the kind of death that the Uley Neoliths knew, and this 'motherly' ambience would be emphasised by the mature women who, it seemed, performed the funerary rites as representatives of the Earth Mother.

One realised that the fivefold symbolism which came to have such prominence in the later Bronze Age and Celtic mysteries had its simple beginnings in places like this. It may be that 'the fivefold death' represented the death of the senses or simply in these early times the life going out of the head and four limbs. Whilst one can 'tune in' and receive place memories and some-times communication at such places, it should be remembered that this tuning is through one's modern human consciousness. What comes to mind, comes to a mind cluttered with con-ditioning and preconception which would probably be incomprehensible to the people of Neolithic Uley. A five fold death ritual with symbolism which would be obvious to them, may seem bizarre to us. However 'psychic' we are, we will always be faced with this problem of assuming that prehistoric people thought in the same way that we do and of translating what we receive accordingly. Even our psychism is a product of our environment and conditioning.

The body was pulled into the tomb with a rope. This was an important part of the ritual because the rope represented a restoration of the umbilical cord that joined the deceased to Mother Earth. The rope also had a practical purpose. Obviously the body couldn't be carried or easily manoeuvred through the very low and narrow opening and had to be roped and dragged in. This umbilical symbolism was carried on when the navel of the deceased was punctured with the point of an antler to, as it were, re-establish the umbilical connection which had been closed when the umbilical cord had been tied at birth. In fact as it turned out I got this slightly wrong! On reading up on this site after the visit, I noted that excavation hadn't found antler, but boar tusk. This actually equated better with the Underworld tradition that was spawned in these prehistoric times and carried through into the mythology of the Celtic era . . . some four and a half thousand years later. The boar tusk being used by women in death/rebirth rites equates very well with the sow mythology of Ceridwen, the Celtic underworld cauldron goddess. These boar tusks may even be the origin of the 'horns of light' referred to in Taliesin's *Prieddeu Annwn* poem, which seems to be structured around the Underworld mythology associated with pre-Celtic burial chambers.

Be that as it may, in this ritual it seems that five mature women occupied the stations of the burial complex to see the deceased into his or her rebirth state. This rebirth would be through merging with the land. The mound is sited with its entrance in the East, and end chamber in the West. The deceased would therefore be going into the west and into the earth . . . just as the sun appeared to, to merge with the earth mother, so that it could be reborn from her each following day. The tiny opening would in this case assure a 'disappearance' to the uninitiated gathered outside who would not be able to look directly into the tomb. When the corpse had been drawn into the tomb (legs first) by a woman crouched with a rope in the end (western) chamber, the navel would be punctured to let the deceased know that the umbilical connection had been restored. This would be done when the corpse was between the stone screens situated between the two sets of side chambers, as

160

these screens represent the transition point at the neck of the womb. This 'divide' offers the traditional three/five symbolism and it may be of some significance that this tomb was sealed after it had received the fifteen burials/skeletons found. I believe that another Neolithic tomb a mile or two up the road may have been built to accommodate further burials or that skeletons were removed and bones dispersed from time to time when it was thought that earlier burials had merged with the land and/or to stop the fifteen figure being exceeded. A later (possibly Roman) burial higher in the mound seems to have upset the spirits of the place, not because it was so much the burial of a later epoch, but because it violated the magickal limit of fifteen which was so vital to the 'earth balance' of this particular tomb.

What happened after the corpse was dragged in and the navel punctured wasn't so clear. It seemed that the women in the side chambers each performed some ritual act over the four limbs and that being done the corpse was dragged further in and some ritual act performed on the head by the presiding woman/priestess in the western end chamber. Part of the rite seems also to have involved heat and sound. The sonics, the echo effects of the tomb appear to have had central significance in this rite. How they coped with the existing burials in the confined space of the tomb when ritually introducing a new corpse was unclear. It was also not clear whether the tomb was for selected members of the tribe or just anyone who died.*

It seems to me that these are very deep levels of insight indeed, and ones that express many of the foregoing themes: the tribal structures and their stellar connections; the eminent role of women and guardian spirits; the notion of the land and the people being one; the sonics, rites and the soul-flight; the idea that these barrows were built in such a way as they actually did something, that they were magickal machines of some sort.

Historically, Hetty Pegler was the name of the seventeenth-

---

* On reading this in the manuscript 'Cass' noted: 'Mike's comment about "something" happening in the last chamber – some action by the priestess: I think that it was the piercing of the top of the skull – the fontanelle point. The soul comes in there, the soul goes out to the stars there, just as the earth connection is through the navel point. Don't ask how I know, but that's what happened.'

century woman whose husband owned the land on which the tump stands. But history and genealogy have, in this local instance, melted into the quicksilver of myth and magick: when we approach such a place and marvel at its meaning and purpose, we *become* this questing feminine spirit, as Wendy wrote, 'because anyone who comes to her house and asks that question in sincerity has come there to find their true Self.'

It is a curious thing, getting involved in the mysteries of the stone circles, barrows, sacred wells and the like. They may well be expressions of cosmic energies that can have transformative effects upon the world and its ways; they could quite possibly be gateways to other dimensions; the secrets of Matter, Energy, Time and Space are quite likely to be locked up within their structures; but even the finest of priestesses can rarely get from them a straight answer to the simple question: Why is life such a bitch?

A number of people have been compelled to seek out the stones or visit ancient sites when under great emotional duress, and, although no obvious solutions were presented in any case, everyone gained an indefinable 'something' that helped them through. Great and smug psychological conclusions can be drawn from such an impulse, but small and humble magickal beginnings may hold the answer more accurately.

'Claire Lucis' is the pseudonym of a woman whose experiences almost encapsulate this impulse. At a period of great personal darkness she visited the Belas Knap chambered tomb near Cheltenham, which is unusual (but not unique) in being oriented north to south. One of the most striking features of this long barrow is the false entrance at the north end, between convex horns edged with dry-stone walling of exceptional quality. No one is sure as to the purpose of the false door, except perhaps as a means of keeping out grave robbers. But in many of the tombs of Ancient Egypt such false doors were prominent features, and were seen as interfaces between the living and the dead – where the indwelling spirit of the tomb could meet with the summoner. The name itself is medieval in origin and means a beacon mound.

After circling the barrow three times with her Anubis-like hound Rhea, Claire entered one of the chambers, where she almost immediately became aware of the site's guardian, which took the form of a powerful golden dragon: a kingly, gracious and kindly presence which appeared to be guarding deeper mysteries than were immediately obvious. We have mentioned dragons before, as images of earth energies, and – again – we will look more closely at the nature of such protective entities in the next chapter; but Claire's perceptions were later awakened at another site, at a place that she would identify only as the 'silvery hill':

> I sat cross legged by a three pronged tree and quickly stilled myself. A silver triangle of energy appeared in front of me, going in from one palm to another and then apexing in line with my forehead. It was a very strong force. I saw myself looking down upon the mound and saw a large Horus symbol. The mound also seemed to be opening into another world. It was very ancient and very safe.
>
> A beautiful silver young girl came out from behind a tree and approached me. She was quite child-like and looked very mischievous. She asked me if I wanted to see the future. I thanked her but declined her offer, telling her that I had enough difficulty dealing with the past and the present. She smiled. I offered her a gift of silvery stone before rejoining the reality of now. In that reality I remembered that in my pocket was a little silvery, white stone that I had picked up when I was in Llangranog. I placed it in the well of the tree.

I asked Claire if this being might not be related to the Arianrhod figure that Arthur O'Neil and I apparently linked with, separately, on Cley Hill. In her case, however, she felt it was more akin to the Child Within: something within all of us which is eternally young yet incredibly old; wise but also child-like. She saw the same (or very similar) being again shortly after that. As she told it:

> One Saturday morning I woke up very early and had an inner need to visit the silvery hill. I had no idea why – but I had to. Rhea came with me as always. She is a beautiful lurcher with

a strong Anubis look about her. It was very very dark, and as we approached a silvery shadow appeared in the middle of the mound. I felt an overwhelming fear and actually started to cry. I called upon Anubis to guide and protect me, and bless him, instantly my panic subsided and a feeling of safety enveloped me. As I approached the silvery shadow appeared to be an opening, a doorway. I had an incredibly strong feeling that I was part of an ancient ceremonial procession, leading up into the mound. Rhea was very close – which is most unusual for her. As we got closer the whole mound seemed to be silver . . . I went where the doorway had been and asked permission to enter. I was completely unsure what to expect and had no idea why I had been called to this ancient and sacred site.

I sat on a tree stump, stilled myself and waited. A silver lady approached me. A beautiful young but somehow ancient woman. She approached me and simply told me to let go of the need for understanding behind the actions of others, and that sometimes the deepest learning comes through pain, and that we had to accept it, for it had to be. She touched my forehead and told me to listen to my own stillness and to trust my intuition. I thanked her.

As I left the mound I felt completely disorientated. I felt really weird. It was as if I was walking in a completely different world. I was in the wrong place!

This last experience is a common one. If we can explain it at all – if we *should* explain it at all – it can only be through metaphor, simile or analogy. A purely rational, scientific analysis of the 'this is nothing more than' kind will simply destroy what is a beautiful, moving, if completely bewildering, feeling – a feeling that is derived from the experience of living in two worlds.

In some ways, on another level, this is exactly what our guide the Reverend Edward Duke did during his journey. He was a man of letters studying the works of the unlettered; a Christian entering the mysteries of the pagans; a rationalist looking at the irrational; a proud Victorian male who was touching upon, in this Orbit of Venus, the mysteries of women; and a mere man of advancing years seeking to fathom the timeless realm of the spirits themselves.

And being a mere mortal, locked into temporal needs – not least being the need to return to Lake House at a reasonable hour – he found it necessary to leave the Orbit of Venus and press quickly onwards to the place that seemed to confirm the veracity of his whole scheme.

And that was Marden.

CHAPTER

SIX

The Orbit of Mars, the Place of the Guardian Spirits and the Mysteries of Men

I was then aware of nothing but a huge electrical
charge in the air which rooted me to the spot. I
first saw a head form from the soul in front of me
in the barrow. A twisted face actually came out in
three dimensions from the earth itself before
shrinking back. In its place there formed a being
of light, approximately the size and girth of a pylon.
He was standing on top of the mound itself. It
was the site Guardian and he wasn't happy . . .
                                            – Poppy Palin

The exasperating thing about any quest is that, if done properly, the questor always finds . . . something. It is never quite the object of the quest itself which would solve all mysteries and bring the miraculous into the mundane, but it is close enough, or allusive enough, to suggest that with just one more turn, one more revelation, the questor would be at the centre of the spiral, clutching something holy. Few questors are ever that good, and the ones who are, such as Galahad and Perceval, clutched their own Grail, waved goodbye to the Wasteland, and were never seen again. The rest of us . . . well, we have to carry on wandering and wondering, as Jack Green tried to express with his spiral glyph.

Another inner pilgrim who experienced this was Michael Everest, one of the unrecognised and unsung frontrunners in the field of 'sacred geometry', whose unpublished work dating back to the 1970s is still far ahead of much in the genre since. Like almost everyone who feels the stones 'calling'

166

to them, and finds themselves involved on personal quests, he also had the sense that some cosmic trickster gets involved.

'I agree with James Lovelock,' he wrote to me, 'call the earth goddess Gaia and see her as she is. All consciousnesses are absorbed into her and reinforce her. At the same time it seems to me she enjoys playing games . . . First of all showing herself and then hiding again. The results are not reproducible. They fall outside the province of science.'

This from a scientist who once worked for the European Space Agency, Sellafield and Woolwich Arsenal. But among his many purely mystical experiences among the neolithic sites he also noticed something that our guide Edward Duke might have appreciated. While tracking the lines and angles of equinoctial and solstitial sunrise, he found that many purely modern housing developments and place names unwittingly echoed and honoured the event. Something that he ascribed to the actions of the collective unconscious, as defined by Jung.

Which brings us neatly to Duke's revelation at the village of Marden, which for him clinched the veracity of his whole scheme. There it was on the map, bold as anything, almost leaping out of the page like a hare. Marden. *Mar* and *Den*. Just *exactly* where it should be, on the orbit of Mars. He must have given a few hallelujahs at very least, and slapped his servant's back as gentlemen were wont to do in moments of passion.

The only problem he found was that the word Marden seemed to be a compound of two quite separate and perhaps mutually exclusive languages, Teutonic and Celtic, and he was too much of a scholar to brush aside the improbability of that pairing. What he desperately needed was to find some linguistic justification, some as yet hidden but impeccable source which might get him out of a hole.

And sometimes, wrapped up as I have been with the perceptions of magicians, mystics and mediums, I begin to wonder in a half-whimsical way if the answer he looked for didn't come from . . . us.

The one thing that magicians, mystics and mediums tend to agree on is that time – whatever it is – seems to be a two-way street. Or perhaps, in more elegant terms, a Möbius strip in which the inside and outside (like past and present) flow into each other and become one.

Just as a mental exercise we can apply it to our dear old guide Edward Duke: as he travelled the highways and byways between Silbury and Stonehenge (whether in his carriage or in his mind) was he aware that our minds rode next to him? Because if ever he needed help on his journey, he needed it then, when he tried to make sense out of that troubling but crucial name Marden. There arose, he lamented, the awkward objection 'of deriving a compound word from two languages'.[1]

We can help him here. Surely, after all the images and magic that have poured through our subconscious on our journey so far, we can suspend disbelief enough to give him a clue, and mentally *will* him across the intervening years to go and look once more through his bookshelves.

And so he did, and, to his delight and relief, through the kind of synchronistic happening that seemed to follow Michael Everest in his own technical research, he stumbled upon the one book that would give him the answer he needed as if by magic: that unforgettable tome the *Ductor Linguorum of Minshieu*. It almost seemed to fling itself at him. Looking through, sensing that his vision had been saved, he coyly confessed to being 'agreeably surprised to find that the planet in question bore the appellative of Mars in the Teutonic, of which the ancient British is a dialect'. The Celtic and Teutonic tongues being twin sisters, he assured us, meant that the word Marden was 'obviously compounded of the ancient British words Mars and den, and may with strict propriety be rendered as the house or temple of Mars'.[2]

Well, not quite. *The Place Names of Wiltshire*, referring back to sources in the twelfth century, identifies two Old English elements, *mearh* and *dene*, denoting a fertile valley with no hint of the red planet that fitted Duke's scheme so perfectly, falling as it did exactly halfway between Stonehenge and Avebury.

But this is the sort of thing that happens all the time when you start, in your own way, to work with the energies of the ancient sites. Tantalising hints and clues. False trails that turn out, years afterwards, to have been true after all. Or broad highways of obvious revelation that eventually prove to have carried you well past the little byways that lead to the real treasures.

The fact is, Marden was such an unusual place that any reasonable mystic would be quite happy to clutch at etymologies if it would support his vision in such a way. As he wrote of it:

> These works consist of an immense tumulus called Hatfield Barrow with a secondary or smaller one to the south, and they are together located on an area of 51 acres of land, the whole of which is surrounded by a rude and irregular circular vallum with its fosse *within side*! This arrangement denotes (as at Abury) that such a fosse and vallum were not purposed for defence.[3]

In 1807 the archaeologist William Cunnington had sunk a pit into it from the top, but failed to find any kind of burial. Echoing Silbury, nothing was found but the bones of red deer, a pig and a large bird, plus two human cremations. Richard Colt-Hoare, an old friend of Duke, was inclined to think that this barrow was 'designed for a hill altar, or a place of general assembly, not a sepulchre'. Duke commented that Colt-Hoare had, in 1809, 'endeavoured with slender success to investigate the inmost recesses of this enormous mass of earth, and on revisiting the spot in 1818 it was gone – with barbarian hands it had been levelled to the ground!'[4]

(Barbarian hands . . . You have to fall just a little bit in love with Duke for that term alone. One of the most extraordinary pagan monuments in the country had been levelled by good Christians with barbarian hands, and the reverend was furious at the sacrilege and loss. If he had been born a few generations later he would have been an eco-warrior.)

But the only recorded folklore from Marden tells how there was once a mighty battle fought there between 'men with red heads and men with black heads' – and the red-headed men won. Whether this related to Neolithic men being defeated by

Bronze Age invaders, or – much later – Danes crushing the native Brits, is matter for conjecture.

By 1818, as Duke raged, this notional temple of the red planet and the God of War was levelled to the ground by the owners. It was once the largest neolithic henge in Britain, but now there is almost nothing to be seen, and it serves the archaeological community at least as the Terrible Warning. When Paddy and I visited we found almost a ghost village, a closed pub with an empty play area. It may have been a pleasant enough village in terms of housing, locale and views, but there was nothing obvious, on that brief visit, that called out to the psyche.

Now John Foster Forbes and Iris Campbell, the psychometrist, never visited Marden. As I said, there would have been nothing to see if they had. But they did visit a similar site near Penrith in Cumberland, known as Mayboro. This ancient earthwork was surrounded by what he termed a vallum, and covered almost six acres. To their perceptions this place was for the upbuilding of mankind, and the energies used had a direct effect on the human lymphatic system. As JFF noted, 'These glands are the storehouses of energy on the etheric plane and in the operation of some forms of magick the priest must have understood their power.'[5]

As for the construction of Mayboro, as determined from the psychometric angle, Iris Campbell had this to say:

> You have here a house which was ordained for the purpose of co-ordinating light for the benefit of the glandular system of man . . . it seems to have been roofed over with some induced condition, possibly hypnotic and was specially induced in order to shut out intruding mental conflict from without . . . The central stone has remained here because it had the highest magnetic content and, being constantly washed by the auras of the officiating priesthood, it combined the energy of the earth with that of the human element around it. The office of the priest is to mediate between one creation and another. Hitherto the human body has been the only reasoning channel through

170

which all creation, including that of the Universe, may be co-ordinated.[6]

Somewhat like a cross between a power station and a specialist hospital, then. A hospital that, by maintaining the health of that corporate known as Man, had direct influence upon each individual.

Could Marden have served the same purpose as Mayboro – whatever that purpose may have been? Just looking at the old map of the former, and reconstructing the complex in the mind's eye, we are left with a kind of British equivalent of Teotihuacan. And, like Duke, we can only rage at its levelling and its loss. If it lives on at all, it does so as Duke's inner Temple of Mars, where we can look at the concepts of men and their gods, of places and their guardians. For, if any ancient site needed a guardian to save it from the depradations of men and the ploughs they wielded, it was Hatfield Barrow at Marden.

The concept and experience of Guardians at sacred sites is one of the most fascinating aspects of the mysteries. In Bob Stewart's experience at the tomb on Jersey he described how the inner chamber, which was used for consultation and initiation, was kept sealed and guarded by a 'restrained soul'. 'This guardian was a deliberately tied sacrifice, a human who was bound for a specific period to remain in an interim state close to the outerworld, to defend the chamber against break-in and tampering. After a certain number of years (solar cycles) the guard was free, and was replaced or rendered unnecessary by the success of the King's merging.'[7]

One school of thought insists that this is not a question of spirits remaining earthbound because of sudden or violent death: these are not souls wandering through some kind of limbo, trapped by their obsessions, nor yet mere astral shells that hover around places through habit. These are humans who have agreed to remain in situ after their death. The guardian was put there to protect the king. The king was part of the land and the people.

Mike Harris, however, who has probably met more guardians in his time than most, tends to disagree. He felt that the companion of the king would be chosen with little notice, and his death a sudden one, although to be thus chosen for the king's discarnate bodyguard was, perhaps at one time, a great honour. However, he and his group had reason to believe that some later 'companions' preferred dishonour to death.

'Either way such companions did not go into the "great turning" as the king did, but "remained" as we would understand a ghost to remain, to guard the chamber. In the technical terms of the mysteries they would be "bound souls". Thus, while the king established his "root" in the sacred land, the soul of the companion/s would be "restrained" to be given quittance at some later time when it was felt that the tomb no longer needed to be guarded.'

Not all guardians throb with ancient wisdoms however, even if the sites they guard are indeed somewhat special. Mike told me about a visit to the votive lake of Llyn Cerrig Bach, on Anglesey, which was a druidic cult centre until the Roman invasion. The weapons and chariot items found within it indicated that it was once a cult centre of national importance. The lake, now dry, was discovered during World War Two when the runway at Valley airfield was being extended. Because most of the lake was actually within the bounds of the airfield, Mike and a friend had to crawl under the perimeter wire, undetected by the nearby guardhouse.

I got a contact there, as we say, with an old Druid who appeared to have presided over the place. Sadly the great revelations that I expected from him didn't materialise. He seemed to think it very important that I knew that the weapons were thrown into the sacred lake to assure victory. Yes, I already knew that! He then wittered on about the types of weapon allowed and was very much taken with his own importance as caretaker priest of a national shrine. The encounter taught me that being dead does not automatically qualify one for a metaphysical diploma nor does it necessarily deflate the self important. By the time I left the site with him hot on my heels continuing to promote himself and 'his' shrine, I reflecte͞ ͞ ͞ ͞ shot may be a merciful release! He was the first o͞ ͞͞ ͞le corps of cosmic windbags that one encounters in ͞ ͞ ͞ork. As experience is gained one develops a way of ͞ ͞ ͞ ͞ ͞uch firmly, but at the time I was too green to tell h͞i. and leave me alone!

Another such encounter with a discarnate and eq͞ally tedious Anglesey druid was at the Iron Age settlement of Din Lligwy:

> As this was a small settlement I hadn't expected it to have any religious significance and I was surprised to find a Druid there. It later transpired that it was probably the estate of a local chieftain of the Romano Celtic period who being something of a traditionalist presumably maintained a 'Druid in residence'. This Druid valued his position and was still defending it, some nineteen hundred years later. He was paranoid about any visitor who gave off any sort of esoteric aura, fearing that his position and prestige would be undermined. He was insecure because he didn't know much, and may only have been a self styled Druid at this late date. He seemed to jump out at me as soon as I got near the village and started making all sorts of absurd threats. It transpired that not only was he 'fixed' in his own time, but that he also maintained a jealous theocratic hold over a small group of discarnate souls. I suggested to him that this was unethical and that the world had moved on since his time. This initiated a heated discussion in which he kept repeating the little Druidic dogma that he knew. It became very tiresome and I could not persuade him to seek quittance for either himself or his little 'congregation'. I left the site feeling very bad tempered and haven't, some twenty years later, been back there since . . .

A young Australian woman told me a marvellous story along such lines about her visit to a long barrow in the company of two of the stately Crones of England, both delightfully humorous individuals with power that could make your fillings ache, and your stomach feel as if it were ripped open, and who could do all the things that *real* witches are supposed to do. The spirit guardian at the mouth of the tomb they visited was so drained of energy, suffering from what one termed 'psychic

anorexia', that he could barely make even the feeblest of menacing gestures. 'Poor old sod,' said the first witch, shaking her
head. The second witch had an idea. A quick trip into the local
town and they came back with some chicken heads and offal
from the butcher's, which they buried next to where the
guardian lurked. Blood, according to occult lore, contains
the etheric material which spirits can use to give themselves
substance. After 'feeding' upon the offering the guardian then
roared and towered over them in the expected manner. 'That's
better,' said the second witch, as they strolled off back to the
car . . .

Poppy Palin, the gifted artist, writer and tattooist, had a far
more intense and disturbing experience with a guardian during
her visit to Stonehenge. While visiting the nearby group of
three round barrows in company with her friends Helen Read
and Mike Prince, she first did a piece of personal psychic
protection which involved putting on a kind of 'astral' suit of
reflective light-blue material, then began to tune in to the site
itself. She listened and let the site 'speak' to her for a little
while about its nature and purpose, and was overcome with a
deep feeling of respect and awe. All was well until she tried to
contact the guardian . . .

> Contacting the site Guardian is another piece of standard
> psychic etiquette when in the landscape. This time when I tried
> to silently ask for a communion with the guardian I was told
> 'To ask for this is very dangerous, do you still wish to do so?'
> At the same time I was aware of being goaded, and challenged
> by something: 'Go on, I dare you to call up the Guardian!' So
> once again I asked to speak with the site Guardian. I was told
> 'If you do this a third time you will not be safe, do you wish
> to continue?' The other voice spurred me on. 'Go on! Ask for
> the Guardian!' Now, either I was being naive or egotistical or
> a little foolhardy but I went on and asked. By this time I had
> processed with purpose to a spot behind the third barrow and
> I stood still. Both Helen and Mikey were elsewhere out of my
> sight. Previously I had seen Helen across the barrows from me
> and I could not reach her. I could feel with my hands a band

of electrical energy (a force field if you will) between myself and her, running across the barrows. I could see that she was experiencing a totally different set of circumstances on her side of the invisible energy barrier. I believe the electrical 'fence' may have been a ley line? I don't know.

I was then aware of nothing but a huge electrical charge in the air which rooted me to the spot. I first saw a head form from the soul in front of me in the barrow. A twisted face actually came out in three dimensions from the earth itself before shrinking back. In its place there formed a being of light, approximately the size and girth of a pylon. He was standing on top of the mound itself. It was the site Guardian and he wasn't happy . . .

After berating her about her attitude, her inability to know what it is like to be dead, and about the stupidity of an age that saw fit to make the A303 run alongside the Henge and barrows, the guardian went on, 'You think you know of our time, you think your calling yourself a Pagan makes you know of our lives here. You know nothing of who we were or what we did. You know nothing of these dead.'

With that the massive figure picked her off her feet and pushed her down on to the ground so that her forehead was jammed against the soil. He continued to speak to her about how she should learn respect, how our whole age should learn respect, and try to understand that, pagan or not, we are not like them!

At the same time Mike Prince, who had been exploring a different part of the site, became aware of the powerful and imposing figure of the guardian also. He saw Poppy staring up, directly ahead, and then sway before falling on to her knees and curling forward. Deeply concerned, he thought of sending for Poppy's own guardian animal spirit, but she started to get up by herself.

The whole group left the area quickly, feeling nauseous, confused and oppressed. They experienced one of the classic 'missing-time' episodes en route, and started to feel better only when more miles had been put between them and the barrows.

In a modern echo of Ernest Butler's account of raising the

SPIRITS OF THE STONES

spirit of a tumulus, Tom Graves describes in his book *Needles of Stone* how a group of students were terrified by the semi-human guardian they all perceived on top of a long barrow (unidentified), and how some of them needed counselling afterwards.

You cannot blame the guardian. It was only doing its job, and very well by the sound of it.

Another extraordinary encounter with a guardian was detailed by Rowan Greenwood. This took place at Corley Rocks, just north of Coventry and out towards the M6, which in fact runs through the area about a mile further on from the rocks themselves.

Although now surrounded by roads and a few houses, Corley Rocks still manages to be an atmospheric Neolithic site, consisting of an outcrop of rock which has a network of caves within it. But from the rocks you can see for miles, and even if it is only pylons and bypasses now, it is easy to imagine how it would have been used as a special place in ancient times. Then, the rocks would have been a massive outcrop standing in a flat low-lying plain and visible for miles around (a bit like a mini version of Australia's Ayers Rock). 'It's easy to see,' wrote Rowan, 'how it might have been used as a religious or ritual focus.'

On the day in question, she, her husband Michael and daughter Sally travelled to them along Burrow Hill Lane, which branches off from the Keresley Road. She took this route because it was probably the original trackway to the site. Burrow Lane, she felt, was probably a corruption of Barrow. The lane actually goes alongside the rocks and they pulled in at the side of the road to climb up towards the summit. And this is when the story begins:

I have only once reached the top of the site before the atmosphere of this site forced me away from it and this visit was no better. I have sensed three separate entities at this place each of whom has a particular role. I have named them the Watcher, the Keeper and the Sentry because of the different aspects that

I have picked up on. It is of course possible that there is only one extremely powerful being involved which has immense power and presence and which fulfils all of these roles, but I have been given the impression of three beings and with three being such a magical number, I've stuck with this theory.

Of these only the Sentry is overtly hostile and then only when you walk within a few yards of one area of the site. In this area there is a deep ravine between where I stood to take a picture and the place I wanted to go. The force coming at me from the other side of this ravine was very strong and actively forbade me to come any nearer. Two things spring to mind immediately: firstly whatever was originally present on this site is clearly still precious enough to be defended Aeons later; and secondly, whatever is defending it knows that those who are sensitive enough to recognise what is there may present some sort of threat to the site.

I have read many articles and accounts about so-called psychic hotspots and also psychic vampirism where those with psychic power are drained of energy by those in need of power, and I believe that whatever is guarding this site is scared of people coming along who may sense the power contained within the place and use it for whatever purpose. There is also the distinct possibility that I have been recognised as a person of 'magical persuasion' and am being warned off another 'patch'.

I also tried to photograph the ravine from the top of the ridge. This is where the Keeper is to be found. The Keeper seems to be a force which is rooted in the one spot whereas the other two tend to follow you around until you get the 'clear off' message. The Keeper is the oldest of the entities and is keeping safe the secrets and power of this site. I got the clear impression that the duty was given and never forgotten – and never will be. Again it is not possible to discover exactly what is at the root of this power as any attempt at probing deeper is met with a hostile reception. On no account would I attempt to climb down into the ravine as I am certain that that would be totally unacceptable and be met with an out and out attack, at least psychically.

The most benign of the three beings is that which I term the Watcher, but this is the one which probably spooks most people just out for a walk, or whatever, because it operates on a very superficial level. Essentially it deliberately puts people off going to the rocks by simply making them feel uncomfortable – by giving them that 'being watched' sensation. However that is exactly what it is doing – watching and probably acting as an early warning system for the other two. It is also the only one of the three which materialises, which adds to the idea that this is the 'spook' of the place. At one point the Watcher was standing on the outcrop of rock beside a thin tree, just observing my attempts at taking a photo. It would have been interesting if someone with all the electronic wizardry that so-called ghost-busters have could take a shot of this place and see what they could come up with, because the image is quite a strong one.

Unfortunately I'm not a ghostbuster and the developed photo only shows the foliage, but I like to fancy that it is slightly less distinct in the area in which the Watcher was standing. I say standing but the entity doesn't possess legs, and is simply a shape, roughly human sized but with no definable limbs. Even without the visible evidence of this being it is enough to make most people get goose bumps, as it projects some very strong sensations of being observed.

I had gone to the site with my husband and youngest daughter but he had stayed in the car [with her] as she was tired. He later got out of the car when she fell asleep, and confessed that he too had felt the hairs on the back of his neck rise as he walked towards the rocks. He is not at all 'sensitive' but my youngest child is and, having been born near the Celtic New Year (Samhain or Halloween), is particularly 'open', and has complained of black dogs in woods, ladies with shining faces etc. from the age of 18 months onwards.

On this occasion when we both got back to the car, she was awake, and calmly stated that she had been talking to 'the man with the hairy coat on'! My husband had kept the car in clear view all the time and had seen nothing, but Sally was able to describe a man with a long white beard apparently wearing an animal skin cloak who had just stared at her, stroked her face and then smiled at her before going back in amongst the trees. Sally wasn't frightened (she never is!!) and I wasn't at all alarmed by this, but Michael completely panicked and we had to leave in double quick time.

Cass, whom we met earlier in connection with Long Meg, had

an encounter with the guardian spirit at Callanish, which might have fazed anyone less stout-hearted.

The custom when approaching any site for the first time is simply to introduce yourself before going in. I did so at Callanish but the Guardian there took on the manner of a night-club bouncer, and it was as though he stood there, muscular and aggressive, with his arms folded, saying something like 'So what!' Well, my response was to tell him in ringing tones that I was a Priestess of Bride, and that I claimed my right to be there; and at once his whole attitude changed, and there was something which came back which might be translated as 'Sorry missus!'

Guardians are not always about inducing fear and terror, however. In fact some guardians draw us to the sites. And once we are drawn there, and inner links made, usually unconsciously, it seems that we feel compelled to protect and preserve and work with them.

Wendy Berg told me about her visit to Wistman's Wood, which has something of a reputation in the Earth Magick community for being not *quite* in this world, and has been linked with the Mythago Wood of Robert Holdstock's astonishing novel of that name, although the author assures me this is not the case.

When I visited Wistman's Wood in the past I had usually been aware of two tall figures standing either side of the path just at the entrance to the wood. On this visit with a couple of friends they appeared to have been replaced by a single bull-finch who was perched just inside the wood and, although clearly aware of us standing only a very short distance away, stayed put and sang the most extraordinary song. I've never heard a bull-finch sing like that before. There was no way that we could walk past it until it had finished and eventually flown away and the effect of the song was to lift the atmosphere up several notches, almost as if (I hope I'm not being too fanciful here) we were being reminded that we also should raise our consciousness before going into the wood. But then this is the purpose of site guardians, of course.

* * *

The late Arthur Shuttlewood was a journalist who found himself at the centre of the UFO mysteries that seemed to plague the Wiltshire town of Warminster in the mid-1970s. He and numerous others came across what he described with some perplexity as the 'slithering snakes or serpents of sound'. He described how he encountered this creature while standing in the fields around Starr Hill, or Battlesbury Hill, and felt that its odd electrical crackling was generated from underground – a subterranean creature that coiled and uncoiled, wound and unwound, as it headed unerringly for the feet of the intruders. Intriguingly, the electrical charge he noticed was strongly reminiscent of the 'huge electrical charge' that Poppy Palin felt in connection with the guardian near Stonehenge. He described his first encounter with the serpent as follows:

> We heard an eerie crackling noise emanating from the rain-soaked soil before us . . . It was somewhat like static on a radio set – with a distinct electrical element involved in the creeping carpet of sound. It was much as if a serpent was uncoiling and thrusting its sinuous length across the ground. A sibilant snake! We saw no rise and fall of the furrowed soil along its inclines, but the humming and hissing sounds came directly at us about slow walking pace . . . Accompanied by a weird whip-cracking, or the sound of a flailing lash descending at speed, the slithering snake of sound, after coiling its invisible loops of skin and as though baring its fangs, pronged toward us once more . . .[8]

Their nerves broke and they ran. After other encounters over a period of time, however, Shuttlewood was able to muse, 'They are nerve-shaking yet harmless, these peculiar serpents or dragons that swish and whine beneath the feet . . . [They] indicate life that, although alien to us, might have been familiar to our ancestors in the long, long ago.'

Some sites, however, seem able to protect themselves in other ways – as if they have a consciousness and purpose which can ensure that, if they don't want someone to visit, then that person will be thwarted at every step.

Jack Green wrote about an attempted visit to Lindisfarne,

that holy island off the Northumbrian coast which can be reached twice a day by road, when the tide is out:

> To be honest, I was in a funny state at the time. Involved in what seemed like a long running saga of group reincarnation which centred around Lindisfarne, dating from the 7th Century or thereabouts. People kept appearing who had similar ideas – including you! The name, image, and history of Lindisfarne kept cropping up everywhere I turned, at the least likely moments. Although I had been there once as a boy, driven by my brother in his old Austin A35, I had never been since, and determined to go there at once, on a sort of Quest-cum-Pilgrimage.
>
> Well, everything went wrong. Every possible obstacle at every level, personal, social, work-related, seemed to be put in my path. When I finally got on the road I had to endure the most vicious squalls which almost pushed my old car into the verge. Storm debris crashed into my windscreen; something seemed wrong with the engine; a lorry nearly smashed into me. Eventually I gave up and turned around, and found that the demonic conditions stopped almost at once when I was heading in the opposite direction.
>
> However, I was so surprised by all this that I decided to do a rapid U-turn on the road, and found that as I aimed toward Lindisfarne once again the calm, clear morning turned into a minor tempest. Another U-turn, back toward home, and it all stopped; then re-started when after a few miles, I decided to put it to the test by heading – for the final time – back toward Lindisfarne. Then I got a flat tyre and took the hint, and gave up.
>
> I never did get to Lindisfarne on that day, but later in the month I drove up on an impulse and got there with no trouble.

Green's impression was that the place itself, for some reason, did not want him to go there on the day in question. And this type of weather phenomenon seems to be separate from those occasions described earlier in which individuals provoked storms by, in some way, touching upon the 'magkical technologies' behind circles and barrows. This was almost a case of Gaia herself saying the equivalent of 'Go away. Not yet!'

Similarly the magus of a Californian group with Hermetic/Templar leanings visited Cley Hill, near Warminster, hoping to link with some of the energies that lie within this hill, and found that the entire, huge mass was completely enshrouded in mist, although the rest of the area was clear enough. It was as if one particular cloud had decided to descend at that particular spot and stay, creating enough discouragement to make her leave without the merest glimpse of its heights.

Christine Hartley, one of the influential frontrunners in the whole New Age movement after World War Two, told me of an occasion when she was just unable to climb Glastonbury Tor – when something from the Tor itself absolutely forbade her to come any further than the lower gate.

Another woman, with a Wiccan/Hermetic background, told me of her experience in an area of Dartmoor where she felt she had been 'pixie-led' and deliberately led astray in a way that felt to her much more like an act of wilful, even a malicious, intent. She wrote of one wood that, she vowed, she would never walk in again:

> It's not a large wood, but I was once led to exhaustion walking in it. I had been walking on a wide, sandy path, well-defined and signposted. For no apparent reason it suddenly began to peter out. As I was carrying an Ordnance Survey map and pride myself on my map-reading I pressed on, only to find that the path then not only faded almost literally beneath my feet but that when I reluctantly decided to turn round and retrace my steps the path now wasn't visible behind me. Events quickly became nightmarish because each way I turned rapidly took me deeper into impenetrable undergrowth, and within the space of a few minutes I simply could not move. I was hemmed in on all sides by branches which I hadn't got the strength to climb through. It was only when I sat down in tears and said out loud, 'Ok, I give up, just let me out', that I saw a stone wall ahead of me. Getting out involved climbing this and many others, mostly covered with rusty barbed wire, before I found the road miles from where I had started and what should have been a one-hour walk had turned into nearly four.

The act of spirits? Or something within the earth conscious-ness of the site itself?

Tom Graves recounts something similar, recalling how a

student of his, while dowsing at the Rollrights, found herself having a giggling fit after tripping over a tiny piece of chervil, which she swears wrapped itself around her ankle, and sobered up – instantly – only when she was helped out of the circle.

Mike Harris wrote about a full-scale ritual at Dinas Bran with a whole host of 'now famous occult luminaries' which involved scripts, patterns, invocations – 'the whole bit'. All did not go well, however. Scripts and invocations were lost in the wind, the rapport between the officiants was lost as they couldn't hear each other, attentions became diverted to trying to follow the procedure and recover those pages of windblown script. And to cap it all a troupe of German girl guides decided to march right through their hallowed pattern! 'A low key, meditative site visit with the ritual done later in private, under cover, would have been better,' he mused.

Dusty Miller told me about an abortive attempt made by an American cameraman from Burbank Studios in Hollywood to film him at the Coldrum circle, which was originally a chambered tomb heaped over with earth and surrounded by a ring of sarsens.

> Over the years, [he wrote] erosion has taken its toll and now it is a roofless, three sided room overhanging a steep drop of about 15 feet (5 m), but still with a complete ring of Sarsens. We go there a lot to honour our ancestors. On one occasion we took an American visitor there and discovered a very interesting effect of the Coldrum Power Vortex.
>
> As he had a car loaded up with big expensive equipment, we (my son and I) ignored the official car park, and took him down the farm track that goes all the way to this famous site, and parked next to it. There are rails around the site to keep visitors off the stones and reduce the erosion caused by countless feet scrambling over the site. The top of the site has an area within the Sarsen ring, and behind the room that is big enough for ritual use, by the various Pagans and Witches who use the site. It was in this area that we decided to do the interview; so I stood by the room with my foot on a large stone. To make it look good, I even adopted a 'Victorian Big Game Hunter's Stance' and smiled at the huge, state of the art, Video Camera

that our American visitor was setting up. It was as large as a weekend suitcase, and powered by huge multi-cell batteries. Soon he had it set up on a tripod and aimed at me like a machine-gun.

However, no sooner had we started the interview, than his batteries went flat. Boyinnnnggggg! Just like that! Mind you, he took it like a man, apologised and went back to the car to get a replacement. I was in position, so I had to stand still and wait, but I couldn't help noticing that the ancient Beech tree that overlooks the back (west) side of the site was quaking with laughter. Its leaves were fluttering about as if in a breeze, but I could feel nothing. The other trees around the sight were also sniggering, but at the time I didn't think too much of it, as trees often find our human antics rather amusing.

Anyway, back comes our man with a nice new battery, and loads it into his super, 'all singing, all dancing' Video Camera. He turns to me, and tells me to start again. Then by the time I'm into my third sentence, he's suddenly hopping up and down, in frustration, on finding that his second battery has lost all its power. So it is back to the car for his third and last reserve battery, whilst I try to keep a straight face. All around me, the Tree Dryads are laughing fit to burst... and I'm getting the impression that the whole thing is a put-up-job.

Then, once again, our now somewhat annoyed photographer is loading his last battery into his video camera, and discovering that the tripod is no longer steady. By the time he has adjusted it and is ready to start the interview again, he discovers to his extreme annoyance that once again his battery has lost its power. This sends him into a terrible bout of swearing and cursing, and I'm getting scared that he will think it is all my fault.

Then he has a brainwave and remembers the very expensive, state of the art, Japanese Camera that he has in the car. So he tells me, we'll record the interview and he'll take some still photos with his marvellous, 'oh look what I've got', camera. So off he goes and comes back with a tape-recorder and a lovely black camera. Both of which are battery operated and have their power drained in no time flat. By now he is so livid that he is hopping about turning the air blue in his anger. Of course, the Tree Dryads are having a whale of a time laughing at his expense and the whole site is throbbing with suppressed mirth. So what could we do? We had to call it a day and go home. He was much too annoyed to come in for a cuppa, and shot off back to London without ever doing the interview.

Thinking about it, after doing some other experiments with batteries at the site, my son and I have come to the conclusion that for some reason best known to itself, the Power Vortex at Coldrum just won't allow man-made competitors onto the site. We're not saying that the Power Vortex is alive, but sometimes it seems to act as if it is.

It was Bill Gray who talked about the 'power perimeter' which he sensed around the Rollrights – an obviously influential and very much alive set of stones; and it may have been this that stopped me getting anywhere near them.

Despite having the sort of map-reading skills and innate sense of direction that allow me to think of myself as Wiltshire's answer to Daniel Boone, I found myself, on a hot August afternoon, completely lost, even though I could not have been more than a few hundred metres from the circle. But there was a moment when, walking along some small road, I had the feeling that something very odd was happening, that I was not quite in the world I knew. I felt that I had entered a kind of Silence, which I realised then was a state that had little to do with absence of noise. Everything was like what would now be termed a virtual-reality landscape: bright and intense – almost supernaturally intense – but not quite real. Or not with the reality that *I* existed in. It was disorienting, and bewildering, but not frightening. Perhaps it was like the artist John Palmer felt when he stepped out of the West Kennet Long Barrow and understood that the landscape around him had changed. Or, as described in the chapter 'Walker's Hill . . .', more akin to what Edna Hedges experienced when she took shelter from the storm in that thatched cottage which, in her own time, no longer existed.

Whatever, taking the hint, I gave up. Whatever was going on at or within the Rollrights that day, my presence was most definitely *not* required.

Something of this other-dimensional feel came across in the

anecdote sent me by a woman whose background is essentially Wiccan. Jan Holden's experience with a guardian covers many of the themes encountered so far, and also anticipates some of the insights in the next chapter. This was in connection with St Nun's Well, which she visited on a dark, misty and damp day with her boyfriend.

As they parked their car at a deserted crossroads, crossed a stile and headed towards the site, the sky was suddenly darkened by scores of rooks that circled overhead, calling loudly, like something from an old Gothic film. Swirling mist, eldritch trees, dampness like jewels, and a smothered sun which seemed to be silently fighting for its life created a mood in which it is hard not to feel the more ancient perceptions rise. They climbed down some old steps with the mist eddying and clinging to them like wraiths, the visibility almost nil in places; and finally even the rooks went silent, although one always seemed to be watching them. Eventually they came to the well itself, covered in grassy turf, which seemed to have a gnarled old oak tree growing out of the roof, adding to the already eerie atmosphere of their visit. Peering through the mists that curtained the entrance, Jan became acutely aware of the 'Elemental Guardian' of the site, which 'felt more masculine than feminine, but somehow more in tune with the feminine qualities within human beings'.

The inner contact was long and deep and complex, interacting on many levels. To her astonishment she felt that she was given three wishes, but added wistfully, 'I can now only remember one, for at the time it seemed that I was in another dimension, the force coming from him was so elemental, so completely alien, but not in a frightening way.' She felt that they were being screened by this elemental creature, which impacted so powerfully on the deeper levels of her psyche. She felt that this complex entity had many faces and could take on many forms – some of which were fierce and forceful – but that he could also be a Weaver of Dreams. She was left in no doubt that, 'This was *his* place, *his* domain . . . and only those who had the right reverence were allowed to enter. I don't think he would hesitate to make things very difficult for anyone who didn't meet his standards.'

We will look at sacred wells as a whole in more detail in the next chapter; but it is just as well to note here, from Jan's experience, that not all entities in connection with these are necessarily female.

If the orbit of Venus at Winterbourne Basset involved something of the Mysteries of Women, the orbit of Mars must necessarily take us towards the Mysteries of Men. In relation to this William G Gray had a clear insight into the techniques and rites involved for the incarnation of a sacred king. When the time came twelve active and potent males were chosen, one for each sign, and each was required to have some outstanding quality that would make him a worthy father. One male might be chosen for his wealth, another for his skill at hunting, another for intelligence, and so on. Together they formed the circle of seed donors, or 'God-fathers' as he termed it. The eventual object of their attentions, the Virgin-Bride, was specially selected for her moral and personal attributes as a fit mother of the god-to-be.

> The men formed the perimeter of the circle, the Maid the centre, and the Old Woman had her peculiar dance-pattern between the two. Procedure varied considerably according to local custom. Sometimes the Maid danced spirally between the men and came to a central rest position embodying the waiting Earth-Womb, or sometimes she was scarcely conscious of the operation at all, being in a state of semi-drugged ecstasy. Elaborations such as music, etc., depended on resources and beliefs. The men might be as still as their staffs, but mostly they evolved a species of on-the-spot sort of jigging movement, possibly accompanied by chanting and drumming.
>
> Each male taking part in the Rite had to work themselves into a condition of consciousness where they were convinced they had successfully embodied their particular God-Aspect. This of course was done by characteristic miming and invo- cations for as long as might be necessary to obtain the effect

needed. Sometimes hours were passed this way before conditions were right.

The focus of it all lay within the Old Woman, who went from one to another with suggestions and commands, weaving the spell, bringing the whole rite to its climax. Whatever ecstatic or trance state the others might work themselves into this Old Woman had to remain in full control, no matter what.

She brought with her a particularly sacred object, 'a fairly small phallic shaped horn from some suitable animal with a pierced point normally kept closed by the Old Woman's own hand'.

> When the time was judged right, the Old Woman of the Cup went deosil around the circle from one male to another collecting their seed into the horn cup as quickly as possible. They donated this not as their human selves, but in the character and on behalf of the God-Aspect they represented.
>
> When the critical moment came, the Old Woman injected this accumulation of seed into the Maid by means of the horn which she blew into from the broad end, thus applying the necessary pressure. This was the 'breath of life' needed for the insemination process.[9]

A dark and cold conception, this, as viewed in the light of our new millennium. If Gray 'saw' true then these pagans are far removed from the present breed who gush at stones, feel each other's pain, exude the ineffable sanctity of the middle classes and talk about the Old Ways – yet who would find such a rite appalling. Not the sort of ceremony they would want their pagan ancestors to have been involved in. Yet not so far removed from the self-insemination or assisted conception techniques that are such big business today.

Perhaps the brutal guardian that Poppy Palin experienced was right: we are not like them; we cannot fully understand them.

In a safe and anodyne society such as ours, which is yet surrounded by those incredible events of international cruelty and oppression that impinge upon us only via the media, we have to work hard at understanding our ancestors from the Neolithic or Bronze Age cultures. The 'Willing Sacrifices' described in earlier chapters that were envisioned by Charles Seymour at Avebury or Bill Gray at the Rollrights were not, when taken in context, simple acts of savagery by simple peoples. Nor, it seems, were they one-off events in a couple of isolated sites.

Mike Harris, co-magus of the Avalon Group, did a great deal of inner and outer work at Moel Ty Uchaf, a Bronze Age stone circle in Merionydd, North Wales, which has been described as one of the best-preserved and least-tampered-with prehistoric sites in Britain. It is an elevated ceremonial burial place which is purposefully constructed on pentagonal/fivefold geometry, which he linked with the constellation of Corona Borealis. He wrote:

> Many sites were used to celebrate the rites of the sacred king and were places where tribal leaders went voluntarily to their deaths to merge with the land and thus mediate the benevolence of the land and the patterns within the land to their tribe. If the sacred king has merged with the land at the site and has not passed to the stars, you may pick up on him. If he has passed into the stellar realms you will have to go through the underworld of that place and tradition and pick up the patterns of the appropriate stellar constellation to contact him This may only be possible at certain times of the year when the stars are in the correct orientation to the earth. In some instances the stellar alignments under which the site was set up have become so obscure that this may no longer be possible. A number of sacred kings, as the Celtic texts indicate, however, merged themselves with the stars of the Corona Borealis.

From his personal experience the sacred king or the spirit of an initiate bard associated with a site can teach you a good deal about the mediation of archetypal patterns to the earth and the technical magick for doing so. However, he insisted that anyone doing this work *must* allow for the fact that the mindset and magical concepts of ancient people were somewhat different from ours, and that they should be flexible enough to

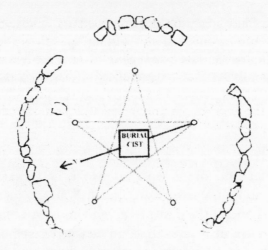

MIKE HARRIS'S STAR

see what is being explained to them. In other words, if you don't prepare yourself for what you might see, you could end being repelled, or scared witless, or judging the rites of our Bronze Age or Neolithic ancestors as being steeped in evil, when it was light they earnestly felt they were working with.

At Moel Ty Uchaf, from his own insight and inner contacts with the spirit and spirits of the place, he was able to determine the rites of sacrificial and sacral kingship that were performed there – and at many similar circles – every five years. Gruesome though they may seem to the modern mind, they were fundamentally concerned with the progress of the tribe, by linking the consciousness of the tribal king to the stars.

The sacrifice, in essence, went like this:

1. The voluntary victim would first be drugged, possibly by snake bite or the administering of venom in some other way. The *Gundestrop cauldron* image of the sacred king (often erroneously called a 'shaman') holding a serpent and a corona shaped torc may be an illustration of this. His eyes are closed which seems to indicate a semi-conscious state which snake bite would, mercifully, induce. In this hallucinatory state, he would be presented at the inner stone at East of North which would align to the Mid Summer sunrise. Here at sunrise the first bloodletting would occur with what Graves describes as

190

scourging. This being the case, the victim would undergo the first stage of shedding his mortality in the symbolism of shedding his flesh. This shedding of skin/changing would also align to the symbolism of his being drugged with venom and 'having the vision of the snake'. This first blood on the ground would also give the goddess the first of five 'fertilisations' aligning to the five years of the victim's kingship as her consort.

2. Moving sunwise, he would then be taken to the next point of the five fold circle facing the ever rising sun and the central of the seven stones representing the stars of Ursa Major. Here he would be blinded and turned back to face inwards into the circle/corona. Thus he would be facing blindly into the corona, the cave of the bear and the secret dark place of the goddess, in darkness, for no man may look upon her directly and live. In this he would also be directly facing his own tomb . . . where, in effect, she was waiting for him, and no man may (normally) foresee his death. This would be the second bloodletting which would rob him of the second facet of his mortality – the ability to see.

3. He would then be dragged to the third point of the summer sun at its zenith, though he would be unable to see it. At this point of the sun at its most potent he would be castrated, his genitals and, again, blood fertilising the earth. Some blood would possibly be preserved at this stage to sprinkle on the tribe to also make them fruitful. This castration, the taking away of the human ability to enjoy the pleasures of the flesh and procreate, would discontinue yet another facet of his mortality.

4. At the point almost at the west of the circle, the place where the sun sets in winter, he would be killed by empalment by an oak spear and thus cease, at the position of the going down of the sun, to be mortal any longer.

5. His limbs would be separated from his torso at the point west of north.

6. Finally, back at the point of origination in the circle, where the rite began, the victim's successor, the 'new' king, standing at the start of the cycle, would cut our victim's head from the torso, thus taking on the 'soul' of the kingship. He would keep the head elsewhere enshrined for oracular or guardianship purposes, possibly burying it beneath a standing stone.

7. Warriors of the tribe would roast and eat particularly signif-

icant parts of the corpse to share in the strength of the ex 'king'. The remains of the corpse might be placed on a flat stone nearby or within the central burial cist, left open to the elements to allow decomposition. This would be for a specified time, probably until the Corona Borealis showed her 'eighth star' to signify that the dead man had joined the stars and was secure in the heavenly cave of the goddess, and had achieved 'the crown behind the north wind'. In token of him then being secure within the goddess's starry cave the remains, including the charred bones from the roasting, but except of course the skull, would finally be buried in a chamber or cist.[10]

Dark and disturbing visions, these, and all the more so because they have the ring of truth behind them, and can be supported by academics working in the established disciplines of archaeology, history, mythology and folklore. Those people still wrapped up in the notion that our ancestors in Neolithic times were gentle souls living in a gently symbiotic relationship with nature must find the visions of some of the present correspondents disturbing in the extreme. But mainstream archaeologists are coming up with equally gruesome findings. Mary Baxter, for example, a postgraduate student at Cambridge University, wrote an article entitled 'Dancing with the dead in a mass grave' for *British Archaeology*, No. 50. As a human bones specialist, she studied the disarticulated skeletons, which led her to conclude that Neolithic communities did not simply dispose of their dead: they handled them repeatedly and shifted them about. She commented, 'I have found that it was frequently not clean bone that Neolithic communities handled for secondary burial – far from it. In reality, the body parts that were jumbled about and reused seem typically to have been part-decayed; rotting, but still hanging together with ligaments, tendons and possibly muscles still intact.'

Another vision/experience, from a man who wished to remain anonymous, concerned a potent megalith in Cumberland, with which he had a particularly strong relationship. 'I had a vision of a deep and narrow hole in the ground, and a body being put into it, and *then* the stone on top. The body was the sacrifice. The body was me.' Over the years the megalith itself would commune with him in much the same way that spiritualists commune with their spirit guides, which again makes us rethink our notions of consciousness. If flesh can be filled with consciousness and awareness and life, then so can stone?

But not everyone saw the Willing Sacrifice in terms of actual ritual killing. One correspondent, of a Rosicrucian background, spoke of an experience at Iona, where he picked up pre-Christian traditions that the mighty St Columba both maintained and developed. In these the Willing Sacrifice did not actually die but was buried within a chamber, existing as yogis are said to exist: scarcely breathing, apparently dead to onlookers, yet roaming free in spirit. At the end of a certain period of time the initiate would be awakened to share his visions with the people, and another would take his place. This is similar to Joan Grant's vision of the young Egyptian girl's incarceration in the tomb/womb as part of her initiation, and links with actual magical practices throughout the world. The chambered tombs, therefore, had continued uses for the living as well as being launching points for the souls of the departed towards the stars.

But we seem to have certain responsibilities towards these guardians, not least being the need to learn respect. They were not exactly helpless wretches brutally slain by a merciless priesthood, and then magically 'chained' to the site like some neglected dog. Perhaps the guardian whose wrath Poppy Palin unleashed had had his fill of those who came to 'save' him, whose motives were no less irksome – and no less dangerous – than Christian missionaries going among what they saw as savages. Even so, Mike Harris argued that there *are* occasions when we are called to do some work in this respect:

> We are all priests and priestesses across time (whatever that is!). This is often why an incarnate priest or priestess is called to a site to release a bound soul. It may, as I have known, be the case that a Bronze Age priest had intended to return to a site to release the unfortunate soul/s, but never managed to. One may therefore find oneself, in taking the job on these many years later, in the position of doing a colleague a favour . . .

even if that 'colleague' is several thousand years away! In doing so one doesn't judge or criticise their original intention . . . We all do what we have to do in terms of the times and culture that we live in and priesthood then as now was essentially about 'the cure of souls' . . . not least the folksoul and the soul of what Dion Fortune would call the Planetary Being.

So it seems that we have responsibilities towards the sites and the peoples who once lived in or at them, or worked with them. The guardians function either by scaring us witless, or else imbuing us with a sense of the site's importance and sanctity, so that in a sense we take over from them, in a way that parallels the releasing of bound souls described above. We may not have the odd talents to see anything at these places with our psychic gaze, but that is not important. We may not hear the stones or the spirits 'talking' to us in words, and giving us philosophies, but all the seers agree that this is often a distraction. Our guide the Reverend Edward Duke, for example, raged about the destruction of Marden, because in a sense its etymology provided the confirmation he needed for the reality of his scheme. Marden made it all true. Marden was the confirmation of, and guardian of, his own vision. If Marden today is nothing more than a levelled field, and its time-lost structures no more than images in our imagination, then we must learn to look at it laterally: for this is a fertile and empty field next to a flowing river which has been cleared of debris and anything redundant, and on which we can build – on which we can build *anything*. Find that place in our own minds and the philosophies will come.

CHAPTER

SEVEN

THE ORBIT OF JUPITER, THE PEOPLE AND
THEIR SACRED WELLS

*As they all had the bathrocranic skulls that are
peculiar to Elves like us, we assumed that they
must have been members of our ancient tribe,
known to modern science as 'The Brünn People'
and therefore ancestors of ours. Normally, we Elves
burn our dead, and then bury the ashes in a basket;
which may have been the origin of the early
Christian term of 'going to Hell in a basket!' Why
these Elves were buried in a heap during the 'Bronze
Age' is a mystery, but it looks like some of our
ancestors fell foul of the 'Dwarves' (Bronze Age
Copper Prospectors) and were wiped out by the
invaders.*
– Dusty Miller

It was the logic of simple arithmetic, and the need to maintain
his orbital ratios, that brought Duke from Marden to Casterley
Camp, on a line nine miles from Silbury Hill. This was his
temple of mighty Jupiter. He quickly pointed out that although
there was no surviving 'gnomion' in the shape of a standing
stone or conical barrow that might make the observation of
this planet easier, the lofty site and the distant hills on the
horizon would have served the same purpose.

But he did not point out much else, and was unable to
find more than a couple of hundred words, with repetitive
observations, to describe this penultimate point on his meridian. In fact there is no evidence within the text that, at the
age of 61 in rugged countryside, with his thesis proven in his
own mind at least, he actually visited Marden or Casterley
Camp in person. The bleak heights of Tan Hill had probably
finished him in that respect, as it does many visitors today.

195

Instead, he did as witches do: he soared, he travelled in his mind.

To the best of archaeological knowledge Casterley itself is not particularly old in comparison with other sites. In fact, it is believed that Casterley dates from no earlier than the early first century CE, when Roman armies under the future Emperor Vespasian were marching through southern Britain, demolishing the hill forts and moving the tribes into new and lower settlements that were more easy for them to control. In fact, the older inhabitants of the village of Upavon passed on the folk memory that their village had once been on the hilltop. This was recorded long before archaeological research determined the precise nature of Casterley Camp. So the old villagers were right: the people had once lived on the hilltop – but during the time of the Roman occupation. You have to be just a little bit staggered by the enduring power of such folk memories.

Casterley has little in the way of legend attached to it, and even less myth, although tradition holds that there is a golden throne buried within. And Duke notes that in the days when it thrived as a large fortified village, it was supplied with water from two wells, which caused Duke (quite rightly) to rage against those who were short-sighted enough to have them filled in. 'Truth lies at the bottom of the well,'[1] he quoted, as he pondered on what coins or votive offerings might have been thrown into these.

And really, carrying on with the present scheme of things, this is realm of the sacred wells and the hill forts – the places of sustenance and security: any well and any hill fort from any part of the country. It is also the realm of the people who drank at their wells, and lived in their forts, fell in love, made babies and protected them, and then worked magick – all of which were aimed at the future.

Duke identified this point on the meridian as the Place of Jupiter. For us, in astrological terms, Jupiter is the quality of largesse, stability, community and amity. It is to do with creating the sort of material prosperity that can set people free to look for higher things, and struggle towards philosophies. After all, shamans, druids, witches and mystics are valid in a society only when the ability to feed and give shelter to the family unit has been achieved, and survival is a reasonable and enduring prospect. It is that safe level beyond the basic fight-or-flight reflexes in which you can sit down and ask serious questions about the meaning of life, and your own potentials. It is that place, or state of mind, where you feel able to yearn towards some form of 'higher education', which is nothing to do with formal college-based degree courses. Jupiter is, according to any astrological primer, concerned with philosophy, belief, faith, and 'Images of God'.

It is also connected with the idea that every human soul is linked to another, to form a single corporate being. When like-souled individuals are drawn towards particular sites, or find their work evolving in the same direction, this is Duke's 'Orbit of Jupiter' in action.

Edna Whelan had a powerful visionary experience at an old Iron Age settlement high on the upper slopes of Pen Hill in Wensleydale. In company with her friend Tom, she lay down in the centre of the ancient site and closed her eyes. All at once she became aware of two strange old-time warriors dressed in rough leggings and fur capes, standing on either side of her as she lay there, each one carrying a long spear. In her vision they thrust their spears into the ground on either side of her neck, crossing them over as they did so and forming an inescapable hold from which she could not move her head. They stayed there looking down at her and she knew that there were many more people of some ancient tribe all standing around and waiting for something to happen. Then the strangest feeling came over her:

> It seemed that my stomach grew and expanded just as in pregnancy but very much quicker; even within minutes, and, with a small amount of effort, I gave birth to a large egg. This, in turn, cracked open and out of it poured rivers and lakes, hills and valleys, fields and moorland, trees and flowers, all

spreading out to form the English landscape which we all know so well.

It seemed then that this was the performance which was expected of me because the two warriors took away their spears and released me and there was jubilation amongst the gathering of people around me.[2]

Edna made no hard-and-fast analyses of her powerful and rather beautiful experience, but it is clear that sometimes the reality of the people who lived at these sites comes surging through in quite startling ways. It is almost an expression of that idea that underlies all 'Earth Magic', which holds that the Land and its People are One. The experience of this always seems to come without warning, no matter how much you might go looking for it. Michael Everest felt this when climbing one of the hills overlooking Weymouth in Dorset.

I decided we should go and climb the White Horse at Osmington, near Weymouth. I was not going deliberately out of my way to visit an ancient site to think great thoughts upon: this particular White Horse, early 19th Century. The car was parked by the riverhead at Osmington and we strode manfully up the path towards our destination. This line of the South Downs is topped by a whole series of round barrows. The climb up to the horse was exciting but uneventful. We could only manage to reach its tail. After taking photographs we made our way back toward Osmington. The others were going ahead of me. They were waiting at a gateway at the corner of a field. Suddenly I was overwhelmed by exaltation. It was as if I were George Best in his heyday, coming out in front of a capacity crowd at Old Trafford, for the start of a game. I seemed to be surrounded by thousands and thousands of approving onlookers. I had to put my hand to my mouth to stop calling out with joy. I did not want to startle my companions. I found later that this point was the closest approach the pathway made to some barrows on the hill above us.

Which leads on to another of the common perceptions: that the people of the Neolithic past are, in a strange sense, still here. Perhaps not floating about en masse as spirits, but as living flesh and blood entities on the other side of time. Who knows how they would have seen Michael as he panted up that hill? Some bizarrely clothed spirit? A wandering madman who promptly vanished before their astonished and satisfied gaze?

Once when I parked my car in the little car park near the foot of Cley Hill, simply intending to eat my sandwiches and read the football news in the paper, a similar rush of awareness almost smashed through the windscreen and I had a sense of the whole community at once, with fragmented visions of the packed dwellings, the timber and thatch, the mud, the small and dark-haired and often tattooed people, and though there couldn't have been more than a few dozen there, logically, it felt like a metropolis, thriving and thrumming, and a sense within me as if an exile were crying exultantly (but a tad embarrassingly) something akin to, 'The people! The people!' as he came home again.

When Mark Aldridge visited the 3,000-year-old stones known as the Balnuaran of Clava he felt a sense of peace and timelessness pervading the whole surrounding woodland. But when he was within the circular chamber of a cairn he felt a deepening, or thickening, of the air, almost like a physical weight. He was overtaken with an intense feeling of kinship and oneness with the ancestors who had lain there and the mysteries they lived with. He also commented that even a week later, when writing notes on this and other connected subjects, he still experienced this 'rooted' feeling, which remains access-ible to him even today, whenever he turns his thoughts that way. Yet another example of the way in which we do not have to be physically present at particular sites to be able to feel their energies and work with them.

A similar experience is described by Jack Gale, as he approached the site of a recently rediscovered Dianic Temple in Greenwich Park:

> As I neared the mound I had a sudden experience which I can only describe as being grabbed by a wave of unconditional love; being grabbed and hugged as if the mound were saying 'Great you're here at last!' The emotion was so overwhelming, in fact,

that I wept as this was the only way that I, as a human being, could possibly cope with it.[3]

Poppy Palin experienced almost a combination of the two experiences above when she approached some barrows near Stonehenge:

> I myself picked up a processional feeling of reverence for the ancestral dead which was powerful. A deep feeling of respect and awe came over me and I began to follow a winding path around the barrows in honour of those spirits.

Iris Campbell pointed out that such feelings do not necessarily mean a previous life spent in the vicinity, but that 'the vital earth currents [of ancient sites] are the same as those which flow through many parts of the earth's body. On this flow of energy are carried the memories of the planetary historical past and so are given forth from these great storehouses of energy, rather like wireless messages from long past days of the earth's history in which the lives of many of the human race now on earth were lived. It is possible for memories to be felt within the mental body of today.'[4]

As Michael Harris pointed out, however, not all sites are still potent, and not all the spirits at such sites are replete with wisdoms from the distant past.

> Psychic and intuitive experience, particularly at ancient sites, can take a number of forms for a number of reasons. Sometimes these are just 'Place Memories'. Such memories may have no meaning or message for us, being simply the replay of ancient events that have been welded into the psychic fabric of a place. It is easy for the naive psychic to, almost voyeuristically, watch the activities of, say, a Bronze Age priest at some stone circle and believe that they are being shown something personally portentous. More often than not this will simply be an incidental glimpse across time.

In his early days Mike was part of a group that frequently explored sites in his native Wales, and performed modest rituals at a number of them. One such expedition entailed a visit to the isolated Carneddau Hengwyn tombs, with his wife and another group member, Mike Waldron. After walking for some miles over high bleak moorland trying to find the site, he realised that his wife, who up until then had been laughing and joking, suddenly started to remonstrate with them and become quite aggressive.

I wasn't phased [sic] by this because she is like psychic litmus paper and sure enough a series of humps in the featureless moorland suddenly appeared and we were there. My wife sat sulking whilst Mike and I explored the wrecked chambers. As we left the site, however, we realised that we weren't alone. We took a circuitous route back and crossed water a number of times, hoping to break up the etheric form of our new and not very welcome inner companion. He wouldn't have any of it and clung on like mad. We got home and he was still around. He didn't seem as much dangerous as 'odd' and very intrusive. The cats didn't like him and stuff seemed to be going badly wrong as my wife attempted to cook dinner. He was almost tangible dancing about and poking his etheric nose into everything.

Mike and I got the impression that he had been some kind of outcast from the tribe, something of a simpleton prone to epilepsy, who had frequented (and continued to frequent) the tribal burial ground. (My evaluation would be different now!) Eventually my wife insisted that we 'do something'. In those days we were hardly experienced but as at the time Mike was a grade higher than I was I told him it was down to him. He went into meditation and called upon what powers he knew to compassionately send our visitor to wherever he needed to be . . . and much to our mutual surprise it worked.

Wendy Berg turned her own formidable powers of inner observation on to Denbury Hill in south Devon. Although not very high, she noted, this hill, which is topped by a hill fort with banks, ditches, a causeway and two tumuli, is visible for some miles in each direction by virtue of its being a little higher than the surrounding landscape. 'The official explanation of "Denbury" is "the homestead of the Devon people" which seems a bit lame, but I have no better explanation to offer.' In fact, her senses told her that this was – is – somewhere special, an impression that she felt was confirmed as she drove near it, and felt herself becoming agitated for no apparent reason. 'It's funny how the magnetism of a place can produce an inward disturbance which results in this sort of mental and emotional agitation.'

As she spiralled her way to the summit she became somewhat sceptical about the official description of this as a hill fort. It seemed to her that a community living in such a visible position would be very vulnerable to attack, and that the purpose of this and many other such places designated as hill forts was actually far more subtle.

The two tumuli appear not to have been disturbed, and the atmosphere inside the fort is wonderful. The invisible barriers between this place and the outside world below are still intact and very strong. I got a clear impression that one tumulus was 'masculine' and the other 'feminine', and working as a pair. This impression was borne out by the few signs of recent activity which suggest that other people have picked up on this. The 'masculine' one had a small standing stone planted in the middle of it, which I don't imagine can ever have been part of the original structure, although there was no way of telling when it was put there. The atmosphere in this tumulus soars upwards with a pure, clean run through of spirit. My mood and spirits soared and I felt remarkably better on all levels just for standing there for a few minutes. It's the sort of place that would lift a congested headache in an instant.

The 'feminine' tumulus had a small and discreet spiral of pebbles in the middle. Here, the energy moves downwards and into the deep earth. But the two work together as a balanced pair – a circuit of force set up by two pillars and the currents flowing between them. I didn't get any impression of site guardians – the whole structure appears to work at a very high and trans-human level. There is also a sensation all over the top of the fort that it functions out of the normal run of time. Of a vast, slow, cosmic movement which I experienced almost as a physical sensation. I got a constant impression out of the corner of my eyes that the trees were dancing in slow motion, or that the whole hill was moving through space and time at its own slow but inexorable speed and to its own laws of time and motion which were not the same as those which applied to

202

the normally perceived world at the foot of the hill. A remarkable place altogether.

Of course, as we have noted, not all spirits are Beings of Light and Wisdom, and not all of the ancient structures were concerned with cosmic energies or the mapping of stellar movements. But our guide, Edward Duke, did point out something that I had not seen mentioned before in respect of the various fosse ways:

> To unite one village with another, they formed a fosse of from four to five feet in depth, and about three feet in width at the bottom, so as to enable two persons to walk abreast; the banks expanding upwards were nicely curved, as they remain to the present day; the chalk thus thrown on the verge of the banks formed a bright and whitened line on either hand, leaving a path in the hollowed centre, from whence with common care they could not easily emerge; thus did they create 'a lanthorn unto their feet and a light unto their paths' and arrived with safety and certainty . . .[5]

However, it might not be too wise to try to create a rigid model of the ancient past in which hairy-arsed Neolithic shamans gave way to sloping-browed Bronze Aged sorcerers, followed by cerebral Druids and then weirdly tonsured Celtic Christians, all living in the appropriate sites in the visualised manner, and summoned into life from the textbooks with the appropriate academic name . . . Because sooner or later you will come up against Dusty Miller. Then everything will get stood on its head.

I stumbled into one of Dusty's lectures in Battersea Town Hall, where they were having something of a New Age fair, while on my way to meet up with a muttering of magicians on some other business. To pass the time I sat at the back of the hall near the exit, with one eye on the people passing outside, trying to effect a subtle blend of the awesome and the blasé. But after the first sentence that came floating from the silver-haired speaker – 'Have you seen a dryad?' – I was completely entranced. Here was a man who 'saw' and communed with the tree spirits, and who could cajole them (willingly) into the wands he made, where they lived like genies in bottles. At the time I was still wrapped up in the works of Carl Jung, smug and superior in my Jungian rationalisation of magickal and mystical experiences, using terms like 'archetype', 'projection', 'collective unconscious', 'anima' and 'animus' to 'explain away' (and thus dismiss) vital and very real human experience. Logically, I should have mocked, but I found myself making a beeline for his stall and catalogues, so taken by what I had heard that I could barely stop myself reaching for my credit card. Years later, I still regard the two wands he eventually gave me as among my most precious possessions.

Dusty, in his own matter-of-fact, nonpompous and very humorous way, sees himself as part of a living tradition, the leader ('the Dusty') of a tribe that existed in what he terms 'the Wild Wood', thousands of years ago.

> In our family, coming as we do from an extremely ancient tribe of 'Tree Elves' (or 'Tree-dwellers' as the Celtic people called us) we have a great sensitivity to Ley Energy and the way a place 'feels' to us. We could 'feel' the presence of Ley Energy, especially the Power Vortex caused by the crossing of Ley-Lines, and so it was natural for us to consider such places as sacred or holy, as they gave us the idea that they were like a direct (phone) line to Mother Earth, known to us in the Wild Wood days as GranMother . . . We were surprised to find that other people weren't Right Brained enough to have a 'feel' for these places, and when they stumbled upon one, they found they had to mark it in some way, so that they could find it again.
>
> One of the other tribes that shared the Wild Wood with us (known to us as 'The Horned Ones') used to mark these places with great lumps of stone, known today as Megaliths. Thanks to our 'Horned Friends' our area has over a hundred sites marked with the type of Megalith known as a Sarsen Stone.

In Dusty's 'magick' the tree spirits and their green energies are as important as anything connected with the stones and sacred sites, interlinking with the ley lines and the people who perceive them to create an organic whole. Harking back to the Coldrum circle described in the previous chapter, he noted that, back in the 1930s, 22 skeletons had been unearthed from this site.

As they all had the bathrocranic skulls that are peculiar to Elves like us, we assumed that they must have been members of our ancient tribe, known to modern science as 'The Brünn People' and therefore ancestors of ours. Normally, we Elves burn our dead, and then bury the ashes in a basket; which may have been the origin of the early Christian term of 'going to Hell in a basket!' Why these Elves were buried in a heap during the 'Bronze Age' is a mystery, but it looks like some of our ancestors fell foul of the 'Dwarves' (Bronze Age Copper Prospectors) and were wiped out by the invaders.

Dusty's insights, and his knack for squeezing real gnosis out of apparent naïveté, have the effect of making the old faery tales and legends both credible and relevant today, and helping us to look at the peoples who once used the hill forts from an entirely different angle.

So, if all spirits are not illumined, and all places not holy, then neither are all the inhabitants at such places necessarily human. The more you read of folklore, the more you hear the first-hand accounts of the psychics, then the more you come to realise that we inhabit a multidimensional universe filled with all manner of beings, not all of whom have our best interests at heart.

When Joan Grant was hiking in the Highlands with her husband Leslie, making a leisurely way towards Aviemore, she was suddenly assailed by 'something' that was quite beyond her own – extensive and bizarre – experience.

Nothing could have been farther from my mind than spooks when suddenly I was seized with such terror that I turned and in panic fled back along the path. Leslie ran after me, imploring me to tell him what was wrong. I could only spare breath enough to tell him to run faster, faster. Something – utterly malign, four-legged and yet obscenely human, invisible and yet solid enough for me to hear the pounding of its hooves, was trying to reach me. If it did I should die, for I was too frightened to know how to defend myself. I had run about half a mile when I burst through an invisible barrier behind which I knew I was safe now, though a second before I had been in mortal danger; knew it as certainly as though I were a *torero* who has jumped the barrier in front of a charging bull.[6]

She quoted others who had also been subjected to the same degree of terror at the same spot; she mentioned, with dates, the unexplained deaths of two apparently healthy young men who had been out hiking in perfect weather. Killed by this 'something', as far as she was concerned.

Could this link back to those entities/energies symbolised by the hill carvings in certain parts of the country? Remember that folk tradition records many instances of locals 'seeing' these creatures taking on almost tangible form at certain times. Were – are – these akin to the totem creatures or 'power allies' of Native American tribes? As we saw earlier, several correspondents felt that these chalk carvings were intellectual-ised and artistic expressions of energies within the land. Some people, however, feel that they may well be representations of actual entities. In the nature of this book, it all necessarily depends on how you look at them.

A troubling tale along these lines comes from Wales. It is troubling because it is bizarre, yet sincerely recorded, and is distinctly reminiscent of those Wiltshire stories of locals 'seeing' their White Horses take on material form and come down from their hills to drink.

JD Davies, whose father was the Rector of Oxwich, told how his oldest brother had been out fishing with their father in Oxwich Bay. When they had finished, and moored the boat, it was nearly midnight. They had just gained the top of the beach, which abuts a narrow path leading to the church, when his brother happened to look behind him and saw what he described to his brother as:

a white horse walking on its hind legs and proceeding leisurely along the path to the church gate; having called my father's attention to this strange spectacle, he turned round for about a minute, and watched the creature, or whatever it was, until it

206

reached the gate, or rather the stone stile by its side, which the animal crossed, apparently without the slightest difficulty, still going on its hind legs. The uncanny thing then disappeared.

Although the father was clearly aware of this creature the only remark he made was a terse 'Come along' as though he knew exactly what the creature was, had seen it often before, yet did not want his son to get involved in its mystery in any way. As the reverend commented:

The strange adventure was never afterwards spoken of by my father, nor alluded to in any way. I have often been on the point of questioning him about it, but some vague feeling of undefined alarm always prevented me![7]

But as JA Brooks, in whose book the tale is told, speculated, it was possible that the rector had not only seen this obviously magickal beast before but had even used him: 'for it was believed that clergymen and ministers of all denominations could ride the water-horse or Ceffyldwr to whatever destination they required.'

Christine Hartley told me that one of her longest and most powerful 'inner contacts' or guides was the half-man, half-horse known as Cheiron, whose presence, when only dimly sensed and scarcely understood by those around her, could provoke real fear. Did Joan Grant stumble upon a renegade version of this type of entity? Was there any link to the Ceffyldwr?

There are many other half-human, half-animal beings in the Otherworld, it seems.

Anne Ross, the great scholar whose inspired yet thoroughly researched books have given such an impetus to the Celtic Revival of the late twentieth century, tells the story of the carved 'Celtic Heads' which she kept in her house for a while, and which seemed to provoke tangible manifestations of dog-headed but human entities that terrified more than just her.

Throughout Wiltshire in particular there are numerous ancient and modern tales of – invariably huge – black dogs

207

whose appearances were invariably presages of death. Black Dog Hill in Wiltshire is typical.

And then there are the faeries. These have cropped up more than once in the experiences of the correspondents, but – it can hardly be overemphasised – these are spirits that have nothing to do with the emotional Enid Blytonism of our childhood, and in fact are sharp-edged and dark enough to creep into the stuff of our nightmares instead.

One typical piece of faery lore comes from the latter part of the seventeenth century, when John Aubrey recorded the story of a shepherd who had been lured into a glowing network of caves beneath Hackpen Hill. He had been lured there by following the irresistible sounds of a faery fiddler who showed him a realm that was alien to, yet clearly coexistent with, ours. Unlike many before and after, the shepherd managed to return and tell what he saw, but the strains have been heard since, magickal and maddening, leading to a green-gold world beneath our own, where time runs at a different rate from that which we know. There are very many stories from folklore that parallel this experience.

The whole concept of 'faery', however, has been so corrupted by the sentimentalism of Victorian artists as they misinterpreted ancient folk traditions that we have to listen very carefully whenever we stumble upon tales like this. Just reading the folklore that has been collected over the centuries we can see that the majority of the faery races are tall and beautiful. The Gwragedd Annwn, for example, are described as tall, blond, proud and immortal – a very old and predominantly female race who are connected with the deep lakes and the underworld places of Wales. However, another tribe, the Tylwith Têg, were described by Giraldus Cambriensis in his *Itinerary through Wales* as long ago as 1188 as being 'of the smallest stature but very well proportioned in their make: they were all of a fair complexion, with luxuriant hair falling over their shoulders like that of women.'[8] With their own laws, own beliefs, and own morals.

RJ 'Bob' Stewart, who has spent many years working with the

faery energies of the Underworld, opines that the faery race is attuned to the land, and that they may 'communicate with and relate to humans, particularly in the context of the vitality of the land or environment'. He goes on to insist that, while they will appear and communicate according to what is in our imagination, they are not *products* of the imagination . . .

One of his first experiences with these beings involved a puzzling ritualised greeting focusing upon a knife. This happened when he was visiting woods near an ancient site in the early 1970s, when he was startled by the sudden appearance of a short man in brown, soft-leather clothing.

> He stood before me, holding out a long green stone or bronze leaf-shaped dagger, with many patterns on the blade. He said 'Brother, I have a good knife . . .' and waited for me to reply. I had no idea what to say, and after repeating the statement twice, he vanished. At the time I thought I had had some vision of a prehistoric native of the region, as I was close to one of the great stone circles of the Wessex culture. In retrospect I now think that this was a faery contact, with some kind of greeting formula to which I should have known a response . . .[9]

The conclusion has to be that there are places in our minds where we can touch upon other orders of existence: fantastical but very real beings and levels of intelligence that are profoundly different from us, and that our own minds try to make sense of by making use of images from the realms of myth, legend and nature.

Wendy Berg stumbled upon a place on the eastern edge of Dartmoor (which she declined to identify too exactly), starting at a deeply fissured tor, which almost melted into the faery Otherworld. This area, she insisted, seemed to act like a living 'path-working'.

> By which I mean that a sequence or collection of various features within a small area is just like the symbolic inner landscape through which one journeys: curiously shaped rocks, mysterious signposts, significantly placed bridges and trees. As you climb up the hill you realise that the Tor is divided into two and forms a deep pass so that you start this journey by walking through a

pylon or gateway into the inner worlds. The path then descends to a deserted mediaeval settlement, rich in memories of a lost culture and where in your mind's eye you can build again on the foundations of the old stone houses. You look up to where a gate appears, just on the horizon, and take the path up to the gate, through, and then steeply down through fragrant pine-woods to a stream crossed by a tiny granite bridge. This bridge takes you, if you have half a mind, into the faery world. The wood beyond the bridge has an extraordinary feel to it which I found was noticeable the first time I went there, but it has built since with each visit, and with the cooperation of the unseen inhabitants, into a place where paradise can be remembered. The light beyond the bridge is a curious otherworldly green; the ground is a series of faery mounds which are covered with thick, soft moss, and at the base of the trunks of the birch trees are funny little heaps of black and white pebbles – quartz and tourmaline – which I haven't seen anywhere else.

I have sat here many times and experienced the most wonderful, peaceful innocence, the bliss which was before the Fall. I have never seen any faery beings here, either with outer or inner sight, yet I know they're there and would not be impertinent enough to ask for a sight of them. It seems that they are willingly and freely offering what they have and it is a very precious experience.

A similar experience, involving an outer entrance to an inner realm, was described by John Crabtree, editor of *Liongate* magazine, who visited a ring of standing stones on Machrie Moor, on the western side of Arran. The stones themselves are impressive, tall, quite thin and knifelike in their shape, and said to mark the grave of a king buried in a 'cist' tomb. Among the ring of granite stones was one distinctly triangular in shape which seemed to call him personally, and allowed him to descend, in vision, to the world beneath the circle.

Entered and descended down a spiral stairway. Below in a cave I visualised the cist – from the tomb a golden figure of a king emerged and abruptly asked me why he had been woken! I remember struggling with this unexpected retort as it threw me for a moment or two. My 'reply' was 'that it was through the past and the future we connect with eternity – it is the lineage

210

of spirit we work – the work of evolution.' Saw a distinct triangular shape that seemed to correspond to the actual physical triangular shaped stone in the circle of stones itself. It seemed to be indicative of an inner/outer gateway to spirit that was [aligned with me] and simultaneously opened within me a conscious and liberating feeling . . .

So the story of that shepherd following the unearthly music into the caverns beneath Hackpen Hill is an extremely important pointer, and just one of many that allude to the ancient knowledge that the Underworld (which is also the Otherworld) was not a place of fear and dread to our ancestors, but a timeless realm of light, where worlds opened into worlds, and overlapped with ours, and where the dead could sing their green songs – and teach those of us in this world who knew how to listen.

This perception is not something that is unique and exclusive to pagans. Canon Anthony Duncan, who has a widespread reputation for being a gifted psychic, spent 25 years in the Deliverance Ministry, wherein – as he put it – he had to learn to be 'as psychic as a brick' most of the time, allowing that level of awareness to open up only in the context of prayer and only when it was appropriate to a particular pastoral situation. With a great and shared passion for the old sites of Northumberland, he commented that the county is 'stuffed full of wonderful West-facing crags with ancient sculptured faces, undercuts, altars and what-not which are blessedly unrecognised for what they are. Old, old, old and nearly all blissful.' Like Terence Meaden with the faces at Avebury, or Iris Scott's awareness of those at Stanton Drew, Canon Duncan's perceptions of the virtually undiscovered faces in those northern rocks indicate that there may be a whole range of prehistoric art scattered across the landscape that we have yet to notice.

Talking about a time back in the 70s, he remembered that he became very much aware of things like fairies and elementals of all sorts and conditions, and would tend to say hello when he bumped into them: 'It was an important stage in my growth in compassion, but I was on a steepish learning curve at the time, and it was all about learning respect and compassion – and knowing when to mind my own business. Quite simply, it was largely about learning good manners!'

The story he told me concerned a visit to Scotland that he made some years ago with his wife and a friend of theirs. Intending to explore Strathbraan, they drove happily about and managed to encourage their panting motorcar up the hairpin bends towards the top of the range of hills on the north side of Glen Quaich. He goes on:

It began to rain. There was nobody else in sight and no other cars on the road. At the very top of the climb we came to a small plateau with a very distinctive rock, quite close to the right hand side of the road. Rain or no rain, we just had to stop and get out of the car. Immediately, we found ourselves in what I can only describe as fairyland!

All three of us were, in different ways, naturally sensitive to things unseen and we were quite overcome by the sheer, breathtaking beauty of little things. It was as if we were being taken by the hand and shown beauty that we could not otherwise have noticed. The rain fell steadily and we were all wet through. It didn't matter in the least.

And then I suddenly became aware that the profound silence was alive and that it was made up of a wonderful harmony. I looked up at the tops of the mountains all round us and realised, with a shock but somehow without too much surprise, that they were all singing! And I heard them, and I heard the harmony of them. And I will never forget it.

And then I became aware of a very powerful presence, quite close to hand. I am seldom clairvoyant – I seldom 'see' things – but the awareness of presence by the rock by the side of the road was almost overpowering. But there was nothing alarming about it and so I did what I always do when confronted by something 'other.' I said 'Peace be with you!' The immediate sense of welcome was tremendous. We were 'friends' at once. I have a mental image of a very large Pan-like figure, an Elemental, but that is an essentially subjective construct, I did not 'see' – except that I almost did!

We were wet through and it was time to get into the car and

212

drive on. We all turned and said 'thank-you' to all the natural beauty and wonder we had experienced, and I gave a priestly blessing to my new acquaintance and his little kingdom. I had the feeling that this was much appreciated and we parted the best of friends!

A beautiful anecdote, and one that shows that the magickal and mystical aspects of the earth and its mysteries are not the sole preserve of the neo-pagan community. He concluded, almost wistfully:

> The road is made up and is much kinder to motor cars these days. It is quite often used by tourists. The rock is still there and it is as magickal a spot as ever but we have only once stopped there again. We could not recapture what we experienced the first time and we did not try. The views, the landscape, they were as beautiful as ever but I did not hear the mountain tops singing, nor did I encounter my friend Pan – or whoever he was. It was not appropriate, not then. These things are 'given', they are not to be sought after. But I left him a blessing just the same before we drove on!

Obviously the one thing needed in any earthly community is water, and, where there are wellsprings, there are people. The wellsprings do not have to be purely outlets for H_2O however: clearly there seem to be wellsprings of other kinds in certain places, that enable all these other-dimensional beings to co-exist with us humans. And as we have seen in the chapters dealing with dowsers, there is a strong belief among the latter at least that many if not all standing stones are sited over underground streams, and that the stones' energies are somehow derived from, or work in conjunction with, water.

Wells have always had a mystical following quite as extraordinary as any stone circle. Communities grew up around them. They became the focus of worship, and – perhaps more important – that everyday feeling of kinship that develops from people going to draw water from the same place, share gossip and news, and then go about their daily business. Whether the benign feeling that is experienced around the site of a spring emerging from the ground is to do with negative ions, mineral richness, some ancestral memory of women going about their business to draw water for the family, or just simple wonder, they can create that resonance within us which can almost *make* them into sources of healing and mystery.

Peter Larkworthy, who has long experience of the Wiccan tradition, commented to me that the Triple Mothers originally connected with the sacred wells gave way to fairies and water nymphs and later to the saints – 'but always it was the waters that carried the special properties to bless or to curse. Such sites and their guardians can still be very powerful and if we approach them in the right way perhaps we can learn to listen again to the voice from the well.'

To him, the well associated with the Church of Our Lady in Sheviock offered the perfect allegory of how the old ways remain: hidden, often neglected, and fading on a byway as the traffic rushed by – yet still exuding peace and sanctity. He and his partner Jan, acting in a way that Edward Duke at the blocked Casterley wells would heartily have endorsed, cleared the rotting leaves lining the well and uncovered a vulva-shaped niche at the back of the chamber from which the waters flowed. A lady's well indeed! They found some flowering gorse and lit a candle; and, although there was no great psychic experience, they both had the feeling that the well was asking for attention and needed to have its waters flowing more freely.

So they came back another time with a shovel and cleared around the well until it was no longer quite so choked, and once again revealed the inner chamber and vulva-like niche. This time as they lit a candle a misty light gathered in the chamber and, as he said, 'the memory of the earth was shared with us.' They saw, with their psychic eyes, the pool that ran off down the valley, and were shown a group of women who would meet there.

A particular emphasis was placed on one of this group, a woman who had the ability to hear the voice of the Goddess embodied in the waters that flowed up from the Underworld and imparted a wisdom she was able to share. She had learned

214

how to listen and to understand part of the secret language of Nature.

They later made another trip, this time to find St Julitta's well near Camelford, which was almost lost within its own little hazel grove in a valley owned by a caravan park. Not quite a hill fort, but a reasonable modern equivalent. As he looked down upon the area and wondered what it must have been like before the artificial pond was built and the caravans arrived, his inner sight opened and he saw the whole place lit up with an earth-light from within.

It was not only stunningly beautiful but it was so crowded. On every hand were other, intelligent, aware forms of life, call them elementals, fairies or whatever, but they were as aware of me as I was of them. They looked nothing like the books suggest. Some were huge and they were very beautiful. Instead of the well there was a bright mass of light from which a spiral radiated out across the floor of the grove. From the centre of this spiral rose a woman, holding a wide and shallow bowl. She identified herself as the Mother of Memory and described the virtue of the well as one of inner seeing and vision. There was a connection with the hazel nuts in the bowl and a simple rite was performed with us in the grove. At the end we were blessed and the grove and all its denizens faded and sank back into the earth . . .

Oddly enough, I first bumped into Peter at the Chalice Well in Glastonbury, near dusk, where he was studying a copy of the Book of Shadows, and read me the Gardnerian 'charge' while hares did the sort of things that hares do on the lower slopes of the Tor, in the long shadows of the setting sun. And it is appropriate that the above vision, one that he plucked at random from his long experience, is almost a summation of many of the themes within this book: the other-dimensional and nonhuman creatures; the mutual awareness; the spiral; the Woman, rising from the earth . . .

One of the best known of such sources is the hot springs at Bath, once a major cult centre which the Romans adapted for themselves, and where the magician Bob Stewart evoked a powerful image of the priestess crouched at the point where the steaming waters poured from the land, giving out her prophecies. Even today, even surrounded by the tourists who throng past, chattering and flashing their cameras in this underground and steamy spot, this is clearly an eldritch place. But I suppose that I first became aware of the power of what might be termed the 'living waters' when we lived down Murhill, on the border between Wiltshire and Somerset. We rented an old, tiny cottage from Sir Hugo and Lady Marshall, who lived in Murhill Manor, whose springs once provided the drinking water for many of the houses on that precipitous edge of the Limpley Stoke Valley. Sir Hugo was an old man when we moved in, kindly but distant, reserved and gentle. We watched him working long hours in the beautiful garden, wrapped up in his thoughts, more often than not carrying a large sickle, so that I thought of him as the Druid of the valley, the focus of all its magick for a long time before we arrived. The water source for the manor itself was actually derived from springs – which had never dried up in anyone's memory or records. Yet at the moment of his death they did. As if the valley itself was trying to say something.

Springs and wells have played a large part in the magick of almost all the people involved in this book.

One man of Wiccan background, who was yet influenced by the Hermetic background of the occultist Dion Fortune also, described a surging vision connected with Glastonbury's Chalice Well. It was triggered by the death of an old man, a complete stranger, whom my correspondent had tended in the lane outside. As he sat next to the well pondering the imponderables of life and death he felt the spirit of the Crone rise from it, 'who is the giver of peace and rest, and also Marah, the Bitter One, Our Lady of Sorrows ... I saw the great sea of space and how life arose therein and how the formless force takes on body to build and grow, and how in this act such bodies may fade and die, outworn so that that which continues may be reborn into greater life. I saw the wheel of death and rebirth, the days and nights of the soul and how death on one place was birth on another. Dark and terrible though She seemed, implacable as the tides of the sea, yet She left me full of peace and gave rest to my troubled mind . . .'

Another person touched by the same well was Angie Barker, who, although initiated into Wicca by Doreen Valiente* herself, has a curious undercurrent of what might be termed 'Gurdjief-fian' insights (after George Gurdjieff, the Russian occultist who died in 1949), which give her own insights a particularly sharp yet also allusive quality, and enable her to act as a kind of spiritual catalyst for a wide variety of people.

She and her partner Richard Eastburn-Hewitt had arranged to meet me in Glastonbury, where (with a lot of others) we took part in a curious shamanic journey conducted by Murry Hope. Still tingling from that, we parted company and she then went on to the Chalice Well, where, mingling with the other visitors, she seated herself in the small rock garden that surrounds the well head. Within a hundred yards to our left, the ground sweeps abruptly upward, about 160 metres (520 feet), to form Glastonbury Tor, beneath which, as legend has it, is the entrance to the Otherworld. The atmosphere of the well itself, which many felt was a place of druidic sacrifice and vision, then began to affect her.

My eyes followed the line of the Tor down to ground level and back to the Well, which, as customary, had its lid down. The ornate cover (a replica of earlier Victorian ironwork) features the ancient symbol of the vesica piscis: two interlocking circles, each with its circumference passing through the center of the other, said to be the basic figure of sacred geometry. I compared it to the similar figure used in mathematical 'set theory,' where it is called a Venn diagram. At this point I experienced an almost unearthly sensation. It was as if my blood were being displaced by a strange and much subtler fluid. Could it really be the case, an inner voice was saying, that an American scientist had, without realizing it, discovered the meaning of the Grail?

As I sat in that magickal garden contemplating the symbolism of the Well's cover, it was as though spectral figures were passing

* Influential founder of the Modern Wiccan movement.

by, each imparting a seemingly incongruous piece of information with which I was already familiar, but in an order that made a meaningful pattern. Overwhelming as the experience was, I was obliged to return to some semblance of normality when my friends said it was time to depart. I mentally sealed all that had happened into a package and stored it carefully for later scrutiny.

Our journey was relatively short, just over thirty miles to a canal wharf close to the city of Bath, where I boarded the 35-foot motor cruiser that is my home. That night I slept and dreamt well, continuing the saga that had been initiated in Glastonbury.[10]

Like the water that flows to the surface, drawn towards the sky, those 'spectral figures' seemed to draw ideas up from the depths and darkness of her own psyche and helped her to formulate ideas connected with the Holy Grail and the nature of human, bicameral consciousness. But there was a knock-on effect. When I coincidentally bumped into her shortly after that, while musing in my obsessive way on the image of Herne the Hunter, the great Horned God of our ancestors, she told me about a well near my village which I knew. Of *course* I knew. As a minor Fertility God myself I had walked there any number of times, pushing my latest baby in a pram and with one or more of my many other children in tow. And then, archly, she told me of its local name, 'The Spring of the Green Man', which (open-mouthed now, you understand) I didn't know. And there was something within me like that thunderclap which attended the opening of Silbury Hill, and – in brief – I spent the afternoon at this same spring and had experiences and insights there that paralleled Angie's own at the Chalice Well, which resulted in my book *Earth God Rising*, which clearly touched a chord in the public mind at that time and sold dozens of copies worldwide.

A quieter experience was when Annie Tod and I tracked down Ela's Well, which was lost within the Friary Woods between our respective homes. Ela was a historical figure, the irritatingly pious and tediously devout Countess of Salisbury, who was

218

renowned for her good deeds and virtue throughout the thirteenth century. As with the vast majority of 'holy wells', it acquired a reputation for healing eye problems, even to the extent of making the blind see again. Even so, blackhearted pagan that I am, I went convinced that the well was locally famous and holy not because Ela had drunk there, after visiting nearby Hinton Priory, but that she went to drink from it because it was already locally famous and holy – for very un-Christian reasons.

In terms of folklore there have been long-standing reports of phantom monks lurking there, while in recent years a forester, just finishing a cold day's work in Friary Wood, looked up toward the well and saw a woman in white standing to one side of it. Terrified, he drove out of the wood as fast as he could.

When we arrived at the barred gate marked 'PRIVATE PROPERTY', Annie pushed on ahead while I followed more slowly, whingeing quietly about the malign alchemy that occurs when cold, moist mud conjoins with warm, dry (and brand-new) trainers. She found it easily enough, a cleft in a hill shored up on three sides by old stonework, from which the stream surged out. A strange and elemental spot, this; and, although there were only we and the sound of distant birds, and the noise of the stream itself, I had the feeling that the place was quite crowded. For a brief moment I glimpsed, out of the corner of my vision, a line of white-clad women on the little ridge directly above the well, looking at us. I had the idea there were seven of them, watching, and that their shades were very old indeed, and predated Christianity.

It came unexpectedly. The moment I focused my conscious mind on the image it went. But I 'saw' them. No more than that. None of the sense of belonging I felt at Cley Hill, but a definite one of being observed. They were not hostile, nor yet welcoming. They may have been what many describe as 'place memories': images that have been stored, somehow, in a particular place, and can replay themselves to the inner eye like recordings on a video.

Edna Whelan told me of a well she had found in East

Yorkshire, a special small well covered by a redbrick well house in a grove of hawthorn trees. With her inner eye she noticed that the ground around the well was covered up to a foot or so by a thin, opalescent mist, 'and standing there beside the well was a tall, slender, female figure dressed in white'. The figure vanished, as those at Ela's Well had done for me. She noticed that on a rise of ground behind this well there stood the remains of an ancient burial mound.

Bill Gray told me a story along these lines, which is important in understanding the whole concept of spirits and their appearance. In essence, when he was a young man he lived in a disturbing and troubled house in Brighton, which seemed, to his psychic senses, to be soaked with the atmosphere of violence. He 'saw' a young woman being brutally beaten in the very room in which he had to sleep. He 'saw' the blood on the walls and floor. He felt the man's rage, the woman's pain and terror, and heard, with his inner ear of course, the shouting and screaming from both parties, and then observed the police and ambulance coming, and the woman's body being carried out.

He did research. What he had witnessed with his psychic powers was absolutely accurate. But when he learned more, from local testimony, he realised that this was not actually a haunting in the usual sense. Because the woman had not died. In fact, she and her husband became reconciled and were living, apparently quite happily, a few streets away!

Of course, I went to Ela's Well with a full knowledge of local lore, and mightily keen to see a Woman in White as the forester had. As it turned out I glimpsed, for the merest fragment of a second, seven of them. Whether they were 'place memories', vital entities connected with the well and its ancient worship, or wishful creations of a fertile unconscious, I am still not in a position to decide.

Wendy Berg did a lot of her early work in the Wiccan tradition in the Nine Wells Wood, which appears on the map as a small, rectangular plantation lying at the foot of the low hills known as the Wandlebury Hills where the dowser Tom Lethbridge uncovered the chalk figure of the many-breasted goddess of the underworld he called Magog.

'The wood is full of surprises,' she wrote, 'not least that when you are inside it appears to be so much bigger than it could possibly be from the outside . . . Even when you near the wood it looks very little – it is edged neatly and regularly and gives no hint of its interior which is something *quite* different . . .' At one edge of the wood, she noted, is a deep semicircular bank at the base of which a single spring bubbles up from under the ground. If you follow this trickle downstream it increases in size as it is fed by further invisible springs until, especially after recent rainfall, it becomes full-flowing and milky-white from the chalk beneath. At the other end of the wood it pauses and collects into a deep pool, which is also often white, especially when children have been playing there and stirring up its depths. 'This,' she felt, 'is such a wonderful example of the white fountain of *awen*, the flow of inspiration and fertile creativity from the inner world . . .'

It was in this wood, and through the streams and pool made milky-white from the chalk beneath, that she forged an ongoing relationship with the 'Lady of the Fountain' and her 'daughter', Luned. When I asked her about the former she replied that she experiences her rather like the fountain itself:

as a pressure which pushes me along in a certain direction and at a speed which is dictated by the amount of pressure – the amount of water springing up, the amount of inspiration, or the urgency with which it comes through. The nature of the pressure is, in essence, inspiration, the urge to create something, to bring something to birth into the world, to sing the song of an inner truth which has its origins deep within the land.

Luned, however, is a very different inner-plane being, as Wendy perceives her, and she told me about hearing her voice in encounters with those who should have been acting as guardians of the fountain but were not, once publicly bawling out someone who had been acting in respect to the sacred waters in a less than acceptable manner.

Her name suggests the moon, but she's not a very lunar soul.

She's forthright to the point of bossiness but she speaks her mind – or the mind of the Lady of the Fountain – very clearly. In fact what she says is very much to the point and she is carrying out the wise and urgent instructions of the Lady without paying much regard for the niceties and conventions of society. Presumably the Lady needs her daughter to speak with a forthright voice in the world to make herself heard above the din of denial.

For Wendy this wood provided her with a magickal training ground for use with a group of friends, now for the most part dead or otherwise departed. 'It holds many fond memories of happy times and youthful magickal endeavour when it all seemed so easy, and I believe that I shall not return there until near the end of my own life which must be returned into her keeping . . .'

Jack Gale described a very different Lady linked with a 'megalithic' fountain next to Lover's Walk in Greenwich Park. This mysterious capped drinking fountain is fashioned from a group of stones which, as he put it, 'look like refugees from some megalithic site, which, in fact, is what they are'. His friend Carole Young, a gifted psychic, visited the cluster and became aware of, and communicated with, the ensouling spirit of the fountain:

> . . . an embodiment of the Wise Crone aspect of the Goddess if ever there was one. The Dark Old Lady of the fountain has a formidable presence; certainly not a force to be messed about with. During this communication we learned that the stone had stood in a vertical position in her original location, having been turned through ninety degrees into a recumbent position when set into the fountain. She had been happier, she explained, when the uncapped fountain water flowed freely although she still quite liked being at the site which was nevertheless close to water.[11]

They were told that the stone itself wished to be consecrated, to undo the apparent 'mismatch' between her energies and those of the surrounding site – perhaps inevitable when an object from a sacred place brings its own power to a site that is already highly energised. Through consecration, it seemed, the two energies would be linked and bring about a state of balance; also giving the stone a fresh start and a new identity in her 'new' home. Part of this ritual involved giving it a suitable name to use during the ceremony: in this case the name 'Motherstone'. Jack was told, via Carole, to use plenty of water from Glastonbury's Chalice Well, so pouring it over the stone from the raised ground behind as he named her. He was also instructed to use this water to trace a fingertip spiral in the quarter-sphere above the fountain bowl which had been cut out of the top stone at the time of installation, in order to heal damage inflicted by this act. 'A "top-up" operation would subsequently involve regularly brushing mud and rain water from the fountain bowl, and pouring a little Holy water into it. To this I have since added the act of burning a candle of dark-red wax, for this seems to be the Lady's colour as seen by my friends and myself . . .'

The ancient places can inspire more than just visions. They can pulse through and touch the Muse also, resulting in song and poetry. We quoted the lovely lines that came through to Rae Beth when she tuned in to a stone circle. John Crabtree had a similar experience at Callanish, when the words poured from him – or from a part of him that he felt was energised by the spirits of the stones, and the elemental forces:

> With dew in my hand
> I have tarried by the cromlech
> With the Watchers the Silent Ones.
> Beneath the Raven's wing
> I have been unto myself
> As stone unto wave,
> As Eagle unto Air,
> As corn unto Sun.
> I have made strong beams within
> The Ancient Heart.
> To hold the stillness,

To weave the song,
To bind the peace.

There can be few people visiting the ancient sites, or in some way trying to get back to nature generally, who have not in some way been touched by the elemental forces. These are, of course, the energies of Air, Earth, Fire and Water that form the basis of all magickal/mystical/alchemical traditions, and are known as Sylphs, Gnomes, Salamanders and Undines respectively. At the seaside, for example, you would experience the sea breeze, the sand underfoot and perhaps the hills behind, the sun above and waves before. At times like this, when these elements are very large within your consciousness, you can feel the inner exultation – the singing – that makes you want to live for ever. Imagine that each of these elemental energies can express itself through a range of beings that coexist with us, which are part of us, and yet which are not – quite – human. So everyone has experienced the elements. But the witches and magicians go a step further and experience the elementals.

One woman had an extremely powerful experience at the foot of Glastonbury Tor, which resulted in an odd and strangely compelling 'Chant of the Elements'. This was the occultist Violet Firth, whose books under the pen name 'Dion Fortune' – a contraction of her Magickal Name, Deo non Fortuna – still rank among the best ever written. In 1926, while working with her group in an old building at the foot of the Tor itself, she went into full trance and made contact with a mighty elemental power, which gave her this chant, which some occultists regard as an extremely powerful ritual/pathworking in its own right. It reads in part:

> The Wind and the Fire work on the Hill
> The Wind and the Fire work on the Hill
> The Wind and the Fire work on the Hill
> Invoke ye the Wind and the Fire.
> The Wind and the Fire work on the Hill
> The Wind and the Fire work on the Hill
> The Wind and the Fire work on the Hill
> Trust ye the Wind and the Fire.

> The Wind and the Fire work on the Hill
> Hail to the Wind and the Fire.
> Draw down the Power into yourselves,
> Work with the Wind and the Fire,
> Sun and Air, Sun and Air, Sun and Air.[12]

The man who transcribed this from the words of the entranced priestess noted that the repetitions glided up the scale in quarter-tones, and ever increasing volume, while the later Earth and Water chants were quieter in nature, and gradually diminished in tone. The unnamed Power went on to comment:

> Do not think about the Nature Forces, work with them, feel with them, they have not mind, you cannot touch them with the mind, feel with them, move with them, sing with them, do not be afraid of them, you need them, you have left them too far behind . . . For they hold the Gates that open to the inner world . . .[13]

Remember that Paddy Slade's impulse to awaken the circles came from a Fire Elemental, of whom she was initially somewhat wary. In contrast Dolores Ashcroft-Nowicki, whose experiences we discussed at Newgrange, had an equally charming tale to tell about sylphs:

> In the early eighties one of the SOL's [Servants of Light] Australian Supervisors came over to visit us. She was a very down to earth person with a quiet sense of humour and endless patience with her students. On her first weekend we all drove out to Gronez Castle on the north side of the island. Gronez is a ruin with just one archway and a few other bits and pieces to show it was once there. The area is bleak and windy for the north side is the highest area with cliffs that fall away into the sea a couple of hundred feet below. On a clear day you can see the beaches of France and at night watch the headlights of cars and lorries as they drive along the coast road leading to St Malo.
>
> It was early in spring and the weather was clear, bright and a little cool. We set off along the cliff path that winds for about three miles dipping occasionally into little places where seats have been placed out of the constant wind. The dog bounded on ahead racing back now and then to make sure we were following. We came to the top of a rise and took a few steps

down into one of these little wind breaks. The dog had stopped and was looking intently in front of her. We looked as well, with our mouths open. Well down in the dip just by the seat a cloud of sparkling lights whirled and eddied in a dance. They were quite tangible, we all saw them at the same time. The cloud was very roughly spherical and within it the lights twisted and turned and made patterns, constantly moving, never still.

We walked very slowly and softly down into the dip, and the lights persisted. We stopped and looked at them asking ourselves just what they could be. They took no notice of us, the dog was flat on the ground and crawled under the seat whimpering. As far as we could see the lights were separate and about the size of this letter (O). They had no shape, no form that we could see but they were definitely there.

Tentatively we put out our hands and tried to catch them, thinking they would vanish . . . but they didn't. They clung to our fingers and skittered around our hands like fireflies . . . but they had no wings and they were not insects. I gathered up a handful and threw them into the air, they came spiralling down and spun more rapidly than ever. I thought to myself: 'they liked that' and did it again.

For a full ten minutes the three of us played with the little sylphs, even to stepping into the cloud with them. It was like tiny pin pricks, not painful but there, on your skin. We were like children with a new and delightful toy as we played with the little creatures, then suddenly, they were gone.

I have never seen them or anything like them again, but I am satisfied in my own mind that on that day the three of us played tag with a cloud of air elementals.

Could you imagine our guide, the Reverend Edward Duke, playing tag with a crowd of air elementals? But who knows what sort of fun they might have had with him all the time? Pricking at things in his mind, pushing him here and there and making him look at things that he might never have noticed otherwise? Actually I think this sort of thing happens all the time, when you visit the sorts of places that we have dealt with here. Beings from other realms impinge upon our psyches in ways that we cannot easily explain, or perhaps don't become aware of until much later, so that during a quiet moment at dusk you can sit and reflect upon the oddest things and say, 'Hmmm, yes, that place touched me.'

Edward Duke was touched by the land, somehow. In fact one of his books bore the telling title: *'Beneath the Surface'* or *'Physical Truths, especially Geological, shown to be latent in many parts of the Holy Scripture'*. The spirit of land – the sylphs, gnomes, salamanders, undines and all those phantasmagorical creatures who share it with us – was calling him all the time.

So really, as he stood on the heights of Casterley Camp – whether in the flesh or in his mind – and mused upon the peoples who had passed through here, and (deeply symbolic, this) raged about the wells that had been blocked, it only remained for him to make his visit to Stonehenge, and then he could go home.

Which might be said about all of us.

EIGHT

King Saturn, Stonehenge and the Womb of Time

*I don't know why the government goes to such
lengths to keep people out of the stones at the
time of the solstice. Let the travellers and the hippies
and the New Age lot into Stonehenge to worship
in their own ways, even if some find it offensive.
Let the people frolic, and dance, and have sex,
and get smashed with drugs and liquor to the sound
of drums and chanting and singing. That's how it
used to be . . .*
– Paddy Slade, *hereditary witch*

And so at last the Reverend Edward Duke came to Stonehenge,
after journeying dozens of miles as measured by the road
system, but millions of miles through that solar system
exploding in his mind. He paused for a while on Knighton
Barrow, named from the farm to which it was attached, and
commented:

An extensive horizon may be surveyed from this elevated spot.
Behind, you have Casterley Camp, the temple of Jupiter, and, in
front, you have Stonehenge, the temple of Saturn, the celebrated
wonder of the West of England. From this eminence, at the
distance of three miles, Stonehenge is seen in the midst of rising
grounds on all sides, whose tops are crowned by ranges of
sepulchral tumuli, a sight unique and captivating to the eye.[1]

He spent some time reassembling his arguments, coming
back once more to the conclusion that Stonehenge *had* to have
been a temple of Saturn, and adding one more observation:

The temple of Stonehenge, and its surrounding fosse, bear the
exact relative proportion as the planet of Saturn, and his sur-

rounding belt . . . My opinion is that . . . the Druids had the use of the telescope.[2]

Just when we start to think that our guide might have been plugged into arcane and esoteric wisdoms, just when you begin to think he might have been a secret Druid, Rosicrucian or esoteric Freemason, he launches into arguments that are based upon mirrors, burning mirrors, glass beads that could easily have been converted into lenses, or yet more mirrors, gems, dioptrons, Pythagoras, Chaldeans, Egyptians and almost any reference, from Diodorus Siculus to Sir William Drummond, that might support his case.

No mystic, this, despite the long journey he has brought us along. Just your average scholarly Victorian dog-collared Man of God who also happened to be – as he thought of himself – a Man of Science.

In astrological terms, Saturn is synonymous with Cronos – or Time – and all its shadows and sorrows. It is to do with past karma, and we can evoke its spirit with those lines from the Rubaiyat of Omar Khayyam:

> Up from Earth's Centre, through the Seventh Gate
> I rose, and on the Throne of Saturn sate,
> And many Knots unravel'd by the Road;
> But not the Master-Knot of Human Fate.

Saturn helps us towards the ability to understand sorrows, and convert them into valuable spiritual experiences. As Bill Gray wrote, drawing on his own and especially his wife Bobbie's astrological insights:

Time is Saturn's Noose. It can be drawn to the smallest point, or paid out until Eternity is encompassed, but it is still fundamentally a Noose, and those who learn how to hold its Knot and manipulate its Cord have mastered the secret of Saturn and achieved immortality. The Knot is NOW, the Cord is ALWAYS. We must never let go of the Knot.[3]

Somewhere within the noose-like pattern of Stonehenge, at Duke's ultimate Temple of Saturn, invariably standing at the edge of consciousness on one level and midway between the road and the hot-dog stalls on another, mystics, mediums and magicians of all traditions have been grasping at that knot that they all feel might unloose the Mysteries of Time and Space, and our relationships therein . . .

Estimates of Stonehenge's age vary considerably, but the general opinion is that it was built between 3100 and 2100 BCE. The first stage consisted of a low circular bank and a ditch of earth surrounding a ring of narrow pits known as the Aubrey holes. The second stage saw the creation of a double ring of standing bluestones (pillars of igneous rock), which some feel may have originally formed part of a stone circle elsewhere, which was dismantled before it had been completed. These bluestones were apparently transported from the Preseli Mountains in West Wales, 220 km (140 miles) away. The heaviest of these bluestones weighs seven tonnes, and is the one commonly known as the Altar Stone – although Meaden preferred to call it the Womb Stone. Had this one still been standing, it would receive the phallus of shadow caused by the sun and the Hele Stone at sunrise on the longest day. The final stage was the present monument, built around 1800 BCE and consisting of an inner horseshoe of five trilithons (each consisting of two upright stones of about 40 tonnes and a horizontal lintel), a central altar stone, and an outer ring of 30 uprights (each weighing about 26 tonnes) joined by lintels, all made of a local sandstone known as sarsen, which came from the Avebury region.

The trilithons of Stonehenge are so striking, so replete with the sense of power, that the world tends to feel that ancient knowledge might be found lurking through and beyond their portals if we could only find the passwords that might allow us to enter in the proper spirit. In fact the very nature of the trilithon creates within anyone a childlike impulse to go through it. Whether we try to do so via body, mind, spirit or all three depends on which level Stonehenge touches us. But it seems that the people who are drawn to Stonehenge tend to have felt the pull from a very early age, without being able to analyse it. When they do visit, it can have troubling effects.

Elizabeth Lepore is a natural psychic and a magician who was brought up on the Eastern Seaboard of America. She was scarcely able to control her feelings when she first went there, with her parents, as a young girl. Even today she can still blush at the way she behaved on that visit:

> Stonehenge was always a fascination with me as a child. When I played in the sandbox as a child my mud pies usually had standing stones in a circle as decoration. When I did my strange rituals, I was very young and always used stones around my circle. I told my grandfather they were for the people who Watched. We took a train to Salisbury and from there a double-decker bus to Stonehenge. I was thrilled to ride on top. It was a beautiful sunny day and I was all smiles. As the bus trip ended and I stepped onto the ground, my attitude totally changed. I became very cold and unbelievably cranky. At the base of the hill there is a stand where a person could get a snack. My mother suggested that we get a bite to eat before we went up to the stones. The thought of eating made me ill and I did not hesitate to let my mother know this. I pitched a royal hissy fit because they had the audacity to prepare my tea incorrectly. Mind you, I've never been picky about lemon or black or cream & sugar before . . . I proceeded to turn into a complete egomaniac. I stormed off and up to the stones I went. I was so incredibly angry. Well you know it's roped off now so I couldn't go inside. That gave rise to a flash and comment from me. I just wanted to lay in the middle for awhile and hated the idea that I was being kept out. I was informed that it was roped off due to tourists taking bits of rock home with them. Naturally, that made me even angrier. I was so cold at this point I was shaking. My mother told me I stood up there walking around the circle for over an hour. I felt like a cat watching a bird in a cage. By the time I went back to the stand to meet my mother I felt complete despair. I was dizzy and nauseous.

Was this caused by 'far memories' which her young psyche could not really assimilate at the time? During the millennium celebrations the local television station did a brief programme about the people who saw the year 2000 arrive amid the stones of Avebury. One of them was a young Canadian man who tearfully confessed his certainty that in a previous life he had

SPIRITS OF THE STONES

helped push and pull some of these stones into position; and now here they were, thousands and thousands of years later, still waiting for him.

A great number of correspondents noted how deeply moved they were when visiting certain circles for the first time, as I was when (after several abortive and exhausting hikes) I finally found my way to the Threestoneburn Circle on the glowering, bleak and beautiful moors of Northumberland. Nothing happened on any obviously mystical level. No visions, no synchronistic events, no symbols other than a Tornado fighter-bomber rising apparently out of the ground and screaming overhead in a (*very*) low-flying exercise. Yet I sat in the midst of the stones, with my head on my knees, and cried – though I couldn't have said why. And in many ways Stonehenge is the summation of all such places, dark and pre-eminent, with the imagery of its trilithons stamped firmly upon the global consciousness.

Quite simply Stonehenge attracts . . . well, everything: Earth Energies, Goddesses, Lords of Light and Darkness . . . Glastonbury may be the evanescent star of the New Age cosmos, but Stonehenge is the unreachable and untouchable superstar. The whole gamut of numinous and phenomenal experience as described in connection with the other sites can be found at Stonehenge. As the Reverend Edward Duke described it, Stonehenge is the Womb of Time. All things end and begin there.

We can list some of it:

Mounting the roof of an automobile in the Stonehenge parking lot, the young investigator gazed toward the circular cluster of massive upright stones that loomed about 200 yards away. He had come to the famous spot to check for emanations of so called earth energy, a mystical force venerated by many people who look beyond traditional science for solutions to the mysteries that surround the great stone monument.

The visitor had brought with him a wire antenna bent into an ankh, an ancient Egyptian cross with a loop at the top. Grasping the two-foot long wire ankh by the loop, he pointed the other end at the giant stones. The result, he reported later,

232

was both startling and painful: A burning jolt of power surged up his arm, hurling him to the ground and knocking him unconscious. When he came to, he found that his arm was paralyzed; it took six months for him to regain its full use. But the experience had proved something to his satisfaction:

The earth energy he had come to discover at Stonehenge was real, and it was not to be trifled with.[4]

When dowsing within the circle, Bob Slade put his fully charged analogue phone against one of the stones at a certain height and saw the charge diminish almost to zero. When he moved the phone to a different level, the charge increased again. Different parts of the stone had different effects on the battery.

When Ray Bailey visited he recorded impressions not appreciably different from those of Uri Geller:

I have been aware of this sort of energy and certainly the sensation of 'light beams' rising (or dropping) to and from the heavens when I have walked around the perimeter of Stonehenge also. However, certainly in the case of circles etc., these chakras act as reservoirs, that if linked to energy lines (ley) feed a grid (National Grid?) Taking energy from one place to another. A distribution of Celestial Energy – into the Earth, providing a sustainable nutrient for people, livestock and agriculture!

This does not preclude those who wish to from celebrating Celestial Events, thus enabling them to feel a greater, more integral part of the process of energy gathering, and additionally absorbing life support energy, and for healing through their own chakra system?

Dusty Miller recorded a typically delightful incident connected with birds:

On any number of occasions, I have done rituals in Megalithic Sites, both locally and in other parts of the country; and have been overjoyed to see birds with their heads on one side watching us. In Stonehenge, there are a group of Jackdaws living under some of the stone lintels, and on one occasion, I looked up whilst leading a ritual to find three of them in a row watching our every move. At the end of the ritual, one bird threw down a small black feather to me, as a sort of thank you for the entertainment. It has been enshrined in my filofax ever since, just to remind me.

Paddy Slade, who visited it regularly for almost thirty years during a period when access to the stones was almost absolute and unconditional, was greatly drawn to the star Capella (which she felt was the northern magical tradition's equivalent of Sirius, in terms of reverence and importance), which seemed to circle it exactly. Her strongest impressions of the people who built the circle came when she had been idly dowsing in the ditch surrounding it, and found information pouring through at a rate almost too fast for her to cope with.

'How were the stones moved?' I asked her.

'By sound. All the stones contain quartz. By tuning in to the quartz, and by use of sounds – chanting, singing, drumming – people could actually manhandle those huge stones as though they were styrofoam.'

Grace Cooke had much the same vision, describing in her chapter on Stonehenge how one of the vast cross-pieces of the trilithons was replaced after an earth tremor had dislodged it: the priests gathered round the stone, joined hands, marched round it, chanting, the stone itself shining from some light within. It was all part of the priests' mastery of the power of sound, by intonation and invocation.

To John Ivimy, Stonehenge was a scientific laboratory, according to his personal vision, and he was quite certain about the earlier form and nature of this complex:

> A wide wooden structure supported on stout oak pillars was erected in a circle outside the wooden ring of stones. On this as a foundation a wooden dome was constructed over the whole area, and a floor was suspended from the dome which provided enough space to house all the research workers and their precious equipment.[5]

One group of visitors told of hearing a strange clicking sound from the stones, which changed into a whirring noise that suddenly shot heavenwards as if a giant Catherine wheel had gone spinning upward. 'Shortly thereafter they saw a vision of a yellow-clad woman wearing what looked like an ancient Egyptian head-dress. This apparition, together with what they had heard near the stones, left the visitors with the sense that they had witnessed "some sort of struggle between good and evil".[6]

Thinking of this yellow-clad woman reminds us yet again that one of the common reactions of people who have glimpsed the remote past, and the rites they felt were being worked, is that in a strange way they were somehow involved. We have touched upon this experience several times in previous chapters, but Stonehenge is where all things coalesce. As we have noted, Mike Harris has spent many years actively researching the Earth Mysteries of Wales in particular, and he feels that in many cases 'it could be very much a "two way street" with *them* being as curious about us as we were about them. We in a sense help them to "remember the future." ' He goes on to comment:

Beyond mutual curiosity and inner attention seeking . . . Many psychics/occultists seem to be drawn to such sites to enable a process of exchange and mutual enlightenment. The Bronze Age priests of, say, Moel ty Uchaf can both benefit and be benefited by the 'priesthood' of a modern occult order or coven . . . So it can come down to a situation where a site visit is nothing more than wizards ancient and modern meeting up to 'talk shop'. We are all priests/priestesses across time (whatever that is!).

In the case of myself, when I was typing up the handwritten Magical Diaries of the adept Charles 'Kim' Seymour, I became so embroiled in the overwhelming images and rhythms of the rites that it was as if I too was part of it all. As if some part of my psyche was a necessary component of the rituals being worked fifty years before – and, in an even more indirect way, of those 'seen' by Seymour at Avebury, several thousands of years before. Like perching on his shoulder as he watched. So, when William Gray saw the magick being worked at the Rollrights, was the tribal hag revealing the future also aware of *him*? Was he an integral part of her 'remembering the future', as Mike Harris believes? Perhaps some of Grace Cooke's lighter-than-light, multinational visions of Silbury, for example, were never of that hill's earthly past at all, but were glimpses of its role within our psyches in future – or of the hill in what has been termed its 'primal essence'.

Gareth Knight puts its more clearly, describing an experience amid the huge standing stones at Hagar Qim on Malta, which is just as relevant to Stonehenge or any other circle anywhere:

> ... the sense of communication across time was particularly strong and, somewhat after the fashion of Alan Garner's book, *Red Shift* [when two time zones coexist simultaneously], it seemed two way! I could pick up something of the attitudes of these ancient priestly people, and they in turn could gain something from me. There is a fascinating speculation here for contemplating how ritual can possibly make windows in time, so that, if evolution in consciousness is conceded, it might be a benefit of a particular type of religious ritual observance to pick up vibrations of a more evolved level of consciousness. For those with a penchant for high flying speculation of a science fiction variety it might be considered that just as we might, consciously or unconsciously, be oracular contacts for ancient man; so, by analogy, 'inner plane' contacts we make could possibly be with men in the future. Accounts of the destruction of Atlantis by such contacts might even refer to the destruction of our own civilisation by someone far in the future!

But he also adds:

> I do not take this speculation too seriously, but its possible element of truth might be worthy of some thought. What may be more likely is a kind of spiral in time with similar events occurring at parallel epochs.

We first noted the image of the spiral in connection with Silbury, and we have in a sense walked a sort of spiral outwards from that centre, looking at themes and experiences that have repeated themselves at different levels, whether triggered by long barrows, bell barrows, stone circles, sacred wells, acts of pilgrimage, lucid dreaming or active magic. But the most striking thing of all is that, by and large, the inner perceptions of people from a wide variety of traditions all fit together.

Rather neatly. The psychic perceptions of the high magician dovetail quite beautifully with the psychic perceptions of the hedgewitch: those of the spiritualist medium dovetail effectively with the insights of the illuminated Freemason. And so on. Which leads me to accept that there are energies within the ancient sites that are tangible and touchable, and that the similarity of people's experiences has very little to do with psychological projection and more to do with actual mechanics.

Of course, the twenty-first century being what it is, there is another whole branch of occultism that has developed a tendency to link all of the above to the awkward question of UFOs, and bring us back to the question of Outsiders again. A whole new generation has begun to speculate that places such as Silbury and Stonehenge were built not by Atlanteans, Mayans or Egyptians, but by beings from other parts of the galaxy – as some of the more radical of the correspondents have insisted.

John Michell, in his influential book *The Flying Saucer Vision*, suggested that the design of Stonehenge actually represented the shape of an extraterrestrial vehicle, and sightings of such craft over the circle are fairly frequent – though we have to take into account the huge amount of military flying that goes on in this area. There have been: columns of light rising from the site; rings of fire hovering over it; whole squadrons of UFOs involved in shape-shifting performances in the sky above; balls of light which danced, flittered, moved at incredible speed, hovered, dematerialised, altered shape, and affected electrical equipment, as well as compasses.

Someone who was heavily involved and experienced in the Hermetic Tradition told me of a group working with a *very* senior magician indeed, who took them through the sort of spontaneous and guided visualisation that is known as a path working. The visualised setting was Stonehenge itself, but at a certain point within the journey the magus in question stopped his narrative and kept silent for a long time, before bringing the journey to a stuttering end. When my informant asked the magus later why he had paused in such an odd way, he confessed that the completely unexpected image (i.e. inner

237

experience) of a huge UFO hovering over Stonehenge floored him so completely that he could not speak. More, he felt that if he had told the rest of the group what he had just envisioned, they would think him such a prat that he felt it best to keep it to himself, and just pushed on without mentioning it!

Arthur Shuttlewood, who estimated that he saw at least two UFOs a week over nearly two decades, came to his own conclusion:

> I am not convinced that the majority of what we see comes from other physical realms of the universe. A minority may come from other planets somewhere in this or another galaxy in the vast Milky Way; but most of what I have seen appears to belong to another dimension or level of existence in universal structure. It strikes me as an age-old force belonging to our environs and surrounds. A force, an intelligence, that is far older than Man and has inhabited the earth world far longer than he.[7]

One first-hand experience of UFOs in connection with Stonehenge itself was given to me by Poppy Palin, who is currently living in Warminster, Wiltshire. Poppy told me about her encounter with the guardian at the barrows near Stonehenge, which we mentioned in a previous chapter. But her very first visit to Stonehenge itself in company with her then partner Tim involved a bizarre experience that, at *first* reading, is more attuned to the classic glowing-light UFO-type encounter than anything from the usual magical traditions. On *second* reading, however, something far more extraordinary took place. More akin to a time slip than anything else, and exquisitely suited to the Saturnian nature of this place.

As she told it in her book *Season of Sorcery*, they drove towards the circle on a bright moonlit night, passing through a strange strip of fog on the way, 'like a defined mist across the road at chest height'.[8] They were astonished to observe the sudden appearance of a huge (house-sized) orange ball of light which started to follow them. As they pulled into a lay-by next to the Hele Stone they found that the glowing object stopped too, then proceeded to demonstrate the usual UFO aerobatics:

shooting upward vertically at incredible speed; flying off at a diagonal; disappearing and reappearing in a completely different part of the sky . . .

Poppy touched the Hele Stone, and it tingled, and felt as if her skin might stick to the stone itself. She looked around for other witnesses: other cars or houses, or security guards within the perimeter fence of the henge, but there was nothing and no one else around but themselves. But Poppy and Tim saw the globe of light and its bizarre antics. What she did not see, which terrified Tim, was the giant male figure, 'big, black and horrible',[9] with no face, no features, but cloaked and entirely dark, and coming right towards him . . .

After he'd yelled at Poppy to get in the car, they drove off. As they drove through a second strip of fog like the first, the globe of light stopped, and they began to leave it behind. Looking at her watch, Poppy saw it was 8.45, even though they had been out of the car for only a few minutes, and had arrived at 8. More, a banana that had been fresh and yellow on their arrival at the henge was now black and split, and in an advanced state of rottenness.

There was more to the story than this, but in essence, when they discussed their separate insights and overlapping (but not totally concurring) experiences, they could only feel that the particular spirit that the nonpsychic Tim had 'seen', and the highly psychic Poppy not sensed at all, had existed in another time from them. 'Our hypothesis was that the figure Tim had encountered was the guardian of Stonehenge, which would account for its menacing protective presence, and for the fact that I did not see it. My attention [was on the globe of light], not on the stones at all, therefore I posed no threat.'[10] In fact, there were so many tantalising anomalies to do with the location of the fence, the Hele Stone, the road, houses in the area and trees they had noticed, that they jointly concluded they had 'seen', or passed by, a very different Stonehenge from that which they visited in daylight, on later occasions.

The sites may be 'spiritual' in the broadest sense but they are not always congenial. Too much of modern paganism seems to be concerned more with politically correct styles and dogmatically twee attitudes than with the raw powers beneath and within the land and ourselves. Too often these attitudes are projected on to the sites themselves. After Poppy Palin made her visit to Stonehenge and encountered that angry and aggressive guardian at the nearby barrows, she modified her own opinions quite sharply:

> I do not personally believe [Stonehenge] to be in the slightest bit benign and 'fluffy'. I think its inherent energies are hostile to my own and that it has the potential to be a dangerous site if you are not careful or if you are sensitive to such emanations. I obviously am. I believe, at this time, that the land around this sacred site is highly magnetised and that Salisbury plain and military influences do not help this negative and powerful charge. I believe the site to have a strong trickster energy and that it can present itself in many ways, depending on what it wants from you. It is a place of desolation and bones for me and I shall not trouble it again as I am aware of its capabilities.

This 'trickster' aspect is an important point, and is another theme that finds its summation at Stonehenge. Arthur O'Neil had this sense when he was involved in the Cley Hill episodes. Jack Green was acutely aware of powers that seem to be playing games with him when he was researching the mysteries of the Northumbrian sites; and there was my own experience of that pocket virtual-reality landscape of the Cotswolds, which so bewildered me when I tried to find the Rollrights.

However, when we look at Poppy's experience in conjunction with others, it almost presents a microcosm of current ideas and experience of Stonehenge: the time slips, the spatial anomalies, the UFO, the disturbing entity... Does the giant figure that her nonpsychic partner 'saw' – 'big, black and horrible' – bear any relationship to what Chris Thomas described as the 'black sentinels' whose role is to guard such interstellar gateways as Stonehenge?

'The black sentinels,' he wrote, 'are a form of constructed "consciousness" who have been programmed to actively seek out new sources of energy. These "beings" are conglomerates of very sticky black energy. This does not make them "evil" in the sense that they are aware of carrying out "evil" acts, but purely machines programmed to carry out particular tasks which they are very efficient at.'[11]

To Thomas, Stonehenge is just one of the global centres linking with higher civilisations from different star systems, ranging from the Pleiades, Sirius, the star system we identify as NGC 584, and four other groups in areas of the universe that are, so far, uncharted by us.

One Australian woman who visited Stonehenge regularly was always struck by the impression of brooding power it holds, and noted that, even if the rest of Salisbury Plain is in bright sunlight, Stonehenge seems to have its own black cloud: ' . . . a bit like the character in Li'l Abner', she noted. Her own feeling is that the energies have been 'so mucked about with over the centuries that the circle has gone into sulk mode'. Her own special expertise as a formidable magician has devolved upon 'release working' – helping earthbound souls or bewildered spirits trapped between the worlds find their proper places in the cosmos. As she commented about Stonehenge, 'Since one of the functions of the ley lines was to provide spirit paths for departing souls to use, stands to reason that the major stone circles are a kind of Central Station for souls waiting to move on.' Going on to discuss the technical aspects of such things she concluded:

> Maybe one of the reasons Stonehenge is so gloomy is because it hasn't been used for its proper purpose (or one of them, at least) for many, many centuries. So the energies which should have circulated and been sent on have stagnated. Now, of course, it's so difficult to get near the stones nobody is likely to attempt it. You would need to stand at the heart of the circle and make a grave-offering (food and drink for the journey onwards, and a formal quitclaim). It would be interesting (challenging?) to do some release work there at Samhain or Midwinter. I suspect one would get trampled in the astral rush!

One woman, who to the very best of my knowledge is unconnected with any of the above, described an experience at

Stonehenge that is almost another summary of the many themes that we have discussed so far.

Helen Belot is another Australian very concerned with the healing energies of the earth. In 1992 she stumbled across an energy system that came from the very early times of Ancient Egypt, which she called Sekhem. 'I have remembrances of being a high priest in more than one life in those times, so it is remembered skills that I started using.' She believes that it is her task in this lifetime to bring those skills into line with the culture and thinking of today, to set the standard and teach the teachers. While working with this system she found herself involved in the work of:

> ... healing the planet and restarting and connecting those communication centres mentioned to the ley lines and magnetic grids. Of connecting the cosmic energies to the earth and from the earth to the cosmos in the manner of perfection before it was tampered with.

And so she came to Stonehenge. After a series of what she intimated were truly amazing synchronicities she found herself standing alone in the dark amid the stones. It was 4.30 a.m. and the security guards, after having escorted her to the centre, melted into the darkness. She explained:

> I had been acting purely on intuition up to this point, but as I stood there I knew exactly what I had to do with a deep inner knowing. So using those skills of very ancient Egypt that I call in this lifetime Sekhem, I proceeded to unlock the circle of stones and then to stand in the middle of them and allow them to speak to me.
>
> I understood that I had been present at the creation of the Henge but at that time I was not a human being but of the Angelic realms. I had placed a cache of very small but powerful crystals deep in the earth below the altar stone and these were to power a communication centre between earth and the star system Sirius. Unfortunately this communication system had been shut down by the spilling of blood from sacrifices of all types, wars etc. within the sacredness of the stones. I was there to reactivate it and was given very specific instructions how to do this. As well as Stonehenge there were four

other major communication centres to be re-activated in America, Egypt, Australia and Tibet, as well as many minor ones around the world.

It was an amazing experience to feel the change in the energy of that place when the ceremony was complete and the communications were flowing again. I felt as if the stones were bowing down in thanks and I honoured them for protecting and keeping the crystals from harm until I could come and re-activate them. There was a mutual recognition of this between the stones and me.

I then went and touched each stone. Some had information for me that I was to carry to other places. I understood that this information was in regard to the timing of the earth changes that would be coming to this planet. These communication centres are connected to the magnetic grids and the ley lines as well as to the cosmos. They needed to be reactivated to assist the earth in the changes that will be experienced in the near future and to restore the magnetic grid around the earth to its intended perfection.

I stood in the centre of those very beautiful stones and learned many things about myself and this very great and wonderful planet of ours. And then I locked it up again.

Over the next two years I took the information to the specific places around the world in the time frame given and was honoured to be part of the group that put the last piece into place in Lhasa in 1997. The original concept of the grid communication system of planet earth is again complete and operating.

If the stone circles were originally the material aspects of a magical technology that was connected with the souls of living things and the cosmos itself, then it seems that the people who built them are back among us, and once more using them as they were meant to be used. Or it may well be that they have never gone away. The dowser J Havelock Fidler recorded a dream which, despite the obvious Freudian overtones of which he was fully aware, he felt was actually a vision of a standing stone being charged, or recharged, dating back several centuries:

I seemed to be standing on the left side of a valley running between rounded hills. At the head of this valley was a circular wall surrounding a tall, white stone, which somewhat resembled

243

a lighthouse. Round the wall was a line of people dressed in what appeared to be early seventeenth century fashions, the men in short black tunics, rather baggy breeches and hose, white collars and tall hats; the women in long skirts, white shawls and caps. I had the impression . . . that they were passing something round in an anti-clockwise direction. There was a gap in the wall at the side facing down the valley and, after some time, something seemed to issue from this gap and rush down the valley with a sound rather like escaping steam or a sudden rush of wind.[12]

He felt that this ceremony was connected with a Wiccan ritual known as 'raising the power', dating back to the time, under James VI, when witchcraft was fiercely condemned, and necessarily conducted in secret. Could this ritual, he speculated, possibly have been some method of raising the group's collective psi count, and of in some way transferring this to the stone in the centre of the circular wall? He noticed the similarity between his dream/vision and Tom Graves's experience at the Rollrights when he inadvertently opened the 'latch-gate' and let out the energy spinning around the circle. And certainly Uri Geller would seem to agree that such stones and circles were very much involved in 'raising the psi count'. Can it be that knowledge of how to work with and maintain the magical technology of the stone circles has been passed down through the generations, via individuals or groups such as Fidler dreamed of? And/or have these spiritual engineers really been reincarnating for the purpose of getting all these devices to work again?

When I asked Murry Hope what she had felt at Stonehenge, she wrote back:

When writing *Atlantis: Myth or Reality* for Penguin Books, I studied in detail the illustration of the capital of the Island Continent, as described by Plato in his *Timaeus* and *Critias*. Symbolised in what is often referred to as the 'Cross of Atlantis', this ancient glyph may be seen recurring in prehistoric stone circles and on sacrificial altars suggesting, perhaps, a surviving memory or emulation of the Atlantean original. Aside from its obvious solar implications, scholars have been trying to probe its secrets for centuries. A recent television programme on the subject, which featured the latest scientific analysis of the stones and their possible meaning, ended with the accidental discovery that the stones responded in some way to sound! Sonics? As for my own feelings, while standing quietly among those silent, monolithic, stone memory-banks, my distinct impression was of a people who were trying to preserve, in the only material available to them – stone – the folk memory of a city their ancestors once lived in and loved.

Which is something that Foster Forbes would wholly have agreed with.

So what are these things that seem to be held in common? What are these beliefs that are derived from the mystics', magicians' and mediums' individual experiences – as opposed to speculative ideas stemming from what must be the fevered activity of the left brain?

- Stones are imbued with energies that can be measured, but that are often dormant.
- Stones are imbued with consciousness, which can be awakened by sonic techniques such as drumming, tapping, song, music generally.
- These energies are connected with the ley-line network.
- These energies are often seen as serpent-like or draconic in nature.
- All such places are profoundly linked with the Mysteries of Time.
- They are all connected with spirits – not just of the ancestors, but with deities and nonhuman beings from other dimensions entirely.
- They seem to act as gates, from one spiritual world into another.
- Ancient sites such as sacred hills, stone circles and barrows of all shapes are linked with the stars, which are seen as the true home of the souls of the tribes.
- Deep emotional reactions are often triggered quite unexpectedly.

So, in respect to the last, it really does seem reasonable in this nonrational realm to conclude that subjective responses are not always mere projections from the unconscious, manifestations of the libido, expressions of divided personalities, simple pieces of wish-fulfilment or whatever . . . By and large they are perceptions of very real energies that link the perceiver with things that are . . . well, very old indeed, and fundamentally part of themselves. It strikes me that, if any one thing does bind them all together at some level, it is the realisation that none of the people I met, spoke to on the phone, read about or corresponded with would take serious umbrage with the concept of Gaia. In varying ways they have all felt themselves, to some degree, an integral part of this great entity known as Earth – not just as it is today, in their ephemeral lives, but as it always has been, through time.

None of the correspondents experienced *all* these revelations, however. And they necessarily have different (though rarely antagonistic) interpretations, which they build into their own belief systems. In fact it is rather like the way that stone circles such as Avebury have had bits and pieces broken off and carried away to make other structures. Sometimes, these stolen or discarded chunks of stone have proved to be the most precious of all, as any mason will testify. Sometimes, as any spiritualist medium will confirm, it is often small pieces of apparently meaningless or seemingly trivial vision that can have the greatest and most unexpected impact on the listener, affecting them in ways that outsiders, watching, can rarely understand. Which is why, when I started collecting examples of people's insights and experience, I assured everyone that everything was important, that there are no degrees of spirituality, and even what they felt were the merest fragments might serve to trigger off processes in someone else. And, if it can be summed up in any way at all, the essence has to be that past, present and future are all one; the Land can join them.

Of course Stonehenge today has taken on the mantle of a Cause. If the rebels of my generation were inspired to violence against reactionary governments for political and humanitarian reasons, then there is a hard and disaffected core today who, at every solstice, charge against police lines at Stonehenge for what they feel are purely religious and ecological motives. And while it is appalling to see the way that a very small minority disrespect the stones in their urge to confront authority, there is a sneaking tendency to respect the others who simply want to worship in their own – often chaotic – way. Or as Paddy said:

> I don't know why the government goes to such lengths to keep people out of the stones at the time of the solstice. *Let* the travellers and the hippies and the New Age lot into Stonehenge to worship in their own ways, even if some find it offensive. *Let* the people frolic, and dance, and have sex, and get smashed with drugs and liquor to the sound of drums and chanting and singing. That's more or less how it *used* to be . . .

To finish the book, we could not do better than read Mike Harris's own description of a rite he worked within the stones that impacted upon him in completely unexpected ways. But that has always been the case when it comes to magickal and mystical revelation: you tend to find what you need – which is not necessarily what you want. When you approach the ancient sites with awesome intent, then quite often it can seem to fall flat. At other times, while you're simply passing by with your mind on other things, they can almost leap out at you. But let Mike tell it himself:

> Stonehenge isn't what it was! Not even the way it was thirty odd years ago, when a fledgling magician could wander among the stones at will and think and do pretty much as he pleased. There were few parameters then, physical or metaphysical, before John Michell, Professor Thom and all those other luminaries told us what we should be looking at. Before New Age travellers, English Heritage and the Country Landowners Association took us down the road of riot, legislation and security measures. Nobody had heard of 'Earth Mysteries' then, before the advent of New Age publishing, and its inevitable dogmatists. The Stonehenge I knew relied for its recognition upon an annual pilgrimage of neo-Druids and nobody was very clear what they thought.
>
> Perhaps I should have left it that way, cherishing the memory of those blue remembered stones some thirty years ago, before Stonehenge and I lost our magickal innocence. But nearly twenty years later, I was on my way back and we had both changed.
>
> I met a group of people, some quite distinguished in these

matters, at that pub in Glastonbury. The American woman whose brainwave this was had gathered us all together, having received permission from English Heritage for us to spend the night at Stonehenge. We were a mixed bag of Americans and Brits. We Brits, occultists of various abilities and traditions, had been summoned to provide some ethnic flavour and doubtful wisdom for the American visitors on their spiritual quest, for our American companions were upon a 'sacred tour' arranged by our Californian hostess. The Stonehenge visit was to be the high point of this magical mystery tour of the UK.

After some discussion of what we were going to do... a magical 'earth healing ritual' and personal meditation (we were to be there through the night), we left the pub by the back door to avoid the TV crew who had been tipped off about 'witchcraft' by some well meaning soul! We all then piled into one minibus and set out towards Wiltshire. I have never visited a site under such bizarre circumstances. We came to the Stonehenge car park at the dead of night and were surrounded by security guards with dogs. Documentation was shown, words exchanged, rules and regulations instilled, and then we had to sit shivering in the minibus until midnight. Some of us actually changed into magickal robes and at the appointed time were escorted on foot to the stones themselves.

As I left the bus and plodded across the dew-damp grass, I found myself reflecting on what the hell a forty-something year old man was doing wandering around the Wiltshire countryside, with a bunch of nutters, in the small hours of the morning, dressed (as I was) in velvet robes and carrying a damn great sword. Then we came to the stones, vast, dark silhouettes against an impossibly star-drenched sky. A feeling of great humility and awe stopped me in my tracks. We may be able to give intellectual chapter and verse on why Stonehenge was built where it was; we can talk about sacred geometry and ley lines, and get it right in our heads; but standing among those stones under a clear night sky explains it all to the heart... instantly.

Ancient sites are often like batteries. Their charge gets depleted, leeched out by constant human contact. By night, however, they recharge – and that night was no exception. I would have been content to sit and meditate then go quietly away, but that was not what was expected of me. I had to lead a magickal ritual.

Now, I was trained to do this sort of thing and to do it well. Magick is not something that can be done by committee. One person (usually called the Magus) has to know and direct the appropriate rite and be responsible for its execution. Practical magick, like practical cookery, is doomed by committees of cooks. In this instance, I was sort of responsible in that I had to open and close the proceedings, providing, as it were, the bookends of the thing. Our Californian lady was, however, in charge of things overall and her sacred tourers had each written their own bit of the rite to throw into the pot along the way. The other Brits were also there to throw in their bit of ethnic seasoning and the result was a bland magickal casserole, albeit stewed in superb surroundings. Truth be told this is why most of the Brits were there . . . none of us having had the gumption to try and hire Stonehenge on our own account!

The ritual staggered along until, having run out of steam, the Californian lady hissed to me 'do something' . . . but the rite was past redemption and so I hissed back . . . 'It's your bloody working, you do something'. She mumbled some invocation or other and I then drew things to the close as previously arranged. As magick it was unfocussed and ineffectual and I think that some us standing there with heads bowed were mourning a lost opportunity. But then what would I have done, if it had been down to me? What if the well-drilled magickal group that I belonged to had been there? The answer is that it would probably have been mayhem. Stonehenge is too serious a site for 'serious' magick.

The place has an aura of sanctity set deep in time, time that goes somewhat beyond the Neolithic beginnings and Bronze Age elaboration of its archaeological history. Even that history, the history of its physical construction, reaches across two epochs and to the geographical limits of mainland Britain. Stonehenge was not built and elaborated to simply serve the passing religious whim of a local Bronze Age tribe, there was nothing parochial about Stonehenge. It was and is perhaps the major pulse point in the earth mysteries of mainland Britain. Even Geoffrey of Monmouth, who first gave the Arthurian saga a universality beyond his native Wales, used Stonehenge as a major location in his 'History of the Kings of Britain'. That was in a Roman Catholic Britain, some four thousand years after the first Neolithic sacred builders came to Stonehenge.

What Stonehenge was, and is, to the British folk soul may not be explained simply by placing it in a convenient celestial context, by saying that it 'represents Saturn'. Elucidating its complex geometry, or its stellar, solar and terrestrial alignments, cannot of themselves explain what Stonehenge was and is all about, any more than finding that Westminster Abbey faces East explains British Christianity. Even so, such places are set out in a way which accelerates an aura. Construction and alignment become important, not for what they are, but for what they *do*. And what they do at any sacred site worth the name is to draw three things together. These three are human nature, all nature, and an archetypal world where angels stride the very boundaries of being. And there is a purpose to this through which the soul and folk soul of these Islands continue and evolve. This is a purpose with which the best of magick may co-operate, but with which it tampers at its peril . . . and there is a very fine line between co-operation and tampering!

Perhaps providence led us to Stonehenge therefore, not as a company of determined magicians, but as that motley bunch doing something so harmless and ineffectual that the stones just smiled to themselves before resuming their venerable contemplation. Even so, there was real magick . . . magick in Sirius rising between the trilithons and the wide swathe of the Milky Way winding its way between worlds that few can even dream of. The stars would of course have been different back in those days when Stonehenge saw its beginnings and the heavens turned on the dragon star rather than the Little Bear, Arthur's star, as they do now. Yet the same curve of the heavens was shadowed in the curve of the stones and the same unity between people, land and stars was as it had always been. And that was magick enough.

And a century before Mike Harris it must have been magic enough for the Reverend Edward Duke also, for he got back in his carriage and went home to Lake House, with his own magnificent vision throbbing and chanting in his head like something the Benedictines might have sung on a good day.

And then, when he got back, dismissed his servant and put pen to paper, he did something mildly astonishing. He finished his thesis with a paragraph that has a completely different style from anything that went before. As if, at the last gasp, he no longer worried what the fellows in the Archaeological Society might think. As if, touched by the magic of his journey, he began to speak with the voices of the stones themselves. Listen to it, and try to see him in his study, enraptured by the things – wonderful things – going on in his head.

[These temples form:] ... one grand astronomical scheme, and typify the *magnus annus* – the cycle of the years of the world – the cycle of cycles; – when after the certain revolution of thousands of years, the planets and all the heavenly bodies shall ultimately, and simultaneously, arrive at the same places from whence they originally received their first impulse of motion; when the Ovum Mundi, the Mundane Egg, reposited within the womb of Time, shall, having received the daily influences of the Sun during its lengthened period of incubation, burst its cerements; when the new world shall spring forth into being, and amidst the tuneful harmony of the spheres, the aera of the revived Platonic cycle shall again begin its new and long-continued revolution![13]

Which is not appreciably different from many of the overtly mystical, visionary sentiments of the correspondents within this book.

Perhaps the spirits of the Neolithic priestesses, the Bronze Age bull-headed shamans, the druids, sorcerers, and nonhuman unearthly creatures from other dimensions taught him things along the way, touched his psyche, and forced him to fall back upon the wild perceptions of the right brain as opposed to the rational analyses of the left. Because, ultimately, I believe that in a nonrational, laterally viewed, mytho-magical and curvilinear sort of way, Duke was more right than wrong.

The old Buddhist puzzler comes to mind: 'First there is a Mountain, then there is no Mountain, then there is ...' When you first read the words of the Reverend Edward Duke you think that here is a visionary. Then, as you get closer to what he is saying, you think, no, he's a pseudo-scientist, a mere rationalist. But closer still and you begin to think that – somehow – he really is, or was, a visionary all along.

And in this dreadful age of the professional mystic, the telling sound bite and the media groupies, we today have to acknowledge that some highly touted mystical and magical traditions are built upon little more than those left-brain noises that are so beautifully described as psychobabble, and have no real roots in the gut experience and raw magical insights of those who truly, quietly – and often quite unexpectedly – work the Earth Magic, and have done for an exceedingly long time. Which is where our guide fits in, I think: as someone who walked/worked his way into the earth energies, and touched upon the Spirit of Place and places of spirit along the way. A true pilgrim in fact.

I think that Duke's journey inwards from the Great Mother to the Great Womb pushed him from one mode of conscious-ness into the other, from left to right, from reason to intuition, and made him closer to the folk whose experiences we have looked at throughout than those dry and dusty fellows he originally sought to amuse.

So what can we take from our inward journey in reading this? Because make no mistake that when images are planted in the unconscious, via the imagination, the former acts exactly like that Womb of Time whose powers Duke so splendidly invoked. Whether we are touched by the lonely circling figure of King Zel, or the proud and priestly figure who came with his unearthly hound to the long barrow at sunrise, or the silent priestesses at the wells, the wrinkled hags of the stones, the fierce guardians, weird beasts and soaring energies which promise to lift us to the stars, be assured that some of these images – some of these energies – will take on a curious life that will grow, stir, and, one day, *become*. All of these figures will have been touching upon our psyches, our ancestral mem-ories, whispering to us in their own and often very odd ways, so that some day we will look up and realise that we too, in a strange manner, have heard the voices of the stones.

NINE

A Site Snooper's Glossary

Mike Harris

BARROW: A generic term for earthen mounds constructed from about 3000 BCE, for the burial of the dead. The first barrows were **long barrows** and the earliest of these were just elongated mounds piled over the dead. As time went on Neolithic burial became more sophisticated, with these long barrows or **long cairns** covering various arrangements of internal stone chambering known as **chambered tombs**. These various internal layouts of tombs had ritual significance (the number 5 appears to have preoccupied the tomb builders along with particular terrestrial, solar and stellar alignments). **Passage graves** tend to have a long passage leading to one 'womb like' burial chamber. **Gallery graves** have a number (frequently five) of chambers leading off a central passage/gallery. The symbolism and ritual significance of such things is discussed in *Awen . . . the Quest of the Celtic Mysteries* by Mike Harris.

Both passage graves and gallery graves, as well as having symbolic construction, also allowed for the burial of tribal notables over considerable periods of time, being reopened to accommodate new burials as necessary. Evidence indicates that many barrows were remodelled and extended during a period of some thousand years, which may even suggest their importance as cult centres. It also indicates use by a settled and stable society.

Geographical concentrations of Neolithic long barrows include the 'Cotswold group' of 85 tombs of which Hetty Pegler's Tump, mentioned earlier in this book, is an outstanding example of a gallery grave. Many excellent examples of passage graves are also found throughout the British Isles. Bryn Celli

Ddu on Anglesey is one of many excellent examples. Perhaps the most impressive of all passage graves is, however, Newgrange in Ireland.

ROUND BARROWS are by far the most numerous of prehistoric burial constructions in the British Isles. With the incursion of the **Beaker people** from about 200 BCE, and the start of the Bronze Age, long-cairn burial tended to give way to burial in circular mounds and stone circles. Some of the later passage graves are within circular mounds. Not all Bronze Age tombs are invariably, however, in round barrows (or **bell barrows** as they are sometimes called, due to their inverted 'bell' shape), and some Neolithic tombs are set in round barrows/cairns, indicating the gradual overlap and blending of Neolithic and Bronze Age cultures. Within these barrows stone **cists** (box-like structures) contained either the body or cremated remains of individual tribal notables together with grave goods. Where internal burial chambers were made out of wood or where the stone cist has collapsed and the ground has subsided a depression in the previously flat-topped mound will often be found. Many round barrows are surrounded by a ditch, which would appear to equate with mythological references, not least in later Celtic literature of 'otherworld islands', the province of the celebrated dead 'across the western sea' (see also **ship burials**). Some round or bell barrows have a flange of flat earth between the ditch and the mound itself, known as a **berm**.

Square Barrows are fairly rare and are generally of Celtic origin. Some cover chariot burials (see **ship burials**).

CAIRNS: Barrows of both the Neolithic and Bronze Age period were covered with heaps of stones and soil. Where, however, the soil and grass have weathered away and the original heaped stones remain, these are known as **cairns**.

CHAMBERED TOMB: See **BARROW**.

COURT TOMBS: Where the entrance to a tomb is flanked by two protusions from the mound, forming a small ritual forecourt.

CROMLECH: The internal chambers of Neolithic tombs were structured from huge stones (megaliths). Where the cairn, the stone mound, has been removed, these huge stones that formed the internal chambers remain and are often referred to by the Welsh word, **cromlech**. Such will frequently be seen as a huge flat **capstone** supported precariously on several great upright stones. These indicate admirably the several distinct types of construction i.e. passage graves, gallery graves (see above) and **portal dolmens** (see below) used in the construction of Neolithic tombs. Although 'cromlech' is the frequently used Welsh name for such structures they are also called **quoits** (in Cornwall) and **dolmens**.

Cromlechs displaying the internal construction of the tombs of an earlier race made from such huge stones probably persuaded the Celts, who came after the Neolithic and Bronze Age peoples, to mythologise that Britain had previously been peopled by giants, hence the Celtic mythology of Bran the Blessed and the named association of giants with some tombs – the Neolithic round cairn *Barclodiad y Gawres* on Anglesey, for example, which translates as 'The Giantess's apronful'.

ENTRANCE GRAVES: Small Bronze Age tombs, almost a simple type of the passage graves that typify the late Neolithic and early Bronze Age. **Entrance graves** are mainly found in Cornwall and the Isles of Scilly

HENGE: Originally a term coined for the specific site of Stonehenge, from the Saxon *hengen* ('hanging') which may refer to the legend of Merlin assembling the stones by levitation or simply for the 'hanging' lintels that still partially adorn the uprights. The word henge has for many years since, however, become a generic term for a pre-Iron Age circular enclosure formed by a ditch and bank and cut by a causeway. This is in fact how Stonehenge had its Neolithic beginnings, with the majority of the stones being erected during the later Bronze Age. Henges dating from about 3500 BCE appear to be an early Neolithic focus of magicko-religious activity, which were frequently later elaborated as stone circles and avenues. The beginnings of Avebury were a henge, or series of henges, with the ditch at one time being some thirty feet deep!

LEY LINES: The rediscovery of the ley-line concept may be attributed to the late Alfred Watkins, who noted that certain ancient sites were aligned across the landscape. He published his findings in *The Old Straight Track*, proposing that these alignments marked prehistoric trackways. Commentators in the last 25 years expanded Watkins's concept after research of their own. This included dowsing to show that these leys were geophysical energy lines. Ideas were subsequently muted to the effect that such leys were rather like the meridians that acupuncture believes mark the energy flows within the human body's energy field. This analogy was then extended to suppose that the earth had a comparable energy field to the human body and that our prehistoric ancestors realised this. It was therefore supposed that they set standing stones and other monuments upon the earth's surface in much the same way that an acupuncturist inserts needles into a patient's skin at specific points to modulate energy flows. Hence the title of the definitive thesis by Tom Graves, *Needles of Stone*.

A recent discovery may in fact help support this thesis. Forensic examination of the body of a Neolithic tribesman found remarkably preserved in an Alpine glacier indicated certain chronic ailments. Small varying tattoo markings on his body appeared to have some religious significance until it was realised that these were at acupuncture points and indeed the acupucture points that would today be used to treat the ailments from which he appeared to be suffering. Not only does this indicate that the conceptual basis of acupuncture was understood in the northern hemisphere some five thousand years ago and may not have been of Chinese origin, but that our ancestors would have been in a position to apply concepts of modulating energy flows by treating specific locations and could well have applied this to the landscape as much as to themselves!

Myriad ley lines may be found by tracing ancient site alignments on maps, some of them extending over hundreds of miles. Few people realise that such alignments occur not only in straight lines. Many locations may be found to fall upon the exact circumference of huge circles upon the landscape, for example. Many also trace astronomical configurations.

The ley-line/geophysical energies theory has lately been given some weight in the western adoption of Chinese Feng Shui, a theory of geophysical energy flow through the landscape and buildings placed upon it, which has official credence in the Far East. If our Neolithic tribesman anticipated acupuncture, we have no reason to doubt that he and his kin also anticipated Feng Shui!

PASSAGE GRAVES: See **BARROW.**

PORTAL DOLMEN: A dolmen or cromlech construction which utilises the two supporting uprights of the capstone to form an entrance 'portal'.

QUOIT: Cornish word for dolmen or cromlech.

ROUND BARROW: See **BARROW.**

SHIP BURIALS: Known in many areas of the world and seeming to confirm mythological ideas of sea voyages into the underworld, abodes of the glorious dead or mythological islands. In Britain this seems to have been Celtic/Saxon rather than earlier practice. Though, mythology notwithstanding, Celtic chieftains appear in practice to have preferred chariots to ships as a form of afterlife transport. Comparisons may, however, be made with ancient Egypt and the journey of the deceased pharaoh through the Duat (underworld) in 'the boat of a million years'. The most celebrated ship burial in Britain is probably the Saxon one at Sutton Hoo.

STONE CIRCLES: There are more than a thousand of these in the British Isles, displaying great variations in shape, size and construction. Some appear to have been made from timber rather than stone and few of them are strict geometric circles, even though they frequently betray a sophisticated grasp of both geometry and astronomy. The geometry of pentagrams and heptagrams set within elliptical shapes has, for example, been found. Some circles contained burials, some were attended by avenues of stones (see **STONE ROWS**), and some were 'filled in' so that their standing stones ended up forming the perimeter of a burial mound. Some were also elaborations of earlier henges (see **HENGE**). A number of what appear at first glance to be stone circles are in fact the exposed uprights of burial chambers from which the capstone has disappeared.

The Bronze Age marked an acceleration in the construction of ritual stone circles and many may be found to contain a burial cist (with no mound) at their centre. Others have a single standing stone at the centre, which would seem to equate with the single standing stones sometimes found within passage grave chambers.

STONE ROWS: While rows of standing stones frequently mark causeways or processional avenues to or even joining stone circles (Avebury, for example), **stone rows** are another matter. In Wales and other areas there are lines of single standing stones that have ritual applications that may be guessed at. These are of mainly Bronze Age construction. The earlier Neolithic stone rows on Dartmoor are more of a puzzle where double rows go for considerable distances, leading nowhere, and sometimes terminated by blocking stones across each end of the row, as if to affirm that they lead nowhere and have no association with other prehistoric sites. Speculation among earth-energy enthusiasts suggests that while stone circles provided a means of energy acceleration comparable with a modern (circular) particle accelerator, stone rows were accordingly a Neolithic version of the linear accelerator.

STANDING STONES: Individual **standing stones** are found in many locations, particularly in Wales. They were mainly placed in the Bronze Age, although one or two **standing stones** were often incorporated into early henges (as in the early/Neolithic phases of Stonehenge). They are frequently aligned one to another and/or with other prehistoric sites, significant natural features and thence to seasonal alignments (solstice sunrise, for example). Some mark Bronze Age trackways and provide speculation about leys and/or energy lines (see **LEY LINES**) and certain geophysical properties within the stones themselves. Some stones within stone circles and burial chambers have decorative markings. Barclodiad y Gawres on Anglesey is an outstanding example.

NOTES

Chapter 1: The Reverend Duke and the Ancient Druids

[1] Edward Duke, *The Druidical Temples of the County of Wiltshire*, p. 4, John Russell Smith, 1846
[2] John Michell, *Megalithomania*, p. 102, Thames & Hudson, 1980
[3] Alan Richardson, *20th Century Magick and the Old Religion*, p. 174, Llewellyn Publications, 1991
[4] Grace Cooke, *The Light in Britain*, p. 4, White Eagle Publishing Trust, 1971

Chapter 2: The Sacred Hills, Mounds and Silbury

[1] Edward Duke, op cit., p. 6, John Russell Smith, 1846
[2] DH Lawrence, *Apocalypse*, p. 126, Penguin Books, 1974
[3] Ibid.
[4] Grace Cooke, op cit.
[5] Paul Devereux, *Symbolic Landscapes*, p. 164, Gothic Image, 1992
[6] Ibid.
[7] John Wood, *An Essay*, p. 148, quoted in *Great Stone Circles* by Aubrey Burl, Yale, 1999
[8] Terence Meaden, *The Goddess of the Stones*, p. 166, Souvenir Press, 1992
[9] Paul Devereux, op cit., p. 160, Gothic Image, 1992
[10] J Foster Forbes, *Giants, Myths and Megaliths*, p. 29, Wm Chudley, 1973
[11] Ibid.
[12] Katharine Jordan, *The Folklore of Ancient Wiltshire*, p. 34, Wiltshire County Council Libraries and Museum Services, 1990
[13] Hamish Miller & Paul Broadhurst, *The Sun and the Serpent*, p. 107, Pendragon Press, 1989
[14] Guy Underwood, *The Pattern of the Past*, p. 34, Abacus, 1972
[15] Ibid., p. 97
[16] Ibid.
[17] William Ernest Butler, *The Mound in the Moor*, Issue 1, *New Dimensions*, April, 1963
[18] Ibid.
[19] Mark Vidler, *The Star Mirror*, p. 153, Thorsons, 1998
[20] Ibid.
[21] Edward Duke, op cit., p. 36
[22] Mark Vidler, op cit., p. 162
[23] Chris Thomas, *The Fool's First Steps*, p. 113, Capall Bann, 1999
[24] Tom Graves, *Needles of Stone – Revisited*, p. 39, Gothic Image, 1985
[25] J Foster Forbes, op cit., p. 45, Wm Chudley, 1973
[26] Jack Gale, *Goddesses, Guardians and Groves*, p. 36, Capall Bann, 1999

Chapter 3: Avebury and the Stone Circles of the Sun and Moon

[1] John Aubrey, *Monumenta Brittanica*, 1665, ed. J. Fowles, Milborne Port, 1980
[2] Joan Grant, *Winged Pharaoh*, p. 123, Ariel Paperbacks, 1989
[3] John Ivimy, *The Sphinx and the Megaliths*, p. 72, Turnstone, 1974
[4] Edward Duke, op cit., p. 14
[5] J Foster Forbes, op cit., p. 17
[6] Tom Graves, op cit., p. 93
[7] Chris Thomas, Essay – 'Merlin, a Biography', *Inspiration* Magazine, 1999
[8] Grace Cooke, op cit., p. 45
[9] William G Gray, *The Rollright Ritual*, p. 54, Helios Books, 1975
[10] Ibid., p. 68
[11] Rowan Greenwood, 'An Unfair Accusation', *Comhairle Cairde#5*, 1999
[12] Edna Whelan, 'Communicating with Stones', *Northern Earth*, Issue 64, 1995
[13] William G. Gray, op cit., p. 69
[14] Rowan Greenwood, op cit.
[15] Terence Meaden, *The Stonehenge Solution*, p. 193, Souvenir Press, 1992
[16] Terence Meaden, *The Secrets of the Avebury Stones*, p. 33, Souvenir Press, 1999
[17] Hamish Miller & Paul Broadhurst, *The Sun and the Serpent*, p. 108, Pendragon Press, 1989
[18] J Foster Forbes, op cit., p. 13
[19] Ibid.

Chapter 4: Walker's Hill, the Inner Orbit of Mercury and the Spirits of the Blissful Dead

[1] RJ Stewart, *The UnderWorld Initiation*, pp. 263–4, Aquarian Press, 1985, Revised edition, Mercury Publishing, USA, 1998
[2] Ibid.
[3] Edward Duke, op cit., p. 79, John Russell Smith, 1846
[4] Kindly excerpted by Gareth Knight from his forthcoming book, *Pythoness*, Sun Chalice Books, 2000
[5] William G Gray, op cit., p. 71
[6] Ibid., p. 72
[7] Rowan Greenwood, op cit., p. 27
[8] Kathleen Wiltshire, *Wiltshire Folklore*, p. 2, Colin Venton Ltd, 1984
[9] Evan John Jones, 'Will of the Gods', *Comhairle Cairde#5*, 1999
[10] Kathleen Wiltshire, op cit.
[11] Edward Duke, op cit., pp. 93–4
[12] Quoted in Ken Watts's *Exploring Historic Wiltshire*, p. 69, Ex Libris Press, 1997
[13] Kathleen Wiltshire, op cit., p. 33
[14] Murry Hope, *Practical Celtic Magick*, p. 69, Aquarian Press, 1987
[15] Kathleen Wiltshire, *Ghosts and Legends of the Wiltshire Countryside*, p. 114, Colin Venton Ltd, 1984
[16] Guy Underwood, *The Pattern of the Past*, p. 52
[17] Christine Hartley, *The Western Mystery Tradition*, p. 88, Aquarian Press, 1968
[18] Teresa Mooney, *Paganism – a Beginner's Guide*, p. 14, Hodder and Stoughton, 1996

NOTES

Chapter 5: The Inner Orbit of Venus, the Godesses and the Mysteries of Women

[1] Terence Meaden, *The Goddess of the Stones*, p. 155 Souvenir Press, 1992
[2] John Wood, 1747, *An Essay*, pp. 157–8, quoted in Aubrey Burl's *Great Stone Circles*, Yale, 1999
[3] J Foster Forbes, op cit., p. 36
[4] Tom Graves, *Needles of Stone – Revisited*, p. 63, Gothic Image, 1985
[5] William Stukeley, *Abury, a Temple of the British Druids*, p. 89, 1743
[6] Paul Devereux, *Symbolic Landscapes*, p. 157, Gothic Image, 1992
[7] Christopher Knight & Robert Lomas, *Uriel's Machine*, p. 132, Century Books, 1999
[8] John North, *Stonehenge – Neolithic Man and the Cosmos*, p. 452, HarperCollins, 1996
[9] Robert Briffault, quoted in: Stan Gooch's *Cities of Dreams*, p. 112, Rider, 1989
[10] David Annwn and Alan Richardson, *Inner Celtia*, p. 91, Capall Bann, 1996
[11] John North, op cit., p. 133
[12] Gareth Knight, op cit.
[13] William G Gray, *The Rollright Ritual*, p. 22, Helios Books, 1975
[14] Lyn Picknett & Clive Prince, *The Templar Revelation*, Corgi Books, 1997

Chapter 6: The Orbit of Mars, The Place of the Guardian Spirits and the Mysteries of Men

[1] Edward Duke, op cit., p. 106
[2] Ibid.
[3] Ibid., p. 103
[4] Ibid.
[5] J Foster Forbes, op cit., p.16
[6] Ibid.
[7] R J Stewart, *The UnderWorld Initiation*, p. 263, Aquarian Press, 1985
[8] Arthur Shuttlewood, *More UFOs over Warminster*, pp. 6–8, Arthur Barker Ltd, 1979
[9] William G Gray, *The Inner Traditions of Magick*, p. 50, Aquarian Press, 1972
[10] Mike Harris, *Awen . . . the Quest of the Celtic Mysteries*, p. 72, Sun Chalice Books, 1999

Chapter 7: The Orbit of Jupiter, the People and their Sacred Wells

[1] Edward Duke, op cit., p. 109, John Russell Smith, 1846
[2] Edna Whelan, from her unpublished manuscript, *Out of the Corner of My Eye*
[3] Jack Gale, *Goddesses, Guardians and Groves*, p. 67, Capall Bann, 1996
[4] J Foster Forbes, op cit., p. 18
[5] Edward Duke, op cit., p. 120
[6] Joan Grant, *Far Memory*, p. 170, Corgi Books, 1975
[7] JA Brooks, *Ghosts and Legends of Wales*, p. 53, Jarrold Publishing, 1987
[8] Ibid., p. 52
[9] RJ Stewart, *Earth Light*, p. 49, Element Books, 1992
[10] Angela Barker, from her essay 'Geography of the Otherworld', *Witchcraft and Shamanism*, ed. Chas Clifton, Llewellyn Publications, 1994

[11] Jack Gale, *Goddesses, Guardians and Groves*, p. 49, Capall Bann, 1996
[12] Dolores Ashcroft–Nowicki, *The Ritual Magick Workbook*, p. 200, Aquarian Press, 1986
[13] Ibid.

Chapter 8: King Saturn, Stonehenge and the Womb of Time

[1] Edward Duke, op cit., p. 120
[2] Ibid., pp. 138–9
[3] William G Gray, *The Ladder of Lights*, p. 168, Helios Books, 1968
[4] *Mystic Places*, p. 80, Time-Life Books, Amsterdam, 1987
[5] John Ivimy, *The Sphinx and the Megaliths*, p. 132, Turnstone, 1974
[6] *Mystic Places*, p. 102
[7] Arthur Shuttlewood, *More UFOs over Warminster*, p. 78, Arthur Barker Ltd, 1979
[8] Poppy Palin, *Season of Sorcery*, pp. 34–41, Capall Bann, 1999
[9] Ibid.
[10] Ibid.
[11] Chris Thomas, *The Fool's First Steps*, p. 131, Capall Bann, 1999
[12] J Havelock Fidler, *Earth Energy*, p.73, Aquarian Press, 1988
[13] Edward Duke, op cit., p. 201

BIBLIOGRAPHY

Annwn, D & Richardson, A: *Inner Celtia*, Capall Bann, 1996
Ashcroft-Nowicki, Dolores: *The Ritual Magick Workbook*, Aquarian Press, 1986
Bauval, R & Hancock, G: *Keeper of Genesis*, Heinemann, 1996
Beth, Rae: *Hedgewitch*, Robert Hale, 1992
Bord, Janet and Colin: *Atlas of Magickal Britain*, Sidgwick and Jackson, 1990
Brennan, JH: *Astral Doorways*, HarperCollins, 1991
Brooks, JA: *Ghosts and Legends of Wales*, Jarrold Publishing, 1987
Burl, Aubrey: *Great Stone Circles*, Yale University Press, 1999
Chadwick, Nora: *The Druids*, University of Wales Press, 1966
Cooke, Grace: *The Light in Britain*, White Eagle Publishing Trust, 1971
Dames, Michael: *The Silbury Treasure*, Thames and Hudson, 1976
Devereux, Paul: *Symbolic Landscapes*, Gothic Image, 1992
Duncan, Anthony: *The Fourth Dimension*, Mowbrays, 1975
Fidler, J Havelock: *Earth Energy*, Aquarian Press, 1988
Forbes, J Foster: *Giants, Myths and Megaliths*, Wm Chudley, 1973
Gale, Jack: *Goddesses, Guardians and Groves*, Capall Bann, 1999
Gilbert, A. & Bauval, R: *The Orion Mystery*, Heinemann, 1994
Gooch, Stan: *Cities of Dreams*, Rider, 1989
Grant, John: *Far Memory*, Corgi Books, 1975
Graves, Tom: *Needles of Stone – Revisited*, Gothic Image, 1985
Gray, William G: *The Rollright Ritual*, Helios Books, 1975
Gray, William G: *The Inner Traditions of Magick*, Aquarian Press, 1972
Harris, Mike: *Awen . . . the Quest of the Celtic Mysteries*, Sun Chalice Books, 1999
Ivimy, John: *The Sphinx and the Megaliths*, Turnstone, 1974
Jordan, Katherine: *Folklore of Ancient Wiltshire*, Library & Museum Service, 1990
Knight, C & Lomas, R: *Uriel's Machine*, Century Books, 1999
Knight, Gareth: *Merlin and the Grail Tradition*, Sun Chalice Books, 1999
Laidler, Keith: *The Head of God*, Weidenfeld and Nicolson, 1998
Lawrence DH: *Apocalypse*, Penguin Books, 1974
Meaden, George Terence: *The Stonehenge Solution*, Souvenir Press, 1992
Meaden, George Terence: *The Goddess of the Stones*, Souvenir Press, 1992
Meaden, George Terence: *The Secrets of the Avebury Stones*, Souvenir Press, 1999
Michell, John: *Megalithomania*, Thames & Hudson, 1980
Miller, H & Broadhurst, P: *The Sun and the Serpent*, Pendragon Press, 1989
Mooney, Teresa: *Paganism – a Beginner's Guide*, Hodder and Stoughton, 1996
Newman, Paul: *The Lost Gods of Albion*, Robert Hale, 1987
North, John: *Stonehenge – Neolithic Man and the Cosmos*, HarperCollins, 1996
Palin, Poppy: *Season of Sorcery*, Capall Bann, 1999
Richardson, Alan: *Dancers to the Gods*, Aquarian Press, 1985
Richardson, Alan: *Earth God Rising*, Llewellyn Publications, 1988
Shuttlewood, Arthur: *More UFOs over Warminster*, Arthur Barker Ltd, 1979
Slade, Paddy: *Seasonal Magick*, Capall Bann, 1999

Stewart, RJ: *Earth Light*, Element Books, 1992
Stewart, RJ: *The UnderWorld Initiation*, Aquarian Press, 1985
Thomas, Chris: *The Fool's First Steps*, Capall Bann, 1999
Underwood, Guy: *The Pattern of the Past*, Abacus, 1972
Vidler, Mark: *The Star Mirror*, Thorsons, 1998
Watson, Lyall: *Beyond Supernature*, Hodder and Stoughton, 1976
Watts, Ken: *Exploring Historic Wiltshire*, Ex Libris Press, 1997
Wiltshire, Kathleen: *Wiltshire Folklore*, Colin Venton Ltd, 1983
Worthington, Cairistiona: *Druids – a Beginner's Guide*, Hodder and Stoughton, 1999

PERIODICALS
Comhairle – the quarterly journal of the Comhairli Cairde, 'dedicated to those of all Paths and Traditions' BCM-Writer, London WC1N 3XX
Inspiration – the magazine of the Capall Bann Publishing house
Liongate – a quarterly journal dedicated to 'Opening the Imagination and expressing the Heart'. 91 Roberts Road, High Wycombe, Buckinghamshire HP13 6XD
Northern Earth – a magazine of the Earth Mysteries
Pagan Dawn – the journal of the Pagan Federation BM Box 5896, London WC1 3XX

WEBSITES & EMAILS
The Dusty Millers: http://pdq.to/thedustymillers
Gareth Knight: www.angelfire.com/az/garethknight
RJ 'Bob' Stewart: www.dreampower.com
Northern Earth Mysteries Group: www.btinternet.com/~andrewmriley/nemg/
Uri Geller: www.uri-geller.com
Order of Bards, Ovates and Druids: http://druidry.org
JH 'Herbie' Brennan: http://homepage.tinet.ie/~herbie
Janet and Colin Bord: http://www.forteanpix.demon.co.uk/
Mike Harris: website in preparation
College of Psychic Studies: www.psychic-studies.org.uk

OTHER GREAT SITES:
www.stonepages.com
www.themystica.com
www.phantasmata-fix.no
www.crystalinks.com/megalith.html

INDEX